The World of E-Government

The World of E-Government has been co-published simultaneously as *Journal of Political Marketing,* Volume 2, Numbers 3/4 2003.

The *Journal of Political Marketing* Monographic "Separates"

Below is a list of "separates," which in serials librarianship means a special issue simultaneously published as a special journal issue or double-issue *and* as a "separate" hardbound monograph. (This is a format which we also call a "DocuSerial.")

"Separates" are published because specialized libraries or professionals may wish to purchase a specific thematic issue by itself in a format which can be separately cataloged and shelved, as opposed to purchas - ing the journal on an on-going basis. Faculty members may also more easily consider a "separate" for classroom adoption.

"Separates" are carefully classified separately with the major book jobbers so that the journal tie-in can be noted on new book order slips to avoid duplicate purchasing.

You may wish to visit Haworth's website at . . .

http://www.HaworthPress.com

. . . to search our online catalog for complete tables of contents of these separates and related publications.

You may also call 1-800-HAWORTH (outside US/Canada: 607-722-5857), or Fax 1-800-895-0582 (out - side US/Canada: 607-771-0012), or e-mail at:

docdelivery@haworthpress.com

The World of E-Government, edited by Gregory G. Curtin, PhD, JD, Michael H. Sommer, PhD, and Veronika Vis-Sommer, PhD (Vol. 2, No. 3/4, 2003). *Presents the experiences and lessons learned from global authorities who have implemented e-government technology in their own countries.*

Communication of Politics: Cross-Cultural Theory Building in the Practice of Public Relations and Political Marketing, edited by Bruce I. Newman, PhD, and Dejan Verčič, PhD (Vol. 1, No. 2/3, 2002). *"Significant. . . . Sets the standard for this newly integrated discipline." (Martin Evans, MMRS, MIDM, FCIM, MA, Editor,* Journal of Consumer Behaviour; *Senior Fellow, Cardiff Business School, University of Wales)*

The World of E-Government

Gregory G. Curtin, PhD, JD
Michael H. Sommer, PhD
Veronika Vis-Sommer, PhD
Editors

The World of E-Government has been co-published simultaneously
as *Journal of Political Marketing,* Volume 2, Numbers 3/4 2003.

NEW YORK AND LONDON

First Published by

The Haworth Hospitality Press®, 10 Alice Street, Binghamton, NY 13904-1580 USA

Transferred to Digital Printing 2009 by Routledge
270 Madison Ave, New York NY 10016
2 Park Square, Milton Park, Abingdon, Oxon, OX14 4RN

The World of E-Government has been co-published simultaneously as *Journal of Political Marketing™,* Volume 2, Numbers 3/4 2003.

The development, preparation, and publication of this work has been undertaken with great care. How-ever, the publisher, employees, editors, and agents of The Haworth Press and all imprints of The Haworth Press, Inc., including The Haworth Medical Press® and The Pharmaceutical Products Press®, are not responsible for any errors contained herein or for consequences that may ensue from use of ma-terials or information contained in this work. Opinions expressed by the author(s) are not necessarily those of The Haworth Press, Inc. With regard to case studies, identities and circumstances of individu-als discussed herein have been changed to protect confidentiality. Any resemblance to actual persons, living or dead, is entirely coincidental.

Cover design by Brooke R. Stiles

Library of Congress Cataloging-in-Publication Data

The world of e-government / Gregory G. Curtin, Michael H. Sommer, Veronika Vis-Sommer, editors.
    p. cm.
    Co-published simultaneously as Journal of political marketing, v. 2, no. 3/4 2003.
    Includes bibliographical references and index.
    ISBN 0-7890-2305-9 (hc) – ISBN 0-7890-2306-7 (pbk.)
    1. Public administration–Information resources management. 2. Electronic government informa-tion. 3. Internet in public administration. I. Curtin, Gregory G. II. Sommer, Michael H. III. Vis-Sommer, Veronika. IV. Journal of political marketing.
JF1525.A8W674 2004
352.3′8′02854678–dc22   2003015574

Indexing, Abstracting & Website/Internet Coverage

This section provides you with a list of major indexing & abstracting services. That is to say, each service began covering this periodical during the year noted in the right column. Most Websites which are listed below have indicated that they will either post, disseminate, compile, archive, cite or alert their own Website users with research-based content from this work. (This list is as current as the copyright date of this publication.)

(continued)

Special Bibliographic Notes related to special journal issues (separates) and indexing/abstracting:

- indexing/abstracting services in this list will also cover material in any "separate" that is co-published simultaneously with Haworth's special thematic journal issue or DocuSerial. Indexing/abstracting usually covers material at the article/chapter level.
- monographic co-editions are intended for either non-subscribers or libraries which intend to purchase a second copy for their circulating collections.
- monographic co-editions are reported to all jobbers/wholesalers/approval plans. The source journal is listed as the "series" to assist the prevention of duplicate purchasing in the same manner utilized for books-in-series.
- to facilitate user/access services all indexing/abstracting services are encouraged to utilize the co-indexing entry note indicated at the bottom of the first page of each article/chapter/contribution.
- this is intended to assist a library user of any reference tool (whether print, electronic, online, or CD-ROM) to locate the monographic version if the library has purchased this version but not a subscription to the source journal.
- individual articles/chapters in any Haworth publication are also available through the Haworth Document Delivery Service (HDDS).

ABOUT THE EDITORS

Gregory G. Curtin, PhD, JD, is Founder and Managing Director of Civic Resource Group, which provides consulting, research, and training in the use of technology in the public sector. He is currently a Visiting Scholar at the Institute of Governmental Studies at the University of California at Berkeley and Stanford University. He has been the architect of a number of innovative technology programs and initiatives in the public sector, and he has emerged as a leading thinker on e-government and the potential for information technology in the broad civic center. Dr. Curtin is Editor-in-Chief for the *Journal of E-Government*. He has years of experience as a government lawyer, professor of government, public school teacher, political adviser, and public sector consultant.

Michael H. Sommer, PhD, is Senior Consultant for Civic Resource Group in Santa Monica, California, and New York City. He presently serves as a Visiting Scholar at the Institute of Governmental Studies at the University of California at Berkeley and Stanford University. He has been a Visiting Fellow at Yale University and a Visiting Scholar at Harvard University, Stanford University, and Columbia University. He is a former Senior Partner of Sheinkopf, Ltd.–leading international political consultants. Winner of the Peabody Award, two Emmy Awards, the Los Angeles Press Club Award, and the California Newspaper Publishers Award, he is a Managing Editor for the *Journal of E-Government* and a commentator for many international publications and broadcast outlets.

Veronika Vis-Sommer, PhD, is Senior Consultant for Civic Resource Group, and is an editor, journalist, scholar, and political consultant for European and American political leaders, political parties, foundations, and NGOs. She presently serves as a Visiting Scholar at the Institute of Governmental Studies at the University of California at Berkeley and

Stanford University. She has been a Visiting Fellow at Yale University and a Visiting Scholar at Harvard University and Columbia University. Dr. Vis-Sommer has also been Lady Jane Franklin Visiting Scholar at the University of Tasmania, Hobart, Australia, and a Visiting Scholar in Politics at the University of Otago, New Zealand. She received a Federal appointment as a Visiting Scholar in national security and politics at The East-West Center, Honolulu, and has twice been a Fulbright lecturer. She currently is a Managing Editor for the *Journal of E-Government*, Senior Contributing Editor of the *Journal of Political Marketing*, and serves on the editorial board of the *Journal of Public Affairs*.

The World of E-Government

CONTENTS

RESEARCHING E-GOVERNMENT

NEW ZEALAND

AUSTRALIA

AMERICA

EUROPE

INTRODUCTION

The World of E-Government

Gregory G. Curtin
Michael H. Sommer
Veronika Vis-Sommer

Civic Resource Group; University of California, Berkeley; and Stanford University

One of the most frequently asked questions about electronic government, or e-government, is "What is it?" Because the study and practice

Gregory G. Curtin, PhD, JD, is Managing Director, Civic Resource Group, Santa
Monica, California, and Visiting Scholar, Institute of Governmental Studies, University of California, Berkeley, and Stanford University.

Michael H. Sommer, PhD, is Senior Consultant, Civic Resource Group, and
Visiting Scholar, Institute of Governmental Studies, University of California, Berkeley, and Stanford University.

Veronika Vis-Sommer, PhD, is Senior Consultant, Civic Resource Group, and
Visiting Scholar, Institute of Governmental Studies, University of California, Berkeley, and Stanford University.

[Haworth co-indexing entry note]: "The World of E-Government." Curtin, Gregory G., Michael H.
Sommer, and Veronika Vis-Sommer. Co-published simultaneously in *Journal of Political Marketing* (The
Haworth Press, Inc.) Vol. 2, No. 3/4, 2003, pp. 1-16; and: *The World of E-Government* (ed: Gregory G. Curtin,
Michael H. Sommer, and Veronika Vis-Sommer) The Haworth Press, Inc., 2003, pp. 1-16. Single or multiple
copies of this article are available for a fee from The Haworth Document Delivery Service [1-800-
HAWORTH, 9:00 a.m. - 5:00 p.m. (EST). E-mail address: docdelivery@haworthpress.com].

of e-government is only in its infancy, a precise definition is hard to come by, and those working in the field will certainly argue about what exactly is encompassed in the concept of e-government. One thing we are sure of, though, is that e-government is far more than simply making some public information and certain citizen services available via a Website.

As virtually all the contributors to this volume on e-government agree, e-government runs wide across all aspects of government, deep within the core of every governmental entity, and will inevitably be a transforming agent for government and governance. For example, Kuno Schedler has developed a framework for e-government that incorporates electronic Democracy and Participation (eDP), electronic Production Networks (ePN), electronic Public Services (ePS), and electronic Internal Cooperation (eIC). Donald Lenihan, our colleague in Canada, identifies the three key aspects of e-government as: (1) Improving service delivery–building a new public infrastructure; (2) Information–a new public resource; and (3) E-Democracy–extending public space. So, our working definition for e-government is broad, but hopefully to the point: E-government is the use of any and all forms of information and communication technology (ICT) by governments and their agents to enhance operations, the delivery of public information and services, citizen engagement and public participation, and the very process of governance. With this inclusive working definition as a framework, the Editors are excited to begin with this publication the methodical exploration of e-government in all its forms and applications across the globe. (Note: Defining e-government will be one of the key subjects of the charter edition of the *Journal of E-Government*, The Haworth Press, Inc., forthcoming in 2003.)

This volume on "The World of E-Government" is in response to what many fellow e-government colleagues throughout the world have advised us for some time could fill a real need: having in one publication, in one place, at one time, some of the very latest results of superlative international research, analyses, and even no-holds-barred opinions– all written by some of the best obtainable researchers and practitioners in the world–about the latest and most important international developments in electronic government.

Heeding this ambitious call, this collection particularly tried to concentrate on the many ways the enormous promise of electronic government is now being used and, indeed, not used, throughout much of the world; how it is demanded or wished for, or not–by citizens, by governments, by businesses–to meet the different and vital needs of our modern times–and all electronically.

At the same time, the collection also wanted to analyze how e-government serves a myriad of purposes and, indeed, is still likely to fulfill many future citizen and commercial needs. Some of these needs may, of course, presently be represented only by faint glimmers of hope, and much may now only be the stuff of which dreams are made.

As practitioners of, and researchers in, e-government, we are fully aware that, despite this fast-charging, fast-changing, ever-more-complex world in which we live, millions of people–even those who by their leadership roles and technological expertise rightfully should probably know more about e-government–may well never, ever have heard of it. And, thus, very sadly and with a consequence in failed performance for millions of citizens, these unknowledgeable persons cannot quite conceive of its great promises. Among them are our politicians and their staffs. But that, we and many other contributors to this volume believe, very likely will soon change. For e-government, in one way or another, directly or indirectly, even now already in countless ways and each day is changing our lives everywhere–in how we live, in how we do business, in how we interact electronically with governments, with businesses, with people–literally trillions of times and ways daily, and with each other. If these goals have not all been fully met, it is our fond wish that this publication will help to achieve these aspirations.

Readers will quickly note that governments, following the lead of commerce, indeed *must* now respond to millions of citizen needs, demands and wishes anew electronically every day. And as they do so, those developments, in turn, of course, will continue to daily change our lives in countless other ways for the better. As proof, if any is needed, we need only look to how the private sector has taken the lead to see how e-commerce has already transformed much of the world. One of the most far-reaching results of "the wired world" so far–for good or bad–is globalization. Certainly businesses everywhere continue to interact electronically with other businesses and their customers online because they *must do so*, in order to remain efficient–indeed in this very highly competitive commercial world, just to survive. (Note: In light of this globalization and in the spirit of e-government's promise to connect individuals, governments and nations across geographic and jurisdictional boundaries, we have chosen to preserve in the articles to the greatest extent possible–albeit in English–the language, spelling, conventions and colloquialisms of the contributor's native country.)

Nearly all contributors hope that the public sector–albeit, we judge somewhat slowly for most often governments by their nature *react* rather than *plan ahead*–will rapidly continue to improve its capacities for e-government.

E-government needs time to develop and learn from early mistakes. As e-government progresses–and this publication indicates it is moving rapidly ahead on all fronts–it may well lead to perhaps the most dramatic change of all: in the very ways we think about our world, in how we act about our futures, in how we transform ourselves. For electronic communication and even just surfing the Web for some daily personal need for valued information has in a real sense already become an essential, indeed an expected extension, of the power of our brains. All of us are bonded by electronic government.

Let's play devil's advocate: Even if this be spin and hyperbole and we are completely wrong about e-government, one thing, as this volume clearly demonstrates, does seem certain: As electronic government is continuing to change everyone's lives in some smaller and greater ways, it will likely continue for a long time to come, because that is its nature. And, we are convinced, as Americans have been convinced of the potentials of other powerful, socially influential inventions before, that when electronic government's vast, full promise truly begins to be fulfilled, the sky will be–indeed should be–the limit. Perhaps, as so many now fervently hope–especially the highly computerized and energized young, and among them by means of personal computers, the less frequently advantaged and even the dispossessed–that e-government may not just help to rapidly change the course of history but will change the course of democracy itself–finally making grassroots democracy *real democracy, instant democracy,* for *all* citizens, everywhere. Because as this collection illustrates, by its nature, e-government makes all government activities everywhere more *responsive* to real citizen needs. And it does so, *irrespective* of whether governments are presently democratic or not.

As it has already changed the course of worldwide commerce, so the hopes and expectations of millions is that e-government will change the nature of government, all of our lives, and make rapid betterment possible everywhere. It is precisely because explosions in curiosity about information are available electronically that they may well lead to explosions in freedom.

An analogy may be in order: E-government offers in its great possibilities and great promises commensurately great hope and good for all peoples. It is certainly good for the future of this precious, troubled and endangered planet–"the Good Earth," as American astronaut John Glenn decades ago movingly called it when this sophisticated, technologically pioneering, man was rightfully dazzled and stunned, viewing the planet and all of us more than a hundred miles below–immersed in beauteous sheer white clouds and seemingly bluest oceans, shrouding varying degrees of civilizations below with their eons worth of collected virtues and vices. Indeed Glenn, admittedly long before e-government was even a dream, saw wonderful truths unfold below from his tiny–and when compared to his companion, infinity–modestly microscopic speck of a space capsule. Two truths were that we are *all* racing along through space at 17,000 miles per second *together* and that the Earth is so unique and so precious.

Today, with e-government, we are able to add a mighty addendum to John Glenn's truths: All of us, everywhere, can all help each other to fulfill our individual and collective destinies and potentials as we share life upon this precious planet–especially when we enlist our PCs to link us with government and information at the much higher speeds than that which the Earth travels–the speed of electricity and light: 186,000 miles per second. We have every right to ask all governments at all levels to respond to what we daily wish and need at electronic speeds, because, as this volume underscores, the technology is here, willing and able. And political will, by extension, simply must follow. In any case, politicians may soon find real citizen pressures to use e-government will likely be overwhelming.

As the Editors of this publication in their research have ventured elsewhere before, the worldwide revolution in e-government that is going on around us is already so vast, so far-reaching, so immensely powerful in so many ways that–and as all the contributions to this collection clearly evidence–it has already affected each and every one of us in some discernable or indiscernible way. Only good can come from this.[1]

The many nooks and crannies of e-government are being actively explored throughout the world, to make it more responsive and better. While the business sector has caught on and is not only responding more keenly to daily experiments and changes in e-government but actively asking for more government services online, this volume notes that, increasingly, politicians seem finally to be getting the message: that e-government cannot be further ignored by them or their staffs. They *must* begin to *understand* how it can and will fulfill present and future citizen needs.

However, as the update on the recent Accenture report on more than twenty leading countries in e-government has already and tellingly underscored in our lead article, "The distance between the leaders and the followers is widening."[2]

Another recent report on e-government developments of *all* member nations of the United Nations, undertaken by the United Nations Division for Public Economics and Public Administration and the American Society for Public Administration, and spearheaded by Stephen Ronaghan, notes that *progressive* governments, at least, "are upgrading their sites regularly; expanding the types and quality of their online services and improving their content daily in an effort to achieve the highest measure of user satisfaction, administrative efficiency and cost effectiveness."[3]

It is because there was such an obvious need to provide a publication in which everyone involved or interested in e-government everywhere could keep up with the latest research results and discussions and book reviews about e-government, and because the publishers of the *Journal of Political Marketing*, The Haworth Press, Inc., and its visionary President, Bill Cohen, agree with our fundamental philosophy and premises, that all three editors of this volume also have been chosen to soon edit yet another needed, permanent professional journal–a new, sister publication to Professor Bruce Newman's path-breaking and vitally needed *Journal of Political Marketing–The Journal of E-Government*, which The Haworth Press will begin to publish in 2003.

Working again together as a team as they have for this publication, the three Editors will become Editors of *The Journal of E-Government.* Gregory G. Curtin, PhD, JD, will serve as Editor and the Managing Editors will be the husband and wife team, Michael Sommer, PhD, and Veronika Vis-Sommer, PhD. All three Editors–Dr. Curtin as Managing Director and the Sommers as Senior Consultants–are currently associated with Civic Resource Group of Santa Monica, California, and New York City, as well as also being Visiting Scholars at The Institute of Governmental Studies, University of California, Berkeley, and Stanford University.

For this collection, the Editors took special care to ensure that peer reviews for contributing articles were undertaken by outstanding, internationally known research authorities and practitioners in e-government. The valuable changes, additions, and corrections suggested by these independent authorities have greatly enhanced this volume. The Editors are especially grateful to Professor Randy Hamilton, Visiting Scholar, The Institute of Governmental Studies, University of California, Berkeley, for his expert and wise counsel and tireless, highly professional assessments of all articles submitted by contributors while he served as one of the peer reviewers for this publication. The Editors also wish to express their great appreciation to the very valued insights on new developments internationally in e-government and the very helpful assistance and advice provided by Professor Revan Tranter and Professor Eugene Bardach, both highly valued colleagues at the University of California, Berkeley. Special thanks also go to many of the Editors' fine Canadian colleagues, especially Professor Sanford Borins at the University of Toronto, and Donald Lenihan at the Centre for Collaborative Government, Ottawa. Particular thanks go to Seah Chin Siong, partner of Accenture's government operating group in Singapore, who has enabled a close insight of the workings of the country's e-government initiative, currently ranked first in the world.

Although e-government has existed for several years, in many ways it is still in its infancy, and the study of it is even younger still. But this new arena of public interest is certainly attracting the heightened attention of governments, technology providers and researchers alike. Hands-on practitioners are learning how to apply technology to better serve both governmental and citizen needs. Meanwhile, the rapid development of technology offers ever more and creative avenues for the average citizens to connect to their governments, and businesses demand to further e-government. And, research in this new field is being conducted across disciplinary lines indicating its widespread importance and potential. Given this rich environment, the best research and knowledge development in the field is being driven largely by e-government practitioners and technology providers, and this volume has thus included their experiences and practical knowledge. To capture this great insight along with the developing research, the Editors chose first to assemble articles directly from practitioners in governments about their "governance of e-government." These are followed by a selection of articles from those focusing on developing satisfactory provider-customer relationships of e-government, and classified here as the " 'Business' of e-government." Last is offered an array of distinguished international research analyses on the topic.

The decision to follow these distinctions was guided by the wish to make clear which perspective guided the authors. However, to be sure, more often than not, these differentiations are not clean cut in this exciting new field. For example, practitioners sometimes venture into research and researchers into the "business" of e-government, or perhaps vice versa. The crucial point is these three fields together, sometimes at breathless speeds, have promoted and witnessed the fast growth and increase in e-government worldwide.

Another goal of the Editors in preparing this collection was to try to ensure that, as much as possible, its title, *The World of E-Government* would, in fact, be backed up in content with salient developments about, and analyses of, variations of e-government on an international scale. A corollary goal was to enable leading researchers around the world to concentrate on *exactly how* e-government works in their various countries, and in what spheres of governmental and commercial activities, and what these developments really mean for the world so far. The results of developments in e-government internationally, as the reader will see, are *still* mixed. But the hope for rapid improvements, in our judgments, are well-justified.

Despite differences for each of the countries studied here, the challenges more often than not seem to be the same. A scrutiny of the e-government challenges and initiatives across national borders and a comparison of individual solutions offered hopefully provides not only a glimpse at the global impact of e-government but a way for all of us to learn from each other.

In our own undertakings as practitioners of and researchers in electronic government, we have often been struck by what Singapore, Canada, and the United States, frequently listed as among the top leaders of e-government along with New Zealand, could indeed, by comparison and analyses, learn from each other. For as has often happened in the history of science and public policy, by reading what others are doing, we can learn so much and accelerate our rate of progress further and faster.

Europe's diversified e-government initiatives are the subject of three articles. The first provides us with the newest developments in the macrocosm of Europe. The second article focuses on Germany's e-government initiative, and the third analyses seven European countries "to examine how the various developments of e-government can be interpreted."

Question: if it is true that the United States may be lagging behind in e-government, why are Singapore and Canada now making such progress in trying to maximize its benefits? To try to get the full answer, we asked key persons responsible in both countries to provide research assessments and analyses.

In Singapore, Lim Siew Siew of the Infocomm Development Authority and Low Yin Leng, e-government executive for the Ministry of Finance, note, as have contributors from other countries, that "remarkable changes have taken place in the business sector with the advent of e-Commerce." However, they write, in Singapore's case, "similar changes are taking place . . . fueled by the rising expectations of citizens and global competition." These expectations may well be critical. As the Editors have found in their research about U.S. e-government practices, demands from younger, computer-wise e-government users in America, probably somewhat like the experience in Singapore, are demanding "their money's worth" in "flexible, creative e-government uses." Lim and Low argue that what is needed for the realization of this goal and "to survive the fundamental transformations taking place today is to transform ourselves in an e-government, one that harnesses ICT to serve citizens in the best possible way." They add, among other necessary steps for fulfilling e-government, this goal "means not asking the citizen for more information than necessary or requiring the citizen to go to more than one agency for a specific service." Importantly, the authors argue, "E-government is not simply adding an 'e' to government." It requires, they say, "fundamentally (to) re-think all aspects of governance and service delivery to see how it can take advantage of technology and new business models to improve the efficiency of internal processes, as well as change the nature and quality of government interactions with both individuals and businesses."

Some recent international surveys of e-government indicate that the United States may have slipped behind Canada and Singapore as a dominant leader in electronic government developments. *Washington Technology*, in reviewing the global overview of the research organization, Accenture, in its third annual report on international developments in e-government–which are analyzed and updated further in this volume– writes that, for the second straight year, the firm rated Canada as the worldwide leader in e-government. The publication states that "the Canadian government is midway through its five-year plan to provide citizens with anytime, anyplace electronic access to all federal programs and services by 2004."[4]

The Editors are particularly grateful to have both the Singapore and Canadian experiences with, and aspirations for, e-government in one publication. In asking Canada to assess its remarkable progress, the Editors went right to the source and asked Michelle d'Auray, Chief Information Officer for the government of Canada, to provide an overview of that country's highly creative activities in providing many and varied e-government services to its citizens. Ms. d'Auray points out that in Canada, the Internet poses an opportunity to connect citizens in the sparsely populated country. She notes that Canada's citizens "want convenient, accurate, one-stop service access–they don't want to have to know which department or agency is responsible or in order to access what they're entitled to, to fulfill their reporting and remittance obligations, or to get the information they need to make important decisions for themselves and their families." In other words, as their American neighbors across the border might say, in e-government, the Canadians want "one-stop shopping." How the Canadians apparently have managed to bring various e-government goals to fruition makes for fascinating reading and, hopefully, once again provides a valuable learning experience.

Over time, the Editors have been particularly interested in the yeoman's work in America of the influential, nonprofit organization, the Council for Excellence in Government, which published the seminal report, *E-Government: The Next American Revolution.* This important document, when first published in 2001, described "a vision of what full electronic government in America could accomplish and offered a blueprint of how to get there." Thus, we asked, and were very pleased to receive from Ms. Patricia McGinnis, President and CEO of the Council for Excellence in Government, and one of the major spearheads behind and key authors of the report, an updated review of how this valuable assessment took place and what resulted. She notes in her contribution to this volume that the Council's report "was the product of an unprecedented collaboration . . . among 350 information technology experts in business, government, research, and the nonprofit sector nationwide." Crucially, in terms of current changes in e-government, recent actions of the Bush Administration and legislative proposals on e-government have, she writes, reflected the blueprint's recommendations. We are confident readers will appreciate reading herein, for the first time, one of the more complete histories and assessments of this important e-government initiative in the United States. (Note: At the time of Ms. McGinnis' submission, the E-government Act had not yet been authorized by the President. It was finally signed into law in December of 2002.)

Hon. Erkki Liikanen, Commissioner for Enterprise and the Information Society of the European Commission, provides an EU perspective on e-government. He argues that EU member "achievements will not fulfill their promises if further challenges are not addressed by the decision makers at all levels of government." Commissioner Liikanen argues that "top-level leadership and commitment is necessary to deepen e-government, not least for the change management needs for re-organisation of government back-offices." Here again, seemingly, political decision-makers and their staffs need to be brought up to speed on what e-government can accomplish. Parenthetically, as the Editors have written elsewhere, the pay-offs for political leaders can be commensurate with their interest levels in e-government if we can agree that "the first obligation of the politician is to get re-elected."[5] So, too, voters in Europe as elsewhere can quickly learn to like politicians all the more for what kinds of electronic services–and how quickly–governments at all levels will provide to them. This finding alone serves as a perfect tie-in for why politics is a key component of e-government, and why the *Journal of Political Marketing* is a wonderful platform to launch the *Journal of E-Government*: If the elected officials don't get it from a political and policy standpoint, then the citizens and agencies literally won't "get it"–it being the benefits of e-government.

While assessing the effectiveness of New Zealand's oft-cited and very promising developments in e-government, we asked for not one, but two, independent research articles and viewpoints. One article–an academic assessment–researches local government Websites which provide access to government information. This valued insight appears later in the volume and was contributed by researchers Rowena Cullen, Deborah O'Connor, and Anna Veritt.

The second assessment of New Zealand's latest and salient national developments in e-government was undertaken by Brendan Boyle, who is Director of New Zealand's E-Government Unit at the State Services Commission, and by David Nicholson, a Wellington-based journalist. They note New Zealand's nomination by the United Nations as the world's third most advanced country in e-government, adding that the country "has always had a rapid uptake on new technology." But, they add, it "has not hesitated to scour the world for best-of-practices solutions and modify them to its own environment." This reinforces the editorial view of this volume: It is precisely by learning more about new, creative developments in e-government practices in various leading countries that e-government practitioners and particularly decision-makers everywhere are enabled to try out new and various e-government practices that make sense to them.

In Germany, Gerd Wittkemper, Senior Vice President of Booz-Allen & Hamilton, and Ralf Kleindiek of the German Federal Ministry of Justice and one of the leading forces behind Germany's BundOnline 2005 project at the Federal Ministry of the Interior, state that e-government is a key element in shaping that country's future. And, they argue, it will create "a quantum leap on the way to an administration centered around the needs of its customers, citizens, (and) enterprises . . ." and further, that e-government is "pivotal" in governmental modernization, so much so, the authors state, that "the German government has launched (a) e-government initiative" whose aim is to ensure that "citizens, businessmen and the administration can access the services provided by the Federal administration easier, faster, and at lower costs . . . " That may well be a tall order, yet perhaps very realizable. Time will tell whether this will be quickly realized. In the interim, readers are provided a fascinating insight into how Germany plans to accomplish its overall goals for e-government.

On the "business" side, Vivienne Jupp, Managing Partner for Global E-government Services for Accenture, reports on the firm's 2000 study, which ranked e-governments worldwide. Jupp's contribution offers a revealing glimpse into e-government constituents–and e-government's performance for its stakeholders–across the globe.

Janet Caldow, Director of the Institute for Electronic Government of IBM, takes aim in her article on yet a new "business" opportunity, mobile e-government, believing that in the future, "the real payoff will be mobile, wireless access to, and interaction with, mission-critical, enterprise-wide applications." She believes two things will probably occur: First, that governments will interact with citizens wirelessly, and second, public sector workforces may stand ready to gain the most.

In noting the newly updated analyses by Accenture, the Editors took some pains to ask several American researchers to try to establish why America may be lagging behind. Thus, in reviewing e-government developments in America, Robert Atkinson of the Progressive Policy Institute and Andrew Leigh of Harvard University assess that American e-government's next phase–which they term "a seamless, customer-oriented Web presence" may face more formidable barriers to development than did earlier advances. One reason: Progress toward customer-focused e-government, in the authors' judgment, requires fundamental organizational changes to existing bureaucracies "so that the government's Web presence can be comprehensive, efficient, and easy for citizens to use." That, as Commissioner Liikanen has noted in the case of the European Union as well, will most certainly not be an easy task.

In New Zealand, e-government researchers Rowena Cullen, Head of the School of Information Management at the Victoria University of Wellington, and her colleagues, Deborah O'Connor of the New Zealand Institute of Economic Research and Anna Veritt of the National Library of New Zealand, in analyzing e-government developments in New Zealand from outside of government, note in assessing citizen uses of about half of New Zealand sites surveyed, that visitors indicate that a good range of information had been provided to them–but only on the better sites. However, some smaller regional or district council sites continued to provide little in the way of basic information to citizens. And, while more than 90% of New Zealand users approached a site seeking specific information, less than half were able to find the information they sought. This article addresses a major gap–noted by the Editors in their own ongoing research in both the study and the practice of e-government: The local and regional levels of government, where the heavy lifting of service delivery and citizen engagement is conducted on a daily basis, is virtually ignored in the research and woefully behind in the application and funding of e-government.[6] In New Zealand, Cullen et al. write, there may be a need to extend e-government in the country to local governments and other agencies–a vast understatement from our perspective.

Meanwhile, with a hop, skip, and a jump across the waters, in assessing nearby Australia's advances in e-government, the collection's contributors found that the country has also made great strides in how it is improving the full potential of e-government. In assessing what lies beyond e-government service delivery in "Down Under," Karin Geiselhart of the National Office for the Information Economy, and her colleagues, Mary Griffiths of Monash University, and Bronwen FitzGerald of the University of Melbourne, pointedly remind us that in Australia "good government is expensive, bad government is unaffordable." The authors note that while some Australian government uses of information technology are maturing, there still remains a growing need to "effectively engage" Australian citizens in all stages of the policy process. The authors investigate the national framework for e-government in Australia, stating that the levels of technology literacy in elected officials remains a continuing problem, and they review some electronic democracy initiatives in several Australian state and territory governments. These findings underscore what we have earlier observed, that one of the greatest promises of e-government–to facilitate citizen engagement, public participation (or consultation as it is widely known outside of the U.S.) and to bolster the very underpinnings of democracy–is still widely unrealized, and definitely understudied.

Associate Dean Dennis W. Johnson of the Graduate School of Political Management at George Washington University, in viewing the e-government activities of the U.S. Congress, notes that the legislative body, "after a relatively slow start" in the 1990s, is now making some progress in meeting the demands of online communication. This progress, Johnson argues, is "fueled (by) the growing use of e-mail by constituents and the development of online grassroots." He notes that while

"Congress has been inundated with e-mail," it is still "several steps behind the private sector," but that it "is attempting to catch up." Finally, Dean Johnson also argues that the future uses of Congressional Web sites may depend "on the attitudes and priorities set by lawmakers and their senior staff."

Professor Kuno Schedler and Lukas Summermatter of the Institute for Public Services and Tourism of the University of St. Gallen, Switzerland, long expert observers of e-government developments in Europe as well as elsewhere, provide another assessment of its activities in Europe, describing e-government activities in seven European countries. They have developed a heuristic e-government model to accomplish this goal. Professor Schedler is particularly qualified to undertake this task and to make international comparisons, spending as he does a good deal of time in the United States.

To our good friend and valued colleague and Editor of the *Journal of Political Marketing*, Professor Bruce Newman, go very special thanks for enabling this volume in the first place. One might ask why a journal on politics, and specifically one about political marketing, would introduce a collection on e-government. But Professor Newman saw what the Editors of this collection have seen for some time now, that e-government is as much about politics as it is about government, and as such candidates for elected office and those already in office at all levels had better embrace it before it overwhelms them. In keeping with our global perspective, just look at the Honorable Tony Blair in the United Kingdom, who made e-government a key plank of his platform early on in his tenure. As UKOnline was rolled out, the Prime Minister was seen sitting next to administrative staff for training in computers and the Internet–and joking when he got things wrong. Political marketing at its best–the leader as a real person willing to expose his own shortcomings in an effort to get popular buy-in for this strange new thing called e-government. Even more tellingly, the Prime Minister of tiny Grenada, Dr. the Honorable Keith Mitchell, based his election campaign on the idea of utilizing information technology and e-government to move his island nation and his people toward prosperity. The country of approximately 90,000 now has a formal E-government Strategy and Action Plan, and is gradually moving forward with e-government operations and citizen services, thus putting the Prime Minister's money right where his candidate mouth is. The city of Geneva, Switzerland, recently conducted direct elections online, and Estonia, a former Eastern Bloc country, now allows citizens to recommend new legislation directly online. And in broader coverage, over a series of United Nations organized international conferences on e-government, one of the strongest themes that has emerged is that e-government is first, second, third and foremost a political issue. In that regard, the Editors are very gratified that the United Nations has chosen our e-government advisory firm, Civic Resource Group, to assist with a new global study and to consult with the UN on how countries–especially in the developing world–may best use all the multiple capacities of e-government and optimally align these with the individual goals of member countries.

And here in the U.S.–how about Michael Bloomberg, the newly elected mayor of New York City, a serious management and efficiency maven from the private sector who regularly highlights to the media the new information and services that his great city is offering online. In his first city budget, the new Mayor spared only information technology from his cost-cutting axe. And as Dean Johnson notes in his contribution to this publication, the fast-growing development of "online grassroots" and the use–or lack of use–of official Websites by elected officials and candidates will no doubt impact both politics and political marketing.

The list of innovative e-government solutions that directly touch citizens (read voters) goes on, and it continues to grow exponentially day by day–one can do the math: Multiply the number of governments, governmental institutions, agencies, commissions, departments, quasi-governmental entities, etc., around the globe by the possible instances of direct online citizen service delivery, public information accesses, and opportunities for "touching" citizens via the Internet, and one starts to get the point. We haven't even seen the tip of this iceberg yet. The bulk of e-government investment will no doubt go toward the acquisition and implementation of new technologies and processes to improve government operations and service delivery. The greatest benefits and value of e-government, however, will be realized over the longer term in the context of enhanced citizen engagement, better citizen services, increased public participation, renewed trust in government, and overall greater participatory democracy. These benefits, fuzzy as they are, have immeasurable political value which will redound directly to the elected officials, candidates, political parties and organizations that move boldly into the world of e-government and make it their own.

We thank Professor Newman for his wisdom and counsel, for his great patience in always standing willing to answer far too many of our questions, and, again, for allowing us to bring the important international developments reported herein to public attention and at the same time to launch a new journal, and we believe a new discipline, that will cover one of the most exciting public sector transformations in recent times–e-government. If all editors had Professor Newman's superb qualities, the world would be a far better place.

Finally, we wish all of our readers good reading, great fun, and, hopefully, valuable learning experiences from all our outstanding contributing colleagues in e-government across the world.[7]

NOTES

1. For an analysis of developments in e-government in major U.S. cities, see Gregory Curtin, Robert McConnachie, Michael Sommer, and Veronika Vis-Sommer, "American E-Government at the Crossroads: A National Survey of Major City Uses," the *Journal of Political Marketing*, Volume 1, Number 1, 2002, pp. 149-192.

2. *eGovernment Leadership–Realizing the Vision*, Accenture, *www.accenture.com*

3. Benchmarking E-government: A Global Perspective–Assessing the Progress of the UN Member States, *www.unpan.org/e-government/Benchmarking%20E-gov%202001.pdf.* (Note: One of the editors for this volume, Dr. Gregory Curtin of Civic Resource Group and the Institute of Governmental Studies, University of California, Berkeley, along with his colleagues, is collaborating with Mr. Ronaghan and the United Nations in the establishment of an annual global e-government survey and research series.)

4. Gail Repsher Emery, "Canada Tops Global E-Gov Study; U.S. Ranks Third," *Washington Technology*, April 24, 2002.

5. Michael Sommer, "Quo Vadis, E-Government," the *Journal of Political Marketing*, Volume 1, Number 1, 2002, pp. 235-238.

6. See, for example, Gregory Curtin, Michael Sommer, and Veronika Vis-Sommer, "Optimal Regional E-Government: Ranking the 'Best' U.S. Planning Web Sites," *The Journal of Public Affairs*, forthcoming 2003; and "Cities on the Internet 2001: E-Government Applied," Civic Resource Group National Report, *www.civicresource.com*.

7. Further information on the Editors and their ongoing research on e-government may be found at *www.CivicResource.com*

GOVERNANCE
BY E-GOVERNMENT

E-Government in Action:
Singapore Case Study

Lim Siew Siew

Infocomm Development Authority of Singapore

Low Yin Leng

Ministry of Finance, Republic of Singapore

Lim Siew Siew is Executive Consultant in the e-Government Planning and Management Division under the Government Chief Information Office (GCIO) of the Infocomm Authority of Singapore (IDA). She heads a team of e-Government masterplanners to research and analyze e-government strategies and trends to enable more effective strategy formulation and decision-making in the public sector. Siew Siew graduated from the University of Illinois at Urbana-Champaign with a bachelor's degree in Computer Engineering and a master's degree in Computer Science. She has more than 10 years of experience in the IT industry.

Low Yin Leng is e-Government Executive at the e-Government Office in the Singapore Ministry of Finance. She formulates e-government policies and strategies to build e-government capabilities in the Singapore Public Sector. Yin Leng oversees the implementation of service-wide e-government initiatives to enhance the delivery of public e-services. She communicates Singapore's e-government strategies to other agencies as well as to foreign governments. Yin Leng undertook her university education in the United Kingdom on a Public Service Commission Overseas Merit Scholarship. She graduated from the Imperial College of Science, Technology and Medicine with a Masters of Engineering degree in Electrical and Electronic Engineering in 2000.

[Haworth co-indexing entry note]: "E-Government in Action: Singapore Case Study." Siew Siew, Lim, and Low Yin Leng. Co-published simultaneously in *Journal of Political Marketing* (The Haworth Press, Inc.) Vol. 2, No. 3/4, 2003, pp. 19-30; and: *The World of E-Government* (ed: Gregory G. Curtin, Michael H. Sommer, and Veronika Vis-Sommer) The Haworth Press, Inc., 2003, pp. 19-30. Single or multiple copies of this article are available for a fee from The Haworth Document Delivery Service [1-800-HAWORTH, 9:00 a.m. - 5:00 p.m. (EST). E-mail address: docdelivery@haworthpress.com].

SUMMARY. Singapore was ranked second in Accenture's e-Government Leadership study in the years 2000, 2001, and 2002. As an innovative leader in e-government, Singapore strives to achieve the concept of "Many Agencies, One Government" by delivering services that are integrated from the customer's viewpoint, regardless of the number of agencies involved in providing the service. The Singapore e-Government Action Plan was launched in June 2000 with the vision of transforming public service into a leading e-government program to better serve the nation in the digital economy. *[Article copies available for a fee from The Haworth Document Delivery Service: 1-800-HAWORTH. E-mail address: <docdelivery@haworthpress.com> Website: <http://www.HaworthPress.com> © 2003 by The Haworth Press, Inc. All rights reserved.]*

KEYWORDS. Singapore, e-government, leader, integrated, vision

INTRODUCTION

Globalisation and the rapid progress of information and communication technologies (ICT) are bringing about fundamental changes in all aspects of our society. With the advent of e-commerce, remarkable changes have taken place in the business sector. Fuelled by the rising expectations of citizens and global competition, similar changes are taking place in governments.

To survive the fundamental transformations taking place today, the Singapore government needs to transform itself into an electronic government, or e-government, one that harnesses ICT to serve citizens in the best way possible. This means meeting the demands for service effectively and efficiently, and in a way convenient to citizens. It means not asking the citizen for more information than necessary or requiring the citizen to go to more than one agency for a specific service. It means government agencies linking their back-end systems and processes to serve the citizen rather than expecting the citizen to interact with multiple agencies at the same time. E-government will help increase the IT savviness of the public and enhance economic competitiveness.

E-government is not simply adding an "e" to government. It requires that Singapore fundamentally rethink all aspects of governance and service delivery to see how it can take advantage of technology and new business models to improve the efficiency of internal processes, as well as change the nature and quality of government interactions with both individuals and businesses. It is about achieving the vision of "Many Agencies, One Government," delivering services that are integrated from the customer's viewpoint, regardless of the number of agencies involved in providing the service.

CIVIL SERVICE COMPUTERISATION PROGRAMME

One of the critical elements of being able to jump-start and scale quickly any e-government initiatives is the presence of a strong ICT foundation. Singapore's move towards e-government is built on a solid foundation established by the Civil Service Computerisation Programme (CSCP). The CSCP was conceived in the early 1980s with a clear direction of transforming the Singapore government through IT. Since its launch, the CSCP has progressively advanced and evolved with the changing technological, business and social climate to bring about exciting changes to the way the Singapore government serves the public.

The first phase of the CSCP was directed at improving public administration through the effective use of IT by automating traditional work functions and reducing paperwork. The emphasis subsequently shifted to interagency communication and coordination so as to provide integrated services to the public. A number of Data Hubs were created to reduce redundancy in data capturing and promote data sharing within the government. The early 1990s saw the beginnings of an adaptive and robust civil service-wide network, and the consolidation of computing facilities in a data centre. Figure 1 below summarizes the evolution of the CSCP during the 1980s and 1990s.

One other outcome of the CSCP is the build-up of a large pool of ICT-competent personnel in the public service. This group of ICT professionals is one of the critical capabilities for the conceptualization and execution of Singapore's e-government programmes.

E-GOVERNMENT ACTION PLAN

Singapore launched its e-Government Action Plan in June 2000 after wide consultation with all levels of the public sector. It charts the Singapore Public Service's key strategies and programmes to transform itself into a leading e-government, while retaining the flexibility to adapt to changing needs.

FIGURE 1. Evolution of Singapore's Civil Service Computerisation Programme

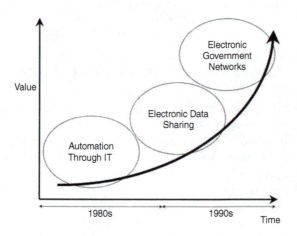

The five Strategic Thrusts of our e-Government Action Plan are:

a. *Reinventing government in the digital economy* through a continuous review of policies, regulations and processes to align them with the rapid developments in the economy and to meet rising expectations from the public;
b. *Delivering integrated electronic services* centred around customers' needs by working across organisational boundaries to integrate information, processes and systems;
c. *Being proactive and responsive* by anticipating citizens' needs and delivering responsive systems and services with speed;
d. *Using ICT to build new capabilities and capacities* for achieving quantum leaps in service delivery; and
e. *Innovating with ICT* by embracing enterprise and experimentation.

We have further identified the following six programmes to drive the Strategic Thrusts:

a. *Electronic services delivery:* This provides a one-stop interface with the public through integration of online services offered by public sector agencies;

b. *A knowledge-based workplace:* This encourages active and collaborative learning and knowledge sharing as part of a culture of continuous learning in the public service;

c. *Technology experimentation:* This pioneers initiatives on a trial or pilot basis to better understand the new capabilities that technologies can offer and how they can benefit the government and its customers;

d. *Operational efficiency improvement:* This encourages radical and fundamental questioning of various functions and processes so as to review their relevance and usefulness in the Internet age;

e. *Adaptive and robust infocomm infrastructure:* This enables the advent of a knowledge-based workplace and the delivery of integrated e-services, in addition to improving operational efficiency; and

f. *Infocomm education:* This endows public sector officers with the capacity to take advantage of growth in ICT capability to revamp internal processes and external service delivery.

Two years into the e-Government Action Plan, Singapore is starting to reap the results of its efforts. In the ensuing sections, several key initiatives and achievements are highlighted.

KEY INITIATIVES AND ACHIEVEMENTS

Putting Public Services Online

To assist public sector agencies in developing their e-services capability, Singapore has identified several levels of e-service maturity based on the depth of interaction between the public and government:

a. *Publish:* One-way; user receives information online but cannot initiate any transaction;

b. *Interact:* Two way; user initiates transaction online but transaction can only be completed offline;

c. *Transact:* Two-way; user completes transaction online, but one transaction at a time; and

d. *Integrate:* Two-way; user completes more than one transaction online with one entry and through a single interface (organizational complexities hidden).

In Singapore's approach to e-services delivery, it strives to deliver electronically every service that can be delivered electronically. In addition, every service shall be delivered at the Transact level online, unless impossible to do so, in which case it shall be offered at the Interact level. Only services that do not involve application from the public shall be left at the Publish level.

A public sector-wide baseline survey was conducted over the period of July-September 2000 to compile a complete listing of all public services offered by the government, and to identify those public services that can be made available electronically. A central tracking system was subsequently developed to monitor the progress of e-services delivery.

As of September 2002, 83% of all feasible e-services were already online. Services are also increasingly being provided at the higher levels of e-service maturity, with over 57% of services available at the Transact level and two integrated e-services launched recently–an Online Donations Portal that provides information about various Institutes of Public Characters and enables donors to make donations online, and a One-Stop Government Job Application Portal that enables individuals to apply for any post available in the public sector. Seven other integrated e-service projects are under development. This includes a business licenses approval system that enables business start-ups to fulfil their business registration and licence requirements at a single Website, and a bill presentment and payment service that enables customers to view and make a consolidated payment for all their government bills and fines online.

The eCitizen portal (*www.ecitizen.gov.sg*) was launched in May 1999 as a one-stop gateway to government e-services that are organized around customers' needs rather than along agency lines. eCitizen requires agencies to work across boundaries to integrate information, processes and systems so as to provide a seamless online experience. The portal currently houses about 600 e-services classifieds into 15 categories and receives about 4.2 million hits each month.

Pivotal to the quick and efficient development and deployment of e-services is the Public e-Services Infrastructure (PSi). It comprises of a highly scalable and secure infrastructure layer, a rapid application development environment and a set of basic services such as payment, authentication and data exchange with legacy systems.

Promoting Public Usage of e-Services

Besides the availability of services online, it is equally important to consider their acceptance and usage by the public. The benefits of e-government can only be reaped if the public regard e-government as the norm in transacting with government. Agencies need to consider how they can enhance the quality of their e-services and encourage their customers to use them. This involves seeking feedback from customers regularly through focus group discussions and demographic surveys, and conducting marketing campaigns to raise public awareness about the benefits of e-services. A large-scale marketing campaign was launched in October 2001 to promote the use of eCitizen and e-services through channels such as newspapers, buses and radio stations.

An e-government survey conducted by the Gallup Organization in March 2002 revealed that 2 out of every 3 Singaporeans who transacted with the government had used e-services in the past year. In addition, 1 out of 3 persons declared the Internet to be their preferred mode of interaction with the government. Some of the popular e-services included the filing of income tax returns, the request for account statements from the Central Provident Fund Board, and the checking of school examination and posting results.

Ensuring Universal Access to e-Services

While we raise the awareness and adoption of government e-services, Singapore is also mindful of IT-illiterate Singaporeans who may not be able to access these services. To increase the ICT literacy of the nation as a whole, the Infocomm Development Authority of Singapore has developed an ICT Training Framework that provides focus on the ICT training needs of the different segments of the Singapore population.

The framework comprises 5 levels of ICT training programmes to meet Singaporeans' specific needs in ICT skills. From basic computer literacy to workforce training to ICT manpower capability development, the framework focuses on different levels of ICT competency to enhance the quality of life and to improve employability. As an example, 'Level 1' focuses on promoting e-lifestyle to the general public, including workers, homemakers and senior citizens. The ICT skills for this level are the essential ICT skills in leading an e-lifestyle, such as basic computing and Internet skills. 'Level 5' focuses on capability development of ICT manpower where continuous skills upgrading is essential in staying competitive and relevant. ICT skills for this level include the critical and emerging (e.g., grid computing, P2P, wireless) skills.

To ensure that all Singaporeans are able to enjoy the benefits of e-government, we are establishing an extensive network of *eCitizen*

Help Centres around the island. Each eCitizen Help Centre is equipped with computers offering free Internet access to government e-services. eCitizen Helpers are on hand to guide citizens, such as the elderly and IT-illiterate, who may need assistance to access government e-services.

Services to Enable e-Business

Government e-services are also an enabler to businesses in their transactions with the government. Aggregating and integrating services essential to the running of a business into a single window helps promote greater productivity, efficiency, and convenience with simplified procedures and faster turnaround times.

The Singapore Public Service has put in place an integrated, one-stop portal where suppliers and prospective revenue tender bidders can interact with the Public Service for procurement activities. Known as the Government Electronic Business (GeBiz), this end-to-end online procurement system now hosts about 2,000 trading partners with an annual transaction value of S$220 million. Currently, all service-wide period bulk tenders have been hosted in the form of electronic catalogues, and procurement is via GeBiz.

Beyond procurement, we are also exploiting the transformational momentum of e-government to streamline the processes and reduce the number of interactions with government that businesses have to deal with. An example would be the online business approval licence system that Singapore is rolling out in phases.

Empowering Public Sector Officers

For e-government to be successful, it needs to be appreciated and embraced by all public sector officers. The Infocomm Education Programme was set up in September 2001 to equip officers with the necessary skills to capitalise on the growth in ICT capability to revamp internal process and external service delivery. A set of ICT competencies and courses has been defined.

To enable public sector officers to better leverage on explicit and tacit knowledge in our agencies, Singapore launched the Knowledge Management (KM) Experimentation Programme in July 2001. The programme provides seed funding to encourage public sector agencies to jump-start pioneering KM projects with the objective of nurturing KM ideas and developing prototypes and trial systems.

In addition to equipping the public officers with ICT knowledge, and creating the fabric necessary for the creation, capture and retention of knowledge, we also want to encourage them to harness the power of ICT in an innovative manner to achieve quantum leaps in service delivery. As such, the Technology Experimentation Programme was launched in July 2002 to support this objective.

Centralised and Adaptive Infocomm Infrastructure

Connectivity is one of the most crucial components in enabling e-government initiatives. A broadband infrastructure for government (BIG) has been put in place to provide public sector agencies with a wider choice of solutions to meet their different connectivity requirements and budget considerations. Singapore's public agencies have successfully migrated to the new infrastructure since July 2001. With the use of a Virtual Private Network solution, public officers can access government networks anytime, anywhere and using any medium.

A Government Data Centre has also been set up to provide centralised expertise and management of critical infrastructure, application and information. This data centre enables public sector agencies to enjoy a greater level of accessibility, security and resilience to potential threats to business continuity.

While Singapore adopts a decentralised ICT management model, it needs to maintain a good degree of interoperability and information sharing within the public service to minimise integration complexity when delivering integrated e-services. To achieve this objective, the Singapore government is developing a Service-Wide Technical Architecture comprising standards, policies and guidelines to guide its agencies in the design, acquisition and management of ICT systems. Besides facilitating interoperability, standardization will also enable agencies to increase operational efficiency by reducing the variety of ICT infrastructures, as well as increase reuse of components amongst their ICT systems; greater economies of scale can also be achieved by consolidating procurement.

Governance and Management

Sponsorship and leadership are extremely crucial for any e-government initiatives to be successful. An e-government office was established in the Ministry of Finance to champion the Singapore Public Service's efforts in embracing e-government. It works closely with the

Government Chief Information Office in the Infocomm Development Authority of Singapore, which provides the technical expertise and advice in the management and implementation of the various e-government programmes.

The e-Government Policy Committee provides strategic directions for e-government and oversees the implementation of the e-Government Action Plan. It is chaired by the Head of Civil Service and comprises of Permanent Secretaries from selected Ministries. The committee is assisted by the Public Service Infocomm Steering Committee, comprised of Chief Information Officers from selected Ministries.

The Permanent Secretaries of Ministries and Chief Executive Officers of Statutory Boards are responsible for the ICT infrastructure and services within their own organisations. Assisted by their Chief Information Officers, they are also expected to align their ICT policies, standards and systems with their business needs as well as the central directions. Service-wide ICT policies are published in the Government Instruction Manual to ensure promulgation and compliance by all public sector agencies.

FUTURE OPPORTUNITIES

Putting all feasible existing services online using the latest ICT tools is costly. In the past, determining the benefits versus costs for any e-government programme is relatively straight-forward as the benefits arising from efficiencies tend to be quantifiable. As Singapore progresses towards the leading edge of e-government implementations, attempts to quantify the benefits of online service delivery and match the development and operational cost to any incremental revenue are becoming challenging. As Singapore raises the standard of service, it also shapes the expectations of its end users. With the younger generation of its citizens more exposed to higher levels of service, Singapore's challenge will be to stay ahead or at least keep up with the growing expectations.

There are also challenges that concern the social fabric and personal desire for privacy and space. The government will continue with its effort to help those who are not IT-literate to benefit from the investment. In addition, the government is mindful of the needs of the public for greater protection and transparency in the management of personal information within and beyond the government.

Looking forward, Singapore sees two key areas as opportunities for future management focus and investment to yield greater value out of the e-government initiative. The two areas are:

a. *Pushing e-services up the maturity curve to provide accessible quality public services.*

   Singapore continues to review the current suite of online services and the needs of the public to identify opportunities for service innovation that will yield greater value for the government and public. Service innovation can come from integration of existing cross-agency related services, streamlining of existing processes and collaboration with private and other nongovernment organisations to invent new services. The use of Customer Relationship Management (CRM) techniques in e-services implementation will be useful to gain insight into user behaviour and needs and to shape services centred on customer needs.

b. *Building capacity for mass engagement of the citizenry through e-governance.*

   The challenge for government is not only to delight the public as customers but also to connect with the public as citizens. The emergence of new technologies offers possibilities of wide interaction with citizens in a way not possible before. Used correctly, e-governance tools can improve the quality of public decisions, enhance citizens' understanding of public policy issues, and build stronger state-society relations. Just as Singapore has identified several levels of e-services maturity, it has developed a corresponding framework for e-governance maturity:

   i. *Describe:* One-way; agency informs citizens of its public policies;
   ii. *Explain:* Two-way; agency explains the reasons for, and objectives of its public policies, and responds to queries and feedback from citizens;
   iii. *Consult:* Two-way; agency seeks views from citizens in the course of developing public policies, both in single agency consultation as well as multi-agency consultation where appropriate; and
   iv. *Connect:* Two-way; agency fosters a network of citizens who proactively offer views and suggestions, and help explain public policies to others.

Moving forward, the Singapore government will focus on establishing basic levels of e-governance and working its way up to establish greater consultation and citizen participation.

CONCLUSION

The current e-government strategies have served the Singapore government well. E-government is an ongoing series of action steps that constantly evolves the current set of services framework. Moving forward, Singapore's direction is to continue to build on the foundation laid by the current Action Plan and leverage on the use of ICT to provide quality accessible public services and to engage its citizens as stakeholders. Singapore's major challenge will be to constantly innovate with ICT and deliver the services expected by its citizens. In the past, it was relatively easy to define the services to be delivered electronically as there were models on which those services could be based. In the future, it will be more challenging as Singapore moves into the forefront of governments in the world in e-government excellence, and it has to lead in the innovation of ICT-based services to its citizens.

NOTE

Prepared by The Infocomm Development Authority of Singapore and The Singapore Ministry of Finance.

CANADA

The Dual Challenge
of Integration and Inclusion:
Canada's Experience
with Government Online

Michelle d'Auray

Government of Canada

SUMMARY. The Government of Canada is leveraging the potential of the Internet and related technologies to offer Canadians user-centered, integrated services when and where they want them, no matter how they choose to access them (online, telephone, mail, in-person). The article

Michelle d'Auray was appointed Chief Information Officer (CIO) for the Government of Canada in September 2000. In that capacity, she is responsible for assuring the sound management of the government's Information Management and Information Technology assets, leading and coordinating the Government On-Line and Service Improvement Initiatives, and exercising functional leadership of the government's IM and IT professionals.

[Haworth co-indexing entry note]: "The Dual Challenge of Integration and Inclusion: Canada's Experience with Government Online." d'Auray, Michelle. Co-published simultaneously in *Journal of Political Marketing* (The Haworth Press, Inc.) Vol. 2, No. 3/4, 2003, pp. 31-49; and: *The World of E-Government* (ed: Gregory G. Curtin, Michael H. Sommer, and Veronika Vis-Sommer) The Haworth Press, Inc., 2003, pp. 31-49. Single or multiple copies of this article are available for a fee from The Haworth Document Delivery Service [1-800-HAWORTH, 9:00 a.m. - 5:00 p.m. (EST). E-mail address: docdelivery@haworthpress.com].

provides insight into the Government of Canada's use of a "whole of government approach" to address the challenges entailed in ensuring that users' needs drive the service delivery agenda. It discusses the key enablers of service transformation, including information management, privacy, security, interoperability and performance measurement. *[Article copies available for a fee from The Haworth Document Delivery Service: 1-800-HAWORTH. E-mail address: <docdelivery@haworthpress.com> Website: <http://www.HaworthPress.com> © 2003 by The Haworth Press, Inc. All rights reserved.]*

KEYWORDS. E-government, Government of Canada, Internet, government online

The tempo of life in our knowledge-based economy and society means that more than ever, Canadians expect to be able to interact with their government with ease. They want convenient, accurate, one-stop service access–they don't want to have to know which department or agency is responsible for what to access what they're entitled to, to fulfill their reporting and remittance obligations or to get the information they need to make important decisions for themselves and their families. They don't want to have to enter the same data over and over again when they deal with their governments. For example, a large percentage of Internet users–75%–agree that they should be able to apply for programs and services from different departments by having to visit only *one* Government of Canada Web site (Ekos 2001).

In tandem with more easily accessible and effective government services, Canadians are also very interested in "e-engagement" or "e-democracy" in its broadest sense. Among the top five priorities for online "services" from government in 2001 were: registering an opinion, participating in a survey and voting in an election (Communication Canada 2001). A more recent consultation exercise with Canadian Internet users showed that they want to use the e-channel to contact their elected officials directly. This expectation is third in their list of priorities after the ability to conduct tax transactions and access health information (Ipsos Reid 2002).

The Government of Canada is committed to e-government that delivers on both counts: It is committed to putting its services online by 2005 and to a 10% improvement in client satisfaction with services by 2005. Canada is a sparsely populated country of 30 million people with two official languages (English and French) spread over nearly 10-million square kilometres and encompassing six time zones. The Internet allows us to bridge the challenges of time and distance, and enables our diverse society to forge a stronger sense of connection both between and among its members and with its governments. The vision guiding the Government of Canada's e-government efforts is to use the e-channel and the technologies associated with it to enhance Canadians' access to improved user-centered, integrated services, anytime, anywhere in the official language of their choice. To implement this vision, we are pursuing a "whole of government" approach that puts the individual or business first, and that directly engages Canadians in a process of continuous service improvement to deliver what they need and want. We have learned that fulfilling this vision demands unprecedented "back end" integration and horizontal management across the full spectrum of what government does. It also means forging a stronger relationship between the citizens of Canada and their government ensuring a high level of transparency and responsiveness.

CANADIANS ARE AMONG THE WORLD'S MOST SOPHISTICATED USERS OF ONLINE TECHNOLOGY

Canadians' expectations for their governments' use of the Internet are rooted in their own experience with the technology. According to recent surveys, 68% of Canadians and 71% of businesses are now connected; average hours online per week climbed to 9.2 in 2001 from 8.8 in 2000; and, among households that are online, high-speed broadband connectivity is climbing, reaching 13% in 2001 from 8% the year before (Ekos 2001).

The Goldfarb report, a national annual study of Canadian socio-political-economic views and attitudes, and also provides insight into Canadians' use of the Internet. According to this research, nonwork-related use of the Internet is increasing, and surfing the net followed by games, word-processing and e-mail are the most frequently mentioned of these usages. Online purchasing continues to grow. Twenty-six percent of Canadians said they have shopped online in the past, up from 21% in 2001 (Goldfarb 2002). The most popular online commercial activities among Canadian Internet users are banking and paying bills, with this type of usage growing from 25% of Internet users in 1999 to 46% in 2002 (Goldfarb 2002). Finally, Canadians' use of the Internet to obtain information from their governments has also risen steadily in recent years, with 62% of Canadians (up from 53% in 1999) reporting this as one of the main online activities in which they engage. This activity ranked 12th among the 27 tested in the study (Goldfarb 2002).

"Information overload" is frequently mentioned as a consequence of the increasing role of the Internet in Canadian society. The 2002 issue of the Goldfarb report suggests that this may be a myth.

The study hints at the literacy effects of new technologies and the "editing skills" that Canadian Internet users are rapidly developing:

> With so much information coming at consumers from so many different sources, it is not surprising that some have suggested Canadians are suffering from "information overload." This does not appear to be the case yet, as Canadians are actually demonstrating a desire for *more* information, whether it be surfing the Internet for product details or gravitating toward news programming on television. We have learned how to efficiently edit out information that we feel is irrelevant to us, and change channels, delete e-mails or throw out bulk mail without a second thought. (Goldfarb 2002)

As millions of Canadians become more sophisticated and discerning users of Internet technology, others–the more than 30% who are not online–may well be falling further behind. While demographic differences such as gender and age are steadily becoming less of a factor in who is connected, household income remains a strong indicator of connectivity. Twice as many Canadians in the $60,000 or more income bracket are connected compared to Canadians with household incomes of $30,000 or less (Goldfarb 2002).

Many of the transactional services that the Government of Canada plans to make available online by 2005 provide assistance to low-income households, or count low-income Canadians among their heaviest users.

To help to bridge the "digital divide" the Government of Canada recognizes that it must make its online services attractive, accessible and intuitive to low-income Canadians. To support this initiative the government is modernizing its entire service delivery network and provides assisted Internet access at its in-person service sites (including some 8,000 community-based public Internet access points). But as it works to achieve a high degree of usability for novice users, it will also be challenged to meet the demands of experienced Internet users, particularly youth and small businesses, who will be looking for rich, multimedia service offerings and increasingly sophisticated "one-stop" interfaces.

THE GOVERNMENT OF CANADA'S
USER-CENTERED, WHOLE OF GOVERNMENT APPROACH

The e-channel offers enormous potential to drive major advances towards customized service delivery that meets the unique needs, expectations and capabilities of each and every individual and business. But, the point is not to simply add another channel to other modes of service provision (e.g., telephone, mail and in-person). This would be neither sustainable because of the added costs of establishing and maintaining parallel service delivery systems, nor likely to fully exploit the enormous potential of the e-channel to support efficient, reliable, and responsive services *across all channels.*

For users, there are important inherent benefits from accessing services online, including increased convenience and timeliness. These benefits will be multiplied as the government leverages the e-channel to create a service delivery infrastructure that becomes more effective, responsive and cost-efficient by providing comparable and complementary, high quality services across all channels (i.e., telephone, mail, in-person and over the Internet).

Since the launch of the Government On-Line in 1999, the Government of Canada has been steadily increasing its use of the Internet to interact with its citizens, including information provision, online consultations, and more recently, "real time" transactional services. Our progress has been recognized by a number of NGO and private sector analysts, including *Accenture*, an international management and technology services consultancy, which for the second year in a row has given Canada top marks of 23 countries for leadership in e-government. (Accenture, 2002)

The Government of Canada is committed to moving forward at a pace and in a fashion that maximizes the inherent transformative potential of the e-channel, meeting the expectations of those who want to conduct business with their government electronically *without disadvantaging* those Canadians who are unwilling or not yet equipped to use Internet services. This inclusive approach is viewed as the best way to strengthen the government's relationship with all its citizens through enhanced services and active engagement.

For example, there are a number of income benefit programs that are undersubscribed because some of the Canadians who would otherwise qualify simply don't know about them and/or are unable to apply. One of more than 50 Government On-Line funded projects is looking at how to use taxpayer data to automatically identify individuals who are eligible for Old Age Security benefits, obviating the need for them to apply directly and substantially increasing the likelihood that these benefits will reach everyone who needs them.

The ultimate goal is to use technology to strengthen Canada's economy and society; reduce the cost and the burden of government processes and transactions; encourage innovation with government as a strategic procurer and model user of new technologies; and, optimize the effective and efficient delivery of government programs and services.

ENHANCING ACCESS AND IMPROVING THE FUNCTIONALITY OF ONLINE SERVICES

The Government of Canada's Five-Part Government On-Line/Service Improvement Workplan

- *Service transformation and multi-channel integration:* Pursuing a user-centered approach to electronic, in-person, mail and telephone service delivery, driven by user priorities and expectations;
- *Common, secure infrastructure:* Building an enterprise-wide electronic service platform that enables integrated services and supports secure Internet, telephone, mail and in-person access;
- *Policy and standards frameworks:* Addressing information management, privacy and security to build confidence in e-services and link service transformation to client satisfaction;
- *Communications and measurement:* Encouraging use of electronic service options in sync with the government's capacity to deliver high quality services, while providing choice of channel; measuring progress according to a comprehensive framework; and
- *Human resources:* Developing the necessary skills in the government's workforce to adapt to change and operate effectively as a provider of user-centered services in a technology enabled, integrated, multi-channel environment.

One of the first Government On-Line achievements was the redesign and launch of the Government of Canada's main Internet portal in February 2001. Since then, the new Canada Site, originally created in 1995, has become a single window to all government programs and services, and its functionality is continuously enhanced (*www.canada.gc.ca*).

The portal organizes information and services under three "gateways" according to the government's three main client groups: individual Canadians, Canadian businesses and international users. The Canada Site has become the *de facto* platform for integrated online service delivery providing access to the full range of programs and services offered by all federal departments and agencies, and in some cases by other levels of government as well (Figure 1).

The Services for Canadians Gateway allows users to access a wealth of information to help them lead their everyday lives. The gateway is organized in an audience-based structure reflecting common client groups such as Aboriginal peoples, children, persons with disabilities and youth. Programs and services are also organized under a dozen sub-

FIGURE 1. Canada Site Homepage

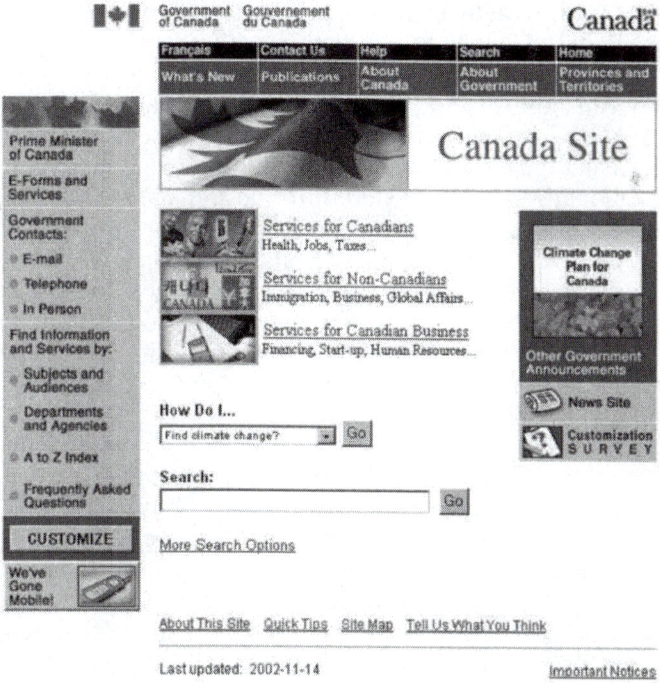

ject-based clusters representing key topics of interest such as consumer information, health information, and public safety (Figure 2).

The Service for Canadian Business Gateway provides information that covers a company's entire life cycle from start-up through wind-down. The gateway has recently been expanded so that entrepreneurs have one-stop access to business support programs offered by provincial and territorial governments, as well as the Government of Canada (Figure 3).

The Services for Non-Canadians (or international users) gateway provides one-stop access to all information and services on investing in Canada, immigrating to Canada and visiting our country and offers navigational information in four additional languages: Spanish, German, Portuguese and Chinese (Figure 4).

Through the Government On-Line initiative, central investments have also been made to assist departments and agencies in providing transactional services online. For example, for the third year running Canadians have had the option of filing their personal income taxes online (2.3 million Canadians or 16% of tax filers used the Netfile service in 2002). Businesses can now file their annual reports on tax withheld at source over the Internet, and a pilot project is underway to allow corporations resident in Canada to file their tax returns online.

Investments to enhance functionality and improve access mean that Canadians can now file for unemployment insurance benefits online and receive other employment information and services at the same time. They can register with the Canadian Food Inspection Agency and receive personalized allergy alert information on food products via e-mail. New online tools enable Canadians to file consumer complaints and direct them to the appropriate regulatory agency and business involved; to post their résumés and receive e-mail notification when job postings matching their search criteria become available; and to calculate their federally provided pension income benefits to help them plan for retirement. The government has also begun to develop an online portal that will allow Canadians to participate in the policy-making process. This pilot portal will provide Canadians with single window access to all Government of Canada consultation and citizen engagement opportunities (both online and offline).

More recently, progress towards supporting secure "end to end" online services that involve the exchange of personal information took a major step forward in September 2002 with the introduction of *epass*. *Epass* is one of the world's first Public Key Infrastructure digital signature services for mass use by individuals, enabling Internet users to exchange information securely and confidentially. Each *epass* is unique,

FIGURE 2. Services for Canadians Gateway

E-Forms and Services

Government Contacts:
- E-mail
- Telephone
- In Person

Find Information and Services by:
- Subjects and Audiences
- Departments and Agencies
- A to Z Index
- Frequently Asked Questions

CUSTOMIZE

Customization SURVEY

Subjects:

Canada and the World
foreign policy, security, aid...

Consumer Information
recalls, safety, complaints...

Culture, Heritage and Recreation
arts, Canadians, sports...

Economy
government's role, statistics, analysis...

Environment, Natural Resources,
Fisheries and Agriculture
air, water, climate change...

Financial Benefits
unemployment, pensions, loans...

Health
wellness, prevention, promotion...

Identification Cards
health card, passport, SIN card...

Jobs, Workers, Training and Careers
employment, learning, workplace...

Justice and the Law
laws, courts, rights...

Public Safety
at home, at work, in your community...

Rural and Remote Services
communities, resources, communication...

Science and Technology
research, funding, institutions...

Taxes
filing, benefits, e-services...

Travel at Home and Abroad
planning, security, passports...

Audiences:

Aboriginal Peoples
culture, resources, health...

Canadian Business
Financing, Start-up, Human
Resources...

Canadians Living Abroad
working, studying, retiring...

Children
parenting, health, learning...

Newcomers to Canada
adapting, working, citizenship...

Non-Canadians
immigration, business, global affairs...

Persons with Disabilities
accessibility, health, aid...

Seniors
benefits, health, care...

Youth
jobs, health, culture...

Search:

Go

More Search Options

About This Site   Quick Tips   Site Map   Tell Us What You Think

Last updated: 2002-10-25   Important Notices

FIGURE 3. Services for Canadian Business Gateway

and is used to authenticate the client and digitally sign documents. The Canada Customs and Revenue Agency is piloting *epass* now with its Address Change Online service, which allows Canadians to input their new address once and avoid having to separately inform the tax and benefits programs administered by the Agency. As more transactional services become available, the Government of Canada intends to make it possible for both individuals and businesses to use their *epass* to access multiple programs and services.

The Government of Canada has made remarkable progress in developing an e-channel that improves citizen access and use of the programs

FIGURE 4. Services for Non-Canadians Gateway

available to them, and in providing "real-time" electronic options for a number of key transactions. Meanwhile, every year since the launch of the Government On-Line initiative the Canadian public's overall rating of the quality of the service or information they receive from their federal government has risen steadily, from 59% saying "good" in 1999, to 67% in 2002 (Communication Canada 2002).

MOVING FROM THE WILD FRONTIER TO THE TOWN PLAN

The Government of Canada is now poised to move to the "next level" shifting from information and services that are grouped together, to those that fit and work together. To achieve this goal, there must be a much more sophisticated horizontal or cross-government governance structure and a higher level of integration at the back end. This involves government-wide business process modeling and development as well as designing and building common information systems and a shared information technology infrastructure. These strategies are advancing user-centered service delivery and are starting to make it possible for multiple real-time transactions across different departments and agencies during the same user session. This involves a significant culture change for the government at every level–one in which territoriality must give way to consultation, collaboration and partnership, and where clear political and senior management accountabilities for government-wide targets will be crucial.

By way of metaphor, the Government of Canada is at the point where the "wild frontier" of online services must begin to make way for a more rational, planned approach to multi-channel, seamless and complementary service delivery. The frontier community is quickly becoming a densely populated town. In response, there is a need to develop a town plan, and appoint a town planner and council to ensure that, as development continues and accelerates, common infrastructure needs are identified and built in a timely fashion. Furthermore, the overall pace and nature of development must be sustainable without exceeding the ability of the tax base to support it. Over the past year, changes have been made in the Government On-Line governance structure to promote the shift towards a broader multi-channel service vision and pave the way for long-term governance of a more integrated service delivery agenda. An interdepartmental committee structure has been established to oversee and provide strategic direction to the Government On-Line/Service Improvement initiative. Senior level governance committees have been created to focus on business process reengineering of program delivery across service channels and departments, while others concentrate on information management and policy issues around multi-channel service delivery.

Over the past year, policy frameworks have been developed in the critical areas of privacy, security, and information management, all of which contribute to building the foundation for more sophisticated online, interactive services, and ensure that Canadians can use them with trust and confidence. To ensure privacy protection is built into the development or redesign of services, the Privacy Impact Assessments policy was adopted in May 2002 (*www.cio-dpi.gc.ca/pgol-pged/pia-efvp/pia-efvp_e.asp*). This policy requires that a Privacy Impact Assessment be conducted for the design or redesign of programs and services that may involve the increased collection, use or disclosure of personal in-

formation, the broadening of client populations, a shift from direct to indirect collection of personal information, and new data matching or
increased reuse or sharing of personal information. Privacy Impact Assessments are intended to promote fully informed policy, program and
system design choices. They assist managers and decision-makers in
avoiding or mitigating privacy risks, as well as ensure that the informed
consent of individuals is obtained concerning how information about
them is used. Recognizing that transparency promotes confidence and
trust, summaries of the assessments are also required to be made publicly available. The Government Security Policy was also overhauled
and issued in February 2002, along with a requirement for new, internationally based information technology security standards.

Improving the state of information management, particularly the
quality of information upon which service managers rely, is also a key
priority in preparing for more integrated service delivery. The existing
information management policy has been significantly updated so that
departments and agencies can better align their needs with modern business delivery requirements, including those associated with providing
integrated, user-centered services. To support the successful implementation of the policy, a Framework for the Management of Information in
the Government of Canada provides practical guidance, and sets out the
principles, standards and guidelines needed to support electronic service delivery in an electronically enabled environment. The Dublin
Core metadata standard has been adopted, and guidelines and controlled
vocabularies are being developed for specific elements, including description, type, format, coverage and audience. The Framework will include content management tools and further metadata standards to
facilitate information access, retrieval, preservation and sharing across
departments and agencies. The Framework will also include guidelines
for the long-term management of electronic records, including encrypted and digitally signed documents. A Web-based information
management resource centre has been established for Government of
Canada employees and business managers at all levels to provide a single point of access to tools, guidelines, standards, case studies and best
practices (*www.cio-dpi.gc.ca/im-gi/index_e.asp*).

Ensuring employees have the requisite knowledge, expertise, skills
and competencies to deliver services in an integrated, user-centered,
multi-channel environment is another critical priority. Strategies for
change in human resources are being developed to support communities
of practice in information technology, information management and
service delivery across federal departments and agencies. The focus is

on capacity building, recruitment, retention and reskilling. (*www. cio-dpi.gc.ca/oro-bgc/index_e.asp*).

The last and arguably most pivotal requirement in preparing for integrated, multi-channel service improvement is interoperability. While governance, policy and human resource frameworks are all critical, they fall flat if the information management and technology systems across departments and agencies fail to enable integration. To achieve this, the Government of Canada is developing a horizontal, cross-government enterprise architecture called the Federated Architecture, which will generate the guidelines and standards for the information technology infrastructure to make systems interoperable across departments and agencies. It is comprised of three "sub-architectures": a technical architecture for interoperable technology systems and processes that protect privacy and strengthen the security of the government's technology infrastructure; an information architecture to facilitate the exchange of information between and among programs to add value and support more intelligent business operations; and a business architecture, to enable programs to be interoperable and to facilitate the reuse of processes and components to support more efficient operations and service delivery. The next iteration of the Federated Architecture will focus on the government's key business processes that can be supported by common and shared technology infrastructure to deliver a higher level of technology and business integration and support customized service delivery.

MAINTAINING MOMENTUM THROUGH ONGOING CONSULTATION AND FEEDBACK

While the Government of Canada focuses on integration at the back end, inclusiveness at the front end has become a fundamental principle guiding service transformation. All online service development and improvement projects involve ongoing consultation with client groups. This approach ensures change is implemented in an iterative fashion, which takes user needs into account every step of the way.

Extensive consultations with Canadians were undertaken to develop the Government of Canada's Common Look and Feel standards, to ensure that all Canadians, regardless of their Internet ability, geographic location or demographic representation have equal access to information and services on Government of Canada Web sites. Thirty-three (33) standards were approved in May 2000. These standards are intended to ensure outcomes such as federal Web sites that accommodate assistive technologies, including text readers and voice activated devices; a clear online federal identity so that Canadians know they are dealing with the Government of Canada; standardized and timely responses to e-mail enquiries; logical and consistent navigational formats; and compliance with all relevant policies of Canada's *Official Languages Act.*

In-depth one-on-one interviews and 20 focus groups in six Canadian centers were held late last year to review the Government of Canada's approach to organizing services by user group, subject and life event, and to identify opportunities for improvements to federal Web sites. Participants validated the approach, agreeing that using several organizing principles supports a "no wrong door" navigation policy, and satisfies the variety of different search strategies that individuals would likely employ. They also made a wide range of suggestions to improve presentation, information "retrievability," personalization and functionality that are currently being implemented (Phase 5 2002).

A total of 4,547 Internet users recently participated as panelists in an online survey and discussion on the Government of Canada's e-services. They generally supported the government's approach and endorsed the goal of putting all government services online and identified areas for improvement such as clarifying navigational instructions, ensuring uniform functionality across Web sites and facilitating direct access to specialists in the public service and their elected representatives (Ipsos Reid 2002). This online panel will be used throughout the remainder of the Government On-Line/Service Improvement initiative to shape and change the online service offerings and their convergence with telephony and in-person services.

IDENTIFYING AND ADDRESSING CITIZENS' PREFERENCES TO ASSURE QUALITY, UTILITY AND SECURITY

Future success depends on staying in sync with the constantly changing expectations and preferences of Canadians. In pursuing a multichannel service modernization agenda, a key factor is the need to move forward at a pace that will ensure Canadians' service expectations of service quality are met. Despite the proliferation of Internet service options and Canadians' increasing use of and reliance on them, service quality still correlates strongly with personal service. For example, while 80% of Canadians feel that computerization either improves or does not affect the quality of products, 50% of Canadians feel that it *decreases* the quality of services (Goldfarb 2002). Human contact matters. The government will need to differentiate carefully between the types and complexity of transactions that can be accessed using a "self-service" approach online and the ones where service satisfaction demands the personal touch. This will be critical to maintaining public support for and confidence in the government's use of technology as well as improving the public's perception of the quality of government services in general.

Equally important is the utility of online service offerings. A recent examination of the factors that have caused some Internet users to "drop out" revealed that 30% of some 232,500 Canadian households that had used the Internet in a typical month but no longer did, reported that they had "no need" of the Internet. Another 17% said they dropped out because it was too expensive. Internet "dropouts" are more likely to be relatively recent users who are less experienced with newer technologies and applications, such as word processing, game playing and data entry. The study suggests that "new" users of the Internet either become frequent users as they gain more experience, or drop out depending on how useful they find it. As the Government of Canada moves to broaden its online service offerings, and, for example, concentrate on older Canadians who tend to be heavier users of many of its programs and services, it will need to ensure that e-service offerings are as intuitive and easy to use as possible. Furthermore, there must be evidence that they will deliver real, immediate and meaningful benefits to keep these newer and less confident Internet users online and engaged (Crompton, Ellison and Stevenson 2002).

Finally, nearly three-quarters of Canadians continue to see electronic records of financial and personal information as a major threat to personal privacy and a somewhat smaller percentage (65%) are concerned about privacy and security related to e-mail and the Internet. The highest level of discomfort at present is around the use of credit cards for online transactions, with 81% of Canadians expressing concern about the security of these transactions. Overall, however, concerns about Internet security and privacy are diminishing as Canadians become more familiar users of the technology (Goldfarb 2002). The percentage reporting they are very concerned has fallen from 31% in 2000 to 26% in 2002, while the proportion reporting they are not very concerned has risen from 20% to 25% (Goldfarb 2002). In this critical area, there is evidence that the Government of Canada has been successful in building trust and confidence around its online services. In 2001, 57% of Canadians agreed that the government wouldn't offer transactions over the Internet unless it was safe to do so, up from 49% the year before (Ekos 2001). Measuring progress on the Government On-Line/Service Improvement initiative in terms of client satisfaction will be critical to provide the assurance Canadians are looking for in terms of the security of their personal information, and to keep abreast of their expectations in terms of quality and usability. Concerted, government-wide efforts to gauge and assess client satisfaction, and determine client preferences, will be essential to encourage take-up of e-services and sustain their use, as well as to demonstrate the value of our investments in service transformation and ensure that departments and agencies realize gains from the efforts they undertake.

Over the past year, the Government of Canada has developed a performance measurement framework for service improvement, which encompasses three main outcomes–citizen/user-centered government; better more responsive service; and, capacity for online service delivery. For each one of these outcomes, specific indicators have been developed (Table 1).

Work is now underway to develop performance measures for these indicators, including a Common Measurements Tool to be utilized by departments and agencies for collecting client satisfaction information across all delivery channels. Standardizing the way that departments and agencies collect this information will support the development of a common, government-wide understanding of citizens' evolving service needs and expectations. This will, in turn, enable the prioritization and timing of improvements to user-centered integrated services, and support consensus on priority areas for further investment. The first version of the Common Measurements Tool is available online through the Institute for Citizen-Centered Services, an intergovernmental research

TABLE 1. Performance Measurement Indicators by Outcome

Citizen/client-centred government	Better, more responsive service	Capacity for online delivery
▪ Convenience	▪ Critical mass of services	▪ Security
▪ Accessibility	▪ Take-up	▪ Privacy
▪ Credibility	▪ Service transformation	▪ Efficiency
	▪ Citizen/client satisfaction	▪ Innovation

body dedicated to promoting excellence in public sector services and delivery channels (*www.iccs-isac.org*).

CONCLUSION

The Government of Canada still has a long way to go to achieve the integration of business processes, information systems and technology that will be needed to fully deliver its multi-channel service vision. However, consistent with the principle of inclusion, these efforts are driven by a strong commitment to client-centricity and engaging Canadians as direct participants in the service transformation and improvement process, and in shaping the policies that drive it. Ultimately, understanding patterns of use and how citizens and clients respond will be critical to building and sustaining trust and confidence in the government's use of the e-channel. Success will depend on moving from serving the early adopters of new technologies, who are relatively easy to engage, to harnessing the full potential of the e-channel to better meet the needs of the entire population so that all Canadians benefit from their government's investments in service transformation no matter how they choose to interact with their government.

REFERENCES

Ekos Research Associates Inc. (2001) Rethinking the Information Highway: Preliminary Results. Ottawa. Vol. 1, pp. 127-128.

Canada Information Office (now, Communication Canada). (2001) Listening to Canadians: Communications Survey. Ottawa. Spring, pp. 48.

Ipsos Reid Corporation. (2002) On-Line Research for the Government On-Line Initiative. (Commissioned by Treasury Board of Canada). Ottawa. Pp. 61.

Ekos Research Associates Inc. (2001) Rethinking the Information Highway: Preliminary Results. Ottawa. Vol. 1, pp. 19.

Millward Brown Goldfarb. (2002) The Goldfarb Report 2002. Goldfarb Consultants Ltd. Toronto. Vol. 2, Book 8, pp. 37.

Millward Brown Goldfarb. (2002) The Goldfarb Report 2002. Goldfarb Consultants Ltd. Toronto. Vol. 2, Book 8, pp. 44.

Millward Brown Goldfarb. (2002) The Goldfarb Report 2002. Goldfarb Consultants Ltd. Toronto. Vol. 2, Book 8, pp. 23.

Millward Brown Goldfarb. (2002) The Goldfarb Report 2002. Goldfarb Consultants Ltd. Toronto. Vol. 1, pp. xiv.

Millward Brown Goldfarb. (2002) The Goldfarb Report 2002. Goldfarb Consultants Ltd. Toronto. Vol. 2, Book 8, pp. 18.

Accenture (2002) E-Government Leadership–Realizing the Vision. Accenture, pp. 44.

Canada Information Office (now, Communication Canada). (2002) Listening to Canadians: Communications Survey. Ottawa. Spring, pp. 31.

Phase 5. (2002) E-Cluster Blue Print Validation Study. (Commissioned by Treasury Board of Canada) Ottawa. Pp. 47-48.

Ipsos Reid Corporation. (2002) On-Line Research for the Government On-Line Initiative. (Commissioned by Treasury Board of Canada). Ottawa. Pp. 61.

Millward Brown Goldfarb. (2002) The Goldfarb Report 2002. Goldfarb Consultants Ltd. Toronto. Vol. 2, Book 8, pp. 35.

Crompton, Susan, Jonathan Ellison and Kathryn Stevenson. (2002) "Better things to do or dealt out of the game? Internet dropouts and infrequent users," *Canadian Social Trends*, Summer 2002. Statistics Canada, Ottawa. Catalogue No. 11-008.

Millward Brown Goldfarb. (2002) The Goldfarb Report 2002. Goldfarb Consultants Ltd. Toronto. Vol. 1, pp. 69.

Millward Brown Goldfarb. (2002) The Goldfarb Report 2002. Goldfarb Consultants Ltd. Toronto. Vol. 2, Book 8, pp. 25.

Ekos Research Associates Inc. (2001) Rethinking the Information Highway: Preliminary Results. Ottawa. Vol. 1, pp. 113.

AMERICA

Creating a Blueprint for E-Government

Patricia McGinnis

Council for Excellence in Government

SUMMARY. In 2001 the nonprofit Council for Excellence in Government published *E-Government: The Next American Revolution*, a vision of what full electronic government in America could accomplish and a blueprint of how to get there. It was the product of an unprecedented collaboration, led by the Council, among 350 information technology experts in business, government, research, and the nonprofit sector nationwide. Recognizing e-government's considerable potential, these professionals were excited by the opportunity to suggest its design and help make it a reality. Administration actions and legislative proposals on e-government in several ways reflect the blue-

Patricia McGinnis is President and Chief Executive Officer of the Council for Excellence in Government, a nonpartisan, nonprofit organization headquartered in Washington, DC.

[Haworth co-indexing entry note]: "Creating a Blueprint for E-Government." McGinnis, Patricia. Co-published simultaneously in *Journal of Political Marketing* (The Haworth Press, Inc.) Vol. 2, No. 3/4, 2003, pp. 51-63; and: *The World of E-Government* (ed: Gregory G. Curtin, Michael H. Sommer, and Veronika Vis-Sommer) The Haworth Press, Inc., 2003, pp. 51-63. Single or multiple copies of this article are available for a fee from The Haworth Document Delivery Service [1-800-HAWORTH, 9:00 a.m. - 5:00 p.m. (EST). E-mail address: docdelivery@haworthpress.com].

10.1300/J199v02n03_04

print's recommendations. This is the story of the initiative and what it achieved. *[Article copies available for a fee from The Haworth Document Delivery Service: 1-800-HAWORTH. E-mail address: <docdelivery@haworthpress.com> Website: <http://www.HaworthPress.com> © 2003 by The Haworth Press, Inc. All rights reserved.]*

KEYWORDS. Electronic government, blueprint, collaborative effort, business, government, research, nonprofit, e-government benefits

Electronic government promises more than fast, accurate transactions and delivery of information and services in the government-to-citizen, government-to-business, and government-to-government modes. E-government also contains the seeds of an even higher value: the greater health and better practice of democracy.

In early 2001, the nonpartisan Council for Excellence in Government published a vision of what fully achieved e-government in the United States could accomplish, what it should look like, and how to get there. Its title was *E-Government: The Next American Revolution.* We at the Council called it a blueprint. It set out guiding principles to help frame choices and actions, plus recommendations in the areas of leadership, strategic investment, collaboration between government and business, an adequate and well-trained work force, privacy, security, interoperability, access, and education.

The 15-page publication (including results of a national public opinion poll on the subject, commissioned by the Council and conducted by bipartisan opinion specialists Peter Hart and Robert Teeter) gained immediate attention from the new Bush Administration and the Congress, as well as increasing notice in the information technology community in and outside the United States.

The story of this initiative–its conception and production, what it proposed, and its impact on the Congress and the Administration–is the subject of this article. It's a story well worth recounting.

TODAY'S REALITIES

Note first, however, that it is still quite early in the era of e-government. Federal law calls for maximum achievement of electronic information and service delivery in all agencies by 2003. But tough issues remain to be resolved. Despite abundant evidence of Web-based technology's impact across the economy and the research community, in law, medicine, and education, and in the private lives of Americans everywhere, government today lags behind other sectors of this country in its capacity to play in this league.

One reason for that is simply the huge amount of information that American government at all levels must generate, update, and manage, often without standardized technology and classification systems that would make information easier to exchange and share. Another plain fact is the difficulty of moving online an organization of government's size and complexity, not to mention a customer base that dwarfs those of the largest multinational corporations.

There are many other reasons. The lack of standardization and information sharing forces government's customers to supply personal information repeatedly while bouncing from one agency to another to get service. And only a small part of government's information and services database can be easily searched because no standardized classification of information and services exists. For the most part, information is organized by agency or service title, not by the needs that bring customers to government for answers or help.

Despite this, Americans are embracing technology to facilitate their interaction with government wherever government makes it possible to do so. They are using government Web sites and see a strong role for e-government, for example, in enhanced homeland security. The Council's most recent Hart/Teeter national poll on e-government, released in February 2002, made these and other points abundantly clear. Americans and leaders in American government are giving significant attention to e-government's potential and the urgency they feel about the strategic leadership and adequate investment to realize that potential. Electronic, online government is clearly moving into the mainstream of American life. Here are the poll's main findings:

- More than 78% believed that e-government would improve preparedness for national emergencies, and enhance homeland security by facilitating better coordination and data sharing.
- Most Internet users (76%) and over half of all (56%) Americans had visited a government Web site.
- Sixty-four percent expected e-government to have a positive effect on the way the government operates. Americans put a higher priority on investing tax dollars in making government services and information available over the Internet (37% vs. 30% a year earlier), and a large number (81%) expressed the desire that these invest-

ments be used to expand systems that help government protect public health and safety.

- Citizens remained concerned about security and privacy, especially identity theft and hackers getting access to information in government systems (65%); yet a large number of Americans (57%) said they were willing to give up some privacy if it strengthens homeland security.

- A large majority of the 400-plus government leaders (federal, state, and local) polled believed that e-government was having a positive effect on how government operates. Most (62%) wanted to proceed quickly to expand it.

E-GOVERNMENT'S PROMISE

In the United States, fully implemented e-government can break down bureaucratic barriers and move to a level of service, protection and connections that Americans want and need, not only for homeland security but in every aspect of the government's work.

It will mean that Americans interested in a regular, tangible role and voice in the process of governing will have that opportunity at their fingertips. An opportunity not just to transact business but to get extensive access to what government is doing and proposing to do, and why, and how.

That will enable more Americans than ever before to participate and exert real impact, in real time, on the course of government decisions and actions and the performance of their elected representatives. Many more people will have the opportunity to become permanent players in the process of shaping and making government work. The gaps so evident, in polls and other research, between what government is, what people think it is, and their belief in it would narrow.

In short, e-government can fundamentally recast the connection between citizens and government. It has the power to put ownership of government truly in the hands of the people. Put another way, government would come closer than ever to realizing the vision enshrined in Lincoln's words: an institution of the people, by the people, and for the people.

CREATING THE BLUEPRINT

The sweeping implications of information technology for efficient government performance and service delivery were apparent at least a dozen years ago. Recognizing this, the Council in 1997 established the

Intergovernmental Technology Leadership Consortium. This coalition sponsors and facilitates results-based projects across sectors and levels of government, serving also as a meeting place where public-sector information technology needs meet with a rich mix of ideas and solutions. Its goal is not just to improve government's service delivery but also to promote economic growth and–like certain other Council programs–to boost citizen participation in governance. (Today the consortium numbers 70-plus public, corporate, and nonprofit organizations, among them AT&T, Microsoft, Bank of America, Xerox, IBM, the Treasury Department's Financial Management Service, the Sustainable Development Extension Network, and the National Science Foundation.)

It was the Council's expanding association within the dynamic information technology sector that in 1999 helped set in motion the idea of a blueprint for e-government. The initiative began in November of that year with a symposium at the Smithsonian Institution, jointly hosted by Morley Winograd, director of then Vice President Al Gore's National Partnership for Reinventing Government, and me. Its participants were leaders and experts in electronic commerce and information technology from government, business, civic groups, and the research community. They came recognizing the urgency of creating a vision of e-government and genuinely excited by the idea of pioneering in the suggestion of its design and how to make it a reality.

Their discussion preceded by just a few days the announcement of closely related e-government objectives published by the White House on December 17, 1999, in presidential memoranda entitled *Electronic Government* and *The Use of Information Technology to Improve Our Society*. The first of those superseded an earlier memorandum (*Electronic Commerce*) and both gave the blueprint project a big push in the right direction.

No one thought that first gathering at the Smithsonian Institution would attract more than 30 people. But interest in the undertaking was already high. More than three times that many actually attended. "There was just a lot of buzz around it," in the words of one of our staff. It was, in fact, the start of a powerful public/private partnership.

The historic Smithsonian Institution was not the only fitting Washington venue for these four sessions. The group met in March 2000 at the Center for Innovative Technology, a futuristic structure in the heart of the Northern Virginia high-tech belt; in June at Decatur Hall, where ambition and influence marked its long history as home to distinguished American pioneers in government and other fields; and in September we unveiled our draft blueprint at the American Institute of Architects.

In these four meetings over ten months, the group concentrated its time on facilitated brainstorming and strategizing. The first questions to be answered were what e-government would look like, who should create it, who would pay for it, who would use it, and what its impact would be. In considering information technology's capacity to help create an e-government culture that crosses boundaries, moves fast, and is responsive to citizens and customers, the experts group also had to confront and navigate the web of complicated, interrelated issues involved.

Their first step was to identify the key agendas in bringing full e-government into existence. These were (1) the roles and responsibilities of the public and private organizations involved in e-government and how they should work together, (2) infrastructure, especially privacy and security, (3) innovation, and (4) the transformation of government, not just its automation. Next, the group broke into four working teams with the mission to develop detailed agendas in each of these areas and specify the necessary tasks called for. The goal in each case was to define where things stood at the time, what they should look like in the future, and how to get there.

The four groups–each with members who were a cross section of the entire group–then worked hard for several months to shape draft recommendations with Council staff, reconvening as a plenary meeting that heard presentations from each task group. At its fourth meeting, the entire group reviewed a first draft blueprint and suggested further refinement. Through the fall of 2000, the Council shaped the blueprint's final version. During their year-long effort, the experts group soon expanded to 150 as word of the undertaking spread and the Council reached out to strengthen and broaden their work. It then gradually grew further. At the end of its work, the group numbered about 350.

A central challenge in the latter stages of the process was to integrate the approaches and recommendations. The problem was not differences in ultimate objective so much as the inherently different nature of assigned tasks. On one hand, for example, there was highly technical material on such issues as privacy and security and implementation of the electronic signature; and on the other, analyses of what needed to be considered in functions like knowledge management. On another level, the work of the group brought to the surface the underlying tensions around certain gray areas where the environments of e-commerce and e-government intersect, requiring a case-by-case approach to distinguish the proper roles of each.

As published by the Council in February 2001, at the end of 15 remarkable and instructive months, the blueprint reflected and included the results of a national opinion poll on public views of e-government, commissioned by the Council and carried out six months earlier. That poll was fundamentally important to the entire blueprint process. We commissioned it to get a clear picture of how Americans saw e-government and what they expected of it, and we used the results as a key guide for designing the blueprint. The poll findings were the basis for several of the blueprint's recommendations.

Conducted by Peter Hart and Robert Teeter, the poll took place in August 2000. Even then, most Americans (73%) thought e-government should be a priority of the new president. Of four possible benefits of e-government suggested by the poll, the largest number of respondents (36%) said it was government that is more accountable to its citizens. Big majorities thought that e-government's impact would be positive and that investing in it should be a priority. Further, because of their current concerns about security and privacy, most Americans wanted e-government to be developed slowly. Sixty-five percent favored the appointment of an e-government assistant to the president. A 65% majority supported the use of government funds to help states modify their voting systems by installing electronic voting machines that work like automatic teller machines. By a 66% majority, the public thought public/private partnerships were the best approach to developing e-government services.

VISION, PRINCIPLES, AND RECOMMENDATIONS

The blueprint first set forth a vision of e-government by contemplating what an e-government world would be like. Imagine, it asked:

- Government where individuals and organizations no longer wait in line between eight and five on weekdays only, but where they can be online at any time or place they wish.
- People in government who are excited about using the Internet to make a difference and produce results. People in business enjoying fast and easy interactions with government that produce results in the public interest.
- People in all sectors–government, business, nonprofits, and the research community–working together to make this happen quickly, creatively, and cost effectively.
- Individual Americans creating customized, one-stop sites for themselves online, where they can choose to get information, con-

duct transactions, or communicate with their elected representatives.

Then the blueprint laid out a set of principles to guide the choices of leaders in pursuing e-government. These specified an e-government that would be (1) easy to use, connecting people with federal, regional, local, tribal, and international governments according to their preferences and needs; (2) available to everyone, at home, at work, in schools, in libraries, and at public locations in their communities; (3) private and secure, with the high standards for privacy, security and authentication; (4) innovative and results-oriented, emphasizing speed and advances in technology, while embracing continuous improvement; (5) collaborative within a framework of government policy, standards and accountability, where solutions are developed collectively, objectively, and openly among public, private, nonprofit and research partners; (6) cost-effective, through strategic investments and results that produce significant long-term efficiencies; and (7) transformational, harnessing technology through personal and organizational leadership to transform government, rather than automate existing practices.

Finally, the blueprint spelled out specific steps to build an e-government that reflects those goals.

In the area of *leadership*, it proposed that the president:

- Appoint an assistant to the president for electronic government.
- Create a public/private council on electronic government, representing business, the research community, the Cabinet, the Congress, and every other level of American government.
- Establish an office of electronic government and information policy as part of the federal Office of Management and Budget, headed by a presidentially appointed, Senate-confirmed federal chief information officer.
- Appoint people to top executive branch positions who will commit themselves to the strategic development of e-government in their departments and agencies.

The blueprint suggested that steps like those carried equal promise for state, local, and tribal governments and urged them to collaborate closely with the federal government and one another in the pursuit of e-government. As other leadership steps, the blueprint recommended:

- That the Congress set up an office of e-government. Among other purposes, this would respond to the Hart/Teeter finding in August 2000 that about 75 percent of Americans thought e-government would improve their ability to connect with elected representatives.
- That Senate committees, in their confirmation process, should highlight all nominees' commitment to e-government.
- That judiciary systems at all levels use information technology to fully open their deliberations, calendars, and decisions to the public.
- That, at the international level, the public/private council lead the way in strengthening relationships and cooperation with other countries that are moving toward e-government.

Because e-government at this scale would need sufficient, carefully applied investment, the blueprint advocated a congressional appropriation of $3 billion over five years for an e-government strategic investment fund–an amount similar to that used to tackle the federal government's challenges in the Y2K episode. The money represented added spending at an average increase of 1.5 percent a year.

The blueprint advanced proposals on four other fronts–broad public/private collaboration to reach full e-government; a skilled workforce to implement it; innovative solutions to questions of privacy and security; and public access and education.

Collaboration. In January 2001, a Hart/Teeter poll supplementing the August 2000 survey showed that sizeable majorities of Americans wanted government and industry to work together, rather than separately, on three key dimensions of the e-government enterprise. Sixty-six percent thought this public/private partnership was the best way to make more government services available on the Internet, 63 percent saw it as the most effective means of expanding Internet access to greater numbers of people, and 70 percent favored the public/private approach to setting standards for privacy and security on the Internet. These findings only reinforced the reality that design, implementation, and management of e-government would need unprecedented and non-traditional collaboration between the public, private, nonprofit and research sectors and within and across every level of government.

Accordingly, the blueprint recommended that government take the lead in setting policy and goals and in strategic investment in e-government initiatives and research, collaborating with the private sector to supply appropriate goods, services, and expertise in response to legitimate need. In partnership with the private sector and others, government should modernize its infrastructure and its electronic accessibility to citizens in order to meet the needs of its consumers. In looking to cross-sector partnerships whenever possible, government should retain its leadership role in issues that are its core competencies.

Work force. The blueprint's framers did not see electronic government as the sole province of technological experts. They felt it should be ingrained in the thinking of government leaders, managers, and workers at all levels. They knew also that the federal CIO Council had recognized specific shortfalls in the supply and quality of the federal IT workforce. Further, Hart/Teeter in August 2000 found a substantial percentage of government executives (26%) believing that the "inability to recruit qualified personnel" was an obstacle to achieving e-government. Among other steps, the blueprint recommended funding of aggressive training to help workers, managers, and leaders apply e-government strategies; that especially for IT positions, the federal Office of Personnel Management encourage hiring that is competitive with the private sector; that federal agencies and the White House design rewards and recognition for highest quality performance in innovation and application of e-government approaches; and that the government offer flexible, entrepreneurial workplaces that attract and help retain the people who know best how to apply e-government techniques.

Privacy and security. The Hart/Teeter August 2000 survey showed that Americans by more than two to one wanted to go slowly in implementing e-government because of concerns about security and privacy. Ease of use and the reliability of technical infrastructure will be one key to the willingness of government agencies to adopt e-government and to the public's ability to use it. Another will be broad public confidence in government's ability to keep personal information private and to make systems safe from inappropriate efforts to gain access. With the development of security and privacy protections lagging behind the development of new software, these issues must be assiduously addressed.

The blueprint proposed that the Strategic Investment Fund support the development and testing of methods to improve privacy, security, and interoperability. It recommended presidential guidelines on getting systems to communicate with other systems efficiently and effectively; the aggressive acceleration of testing solutions to technical challenges, based where possible on multi-agency functions that link readily, rather than on program or agency-specific ideas; the provision of adequate technical infrastructure to support easy, reliable access to online operations; and that the public be able to search directly for answers to problems, not have to find its way first through agency or program portals.

Access and education. Americans see the benefits of e-government as more than simply better or more cost-efficient services; they see it as a means of empowering citizens. The Hart-Teeter survey showed that that a majority thought e-government would raise government's level of accountability to citizens. But too many Americans remain electronically disconnected. While the numbers of Americans with public or private access to the Internet is growing rapidly, the Hart/Teeter poll reported that a third of the public still did not use it. Hart and Teeter also found a third of adults concerned that people without Internet access would receive fewer government services.

In this area, the blueprint recommended that the president establish a goal with a deadline to assure that all Americans have access to the Internet in their homes, regardless of income, disability, or educational background. In the interim, it proposed a broad effort to expand public access to the Internet through libraries, community centers, and other locations. It advocated a White House-led campaign to educate the public on the value of electronic communications and how to use them to interact with government, conduct transactions, and receive services. It recommended a national series of public forums on electronic government, including electronic forums, to obtain maximum public input into e-government strategy, and to map a set of long-term policy goals with measurable objectives for the public, among them the potential for uniform electronic voting methods in which the public can have complete confidence.

IMPACT OF THE BLUEPRINT

Bush Administration actions in the e-government area have in several ways reflected the thinking that informs the blueprint. One example is the decision to appoint an associate director of the Office of Management and Budget for Information Technology and e-Government. This is a new senior-level position with central authority and responsibility for citizen-centered e-government solutions across the federal government and for earmarking financial resources for that effort. Second, the President's Management Agenda, set out in August 2001, established e-government as a cornerstone for making citizen-focused, cross-functional government a reality.

Third, the focus of e-government is beginning to shift from a collection of Web sites to integrated customer service delivery. The 24 major crosscutting e-government initiatives underway show how the Internet can be used to transform service delivery to citizens and businesses. Examples of this–On-Line Rulemaking System, Recreation One-Stop, the E-Grants portal prototype–all show how the approach to citizen interaction with government is changing and will continue to do so.

On Capitol Hill, the Senate in 2001 passed legislation on e-government but the full Congress did not act on it. After reworking the legislation, its sponsors reintroduced it as the E-Government Act of 2002 and it is now working its way through the Congress.

The legislation is consistent with the recommendations contained in the blueprint and provides a valuable framework for building e-government. It would establish an Office of Electronic Government in OMB and the creation of an e-government fund for cross-agency initiatives. It provides a framework for executive branch leadership and the flexible funding required to meet these challenges. It expands public access to government by institutionalizing an Internet portal putting the federal regulatory process and federal court dockets and documents online. The bill calls for standardized approaches to e-government, including e-authentication, geospatial data, and electronic records retrieval and access. It increases the use of share-in-savings contracting, which if designed and managed well, can fuel more effective public/private partnerships and provide much needed incentives for agencies to invest in innovative approaches that will yield long-term cost savings. It also encourages and supports additional research and pilot projects in the areas of Internet access, integrated reporting, and crisis management.

In sum, the proposed legislation is a big, constructive, and important move in the right direction. I am also pleased that the Council was able in various ways to play a role in the process that produced it. In 2001 and 2002, for example, I testified to the congressional panels with jurisdiction over the bill (the Senate Governmental Affairs Subcommittee on Oversight of Government Management, Restructuring and the District of Columbia; and the House Government Reform and Oversight Subcommittee on Technology and Procurement Policy). Senate Governmental Affairs committee counsel Kevin Landy participated in the work of the experts group that shaped the blueprint. And Congressman Tom Davis, who chairs the House Reform and Oversight subcommittee, was a panelist in the discussion that accompanied our public release of the blueprint.

Beyond the quantum improvement e-government can make in the range, quality, and speed of public-sector services across the board, those who created the blueprint knew it could bring a host of other benefits, including truly extraordinary cost savings, to government and to every entity dealing in any way with government. Even more compelling, however, they recognized the unmatched opportunity to encourage Americans of every age, especially young Americans, to help design and build e-government and to own and enjoy it. The measures developed by these information technology leaders were not therefore intended to automate government, but to transform it.

The authors of the blueprint were under no illusion that bringing complete e-government into existence would be simple or quick. The blueprint was not a detailed road map with all the answers. But it posed the fundamental challenge of creating e-government, offered specific proposals to meet it, and identified the resources required. Its creators believed that realization of e-government would have much to do with the future vigor and effectiveness of government everywhere in this country. E-government requires the forging of unusual collaboration and partnership between the private and public sector, not only to create and sustain e-government but also to offer access and education to all Americans and achieve genuine e-democracy.

When the Council published the e-government blueprint, we described it as "not just another policy recommendation or a vision unconnected to reality." Rather, we said, "it is about really dramatic change made possible by information technology, a change whose time has come." Certainly, e-government offers an unprecedented opportunity to make government and democracy work in new ways our forebears could never dream of–and work better than ever.

THE EUROPEAN UNION

*e*Government: An EU Perspective

Erkki Liikanen

European Commission, Brussels, Belgium

SUMMARY. This article gives an overview of policies and progress on *e*Government in Europe. Propelled by the implementation of the *e*Europe 2002 Action Plan, collaborative R&D work and the establishment of trans-European telematic networks between EU national administrations, *e*Government applications have developed dramatically in Europe. However, the first achievements will not fulfil their promises if

Commissioner Liikanen is the member of the Commission of the European Union (EU) responsible for Enterprise Policy and Information Society. From 1995-1999 he was the Commissioner responsible for the budget of the EU, personnel and administration. From 1990-1994 he was Ambassador Extraordinary and Plenipotentiary from Finland to the EU. From 1987-1990 he was Minister of Finance of Finland. He was elected to the Finnish Parliament in 1972 at the age of 21. He has been a member of the Supervisory Board of Televa, a telecommunications company and has chaired the Supervisory Board of Outokumpu Corporation, a multimetal and technology company. He has a master's degree in political science specializing in economics from the University of Helsinki, Finland.

[Haworth co-indexing entry note]: "*e*Government: An EU Perspective." Liikanen, Erkki. Co-published simultaneously in *Journal of Political Marketing* (The Haworth Press, Inc.) Vol. 2, No. 3/4, 2003, pp. 65-88; and: *The World of E-Government* (ed: Gregory G. Curtin, Michael H. Sommer, and Veronika Vis-Sommer) The Haworth Press, Inc., 2003, pp. 65-88. Single or multiple copies of this article are available for a fee from The Haworth Document Delivery Service [1-800-HAWORTH, 9:00 a.m. - 5:00 p.m. (EST). E-mail address: docdelivery@haworthpress.com].

10.1300/J199v02n03_05

further challenges are not addressed by the decision makers at all levels of government. Top-level leadership and commitment is necessary to deepen *e*Government, not least for the change management needed for reorganisation of government back offices. The transfer of *e*Business practices into the public sector can help to achieve increased productivity and inclusion, by ensuring access for all to government *e*Services. The Brussels *e*Government Conference in November 2001 highlighted both the quality of existing *e*Government applications and the potential of European cooperation. European administrations are setting new standards as a basis for further progress. *[Article copies available for a fee from The Haworth Document Delivery Service: 1-800-HAWORTH. E-mail address: <docdelivery@haworthpress.com> Website: <http://www.HaworthPress.com>*

KEYWORDS. *e*Europe, productivity, inclusion, security, privacy, pan-European *e*Services, best practice, private-public partnerships, governance, back office reorganisation

Our contemporaries are . . . much less divided than is commonly supposed; they are constantly disputing as to the hands in which supremacy is to be vested, but they readily agree upon, the duties and the rights of that supremacy. The notion they all form of government is that of a sole, simple, providential, and creative power. . . . It originates, therefore, in no caprice of the human intellect, but it is a necessary condition of the present state of mankind.

–Alexis de Tocqueville
Democracy in America
section 4, chapter II

INTRODUCTION

Public administrations in the industrialised countries have started to embrace new information and communication technologies and are coping with the challenges of establishing "electronic government"– *e*Government. It is a broad challenge: The Internet has the potential to transform not only the way in which public services are delivered, but also the fundamental relationship between government and citizen. After *e*Commerce and *e*Business, *e*Government may be a field of profound changes in the way public administrations operate, making them more responsive and more accessible. *e*Government is thus not only about online public services, it is also about the ensuing changes in the organisation and the workings of government.

First, the access and use of public sector information–economic, legal, health, transport or education–is made easier. Public sector information on the Web may contribute to a broader use of the Internet. Second, public services can be made faster and more available. As with business transactions, citizens will be expecting convenient, round-the-clock interactions. Third, the Internet can increase efficiency in the public sector, cut costs and speed up administrative processes, benefiting citizens both as consumers and taxpayers. However, these benefits will not come about by themselves. They need to be guided by a vision. Technology is merely a tool; the real changes will emerge from new ways of communication and transactions by government–and the acceptance and active use of these by citizens and businesses. Achieving this often involves major changes to the internal workings of administrations–which can be complex to manage.

These challenges are common to the European countries and it is therefore natural that the EU is an arena for addressing *e*Government. A manifestation of the role the EU can play was the *e*Government conference in Brussels in November 2001. The conference showed a strong commitment to *e*Government in Europe, at all levels of government, as well as the political will in the EU accession candidate countries to match the standard set by the Community. However, the conference also showed that a number of issues will have to be addressed before *e*Government becomes a reality.

Against this background, this paper addresses the following issues:

- What is the role of the Commission in the development of *e*Government?
- What has been achieved so far in Europe?
- What are the next steps?

THE ROLE OF THE EUROPEAN COMMISSION

The role of the European Commission ("Commission") in *e*Government is manifold.

- Forward–looking-driving and co-ordinating the policy process, monitor progress,
- Forum–hosting discussions and exchanges of practices and mutual learning, and
- Funding–launching European-wide projects.

Key Elements of eGovernment

A policy for *e*Government must be based on a vision. In the elabora-
tion of a vision, certain elements are relevant as fundamental building
blocks. These elements present a range of emerging issues and challenges. Some of the critical elements in my view are:

Productivity. Over the last ten years, the Internet has had an unques-
tionable and unprecedented pervasive impact on the way individuals
communicate and spend time and organisations manage information
and knowledge to create wealth or implement societal goals. The new
*e*Business philosophy of collaborative commerce–in the broadest sense–is
bringing Enterprise Resource Planning, Customer Relationship Management, Business Intelligence, Supply Chain Management, and *e*Procurement
together to form one intelligible system within and between enterprises.
Productivity growth is the engine of improvement in living standards.
Further development of the Internet could drastically enhance productivity through cost reductions in standard products and steady introduction of new products and services on the market. This is fairly
recognized. What is less publicised is the potential impact of the
Internet on the productivity of the public sector. If businesses benefit
from the Internet, can government organisations take advantage as
well? In my view, the answer is yes. Electronic government is essen-
tially the opportunity offered to governments to empower citizens,
through the use of the Internet, to improve communications with government, lower transaction costs, shorten lines, and, of course, eliminate
burdensome paperwork. This is not insignificant. If 24-hour, seven-
days-a-week availability and convenience, interactivity, customer focus
and personalization are to become the norm in the public sector, it will
not just make life easier, it will fundamentally change the way that people view government itself. Electronic government offers tremendous
advantages for the government itself by improving productivity and employee satisfaction, for the citizens who get fast and user-friendly access
to the services they need, and for the taxpayers who get better governance for each tax euro contributed. However, putting public services
online isn't enough to achieve efficiency gains. As in the private sector,
change in the front office goes hand in hand with back office reorganisation and investment in human capital. We can do this by creating a culture within public service which is not suspicious but supportive of
innovation.

Equity. Government must indiscriminately serve all citizens. Europe
is committed to developing the standards and methods to ensure that

people with disabilities, people in lower socioeconomic classes or who live in rural areas on low-speed connections, etc., have access to *e*Government. This covers the issues known as the "Digital Divide," a term increasingly used to describe the social implications of unequal access of some sections of the community to information and services and to the acquisition of necessary skills. Since the Internet is still in a relatively early stage of commercial deployment, socioeconomic and geographic differences in Internet usage are not surprising and may not be long-lasting. The challenge for policy-makers in Europe will be to determine whether any continuing disparities in the availability and use of the Internet among different groups of Europeans threaten to deepen the divisions within our society. We are committed to achieve an open, inclusive and democratic information society. This is what was started with the *e*Europe 2002 Action Plan and what is going to be continued with *e*Europe 2005 (see "The Policy Framework" section below). The focus in *e*Europe 2005 will be the user and usage of the Internet. The objective is a widespread, more profound and inclusive use of the Internet to improve quality of life and also–the two elements converge-to raise productivity in the private and public sectors. Therefore, emphasis will be on reinforcing the pillars of an information society for all–*e*Learning, *e*Health, *e*Government–and ensuring the roll-out of key technological enablers, such as secure broadband networks and the next Internet Protocol.

Security and privacy. As we increasingly rely on the Internet to support critical operations in both public and private spheres, we need to improve access, affordability and dependability of information systems. The problems to solve can be caused by internal factors (e.g., system vulnerabilities) or by external factors (e.g., intrusions launched by malicious hackers). Directive 1999/93/EC of the European Parliament and Council establishes the requirements for qualified certificates, those for the providers of certification services issuing qualified certificates, and those for the means of creation of a secure electronic signature. Security issues are indeed of much concern, yet a level of pragmatism is required–the level of security needs to be appropriate to the transaction. EU Member States have recognized the need to focus on security as a basic condition for *e*Government, and they have invited the Commission to survey national electronic and authentication systems and tools and to explore the possibilities to promote policy experience. Furthermore, people need to be sure that privacy is guaranteed on the Internet. The threats to personal privacy of communication technologies must be addressed. Invasion of privacy is not acceptable, and least of all in the context of *e*Government, where the information managed is typically personal, confidential or sensitive. However, a level of pragmatism is also required–not all transactions require the same degree of security (health data, in particular, is very sensitive). A balance should therefore be found between the need for identification and personalization and the counter-requirement for privacy and security.

A global approach. As a member of the UN High-Level Panel of Advisors for ICT and development, I attach a particular importance to this subject. The international *e*Government events held in Naples[1] and Palermo[2] demonstrated that *e*Government is an opportunity for both developed and developing countries–by improving communication and exchange of information, they can create powerful social and economic networks, which in turn provide the basis for major advances in development. However, technology is no panacea for all development problems. Also, not everything can be done everywhere. What should be chosen depends on the level of development and on the commitment of key people and institutions. Efforts have to be made to coordinate technology cooperation and assistance. When support for IT infrastructure development comes from a variety of sources, it can become inefficient, by duplication and incompatibility between technological systems. Last year's Brussels *e*Government conference brought witness of the challenges facing countries like South Africa and Brazil in terms of infrastructure and accessibility, but also of the enormous potential of *e*Government for contributing to solutions to global problems of development and democracy. There is truly a need for worldwide cooperation, coherence and inclusion in this field.

The Policy Framework

The work on *e*Government at European level took a leap forward when the Commission in December 1999 launched the initiative "*e*Europe–An Information Society for All." This plan proposed ambitious targets to bring the benefits of the Information Society within reach of all Europeans. European Commission President Romano Prodi stated that "these (technological) changes, the most significant since the Industrial Revolution, are far reaching and global," and "they will affect everyone, everywhere." Managing this transformation represents one of the main economic and social challenges facing Europe today. The *e*Europe initiative was launched to address these challenges, thereby accelerating the European economy's modernisation and contributing to employment, growth, productivity and social cohesion. While Europe had a leading role in mobile communications and digital TV, the uptake of the Internet was still relatively slow. The *e*Europe initiative was therefore timely for giving Europe the opportunity to capitalise on its technical strengths and to lead the next great leap to a multi-platform Internet world.

The key objectives of *e*Europe are to bring every citizen, home, school, business and administration online and into the digital age, to create a digitally literate Europe, supported by an entrepreneurial culture ready to finance and develop new ideas, and to ensure that the whole process is socially inclusive. To achieve these objectives, the Commission proposed 11 priority areas for joint action for the Commission, the Member States, industry and citizens. The priority areas include youth, the disabled, education and research, health, *e*Commerce and *e*Government.

The European Council (EU Heads of State and Government) in June 2000 endorsed the comprehensive *e*Europe 2002 Action Plan. The *e*Europe initiative became an integral part of the so-called "Lisbon strategy," established at the extraordinary European Council on Employment, Economic Reform and Social Change in Lisbon in March 2000. This Council defined for the Union an overall strategy designed to boost competitiveness and innovation, complete the internal market, modernise the European social model by investing in human capital and combating social exclusion, and promote sustained economic growth. Subsequently, the EU supported the so-called *e*Europe+ Action Plan for candidate countries, to bring their preparations in terms of the Information Society in line with the EU. By the end of 2000 *e*Europe had thus become the common strategy to accelerate the transformation of Europe into a knowledge-based economy.

As a tool for realising the *e*Europe targets and objectives, the so-called open method of coordination is used. Rather than the traditional legal initiatives proposed by the Commission, this method consists of establishing policy objectives coupled with time targets, jointly by the Commission and Member States. Convergence towards the objectives of the Union and respect of the deadlines is assured by benchmarking progress and an active exchange of best practices, supported by the Commission. The use of this more informal and flexible method of cooperation in *e*Government is partly due to the fact that the European Treaties do not anticipate Community powers regarding the organisation of public administrations, and because substantial differences remain in the culture and administrative systems of the Member States.

EU-Funded Cross-European Projects– Catalysing the Necessary Changes

A number of EU-funded programmes deal with developing *e*Government through cross-border projects and research. Below are some of the most relevant programmes (Figure 1).

The *IDA programme* (Interchange of Data between Administrations) promotes trans-European telematic networks between European administrations and provides horizontal measures in support of interoperability within and across government networks. Furthermore, the effective implementation of such *e*Services requires interoperability of administrations' back office. Here, IDA represents an opportunity for projects as it can use this instrument to deploy solutions in all EU Member States.

The *eTEN* programme is designed to support the deployment of telecommunication networks-based services with a trans-European dimension. The programme focuses on public services, particularly in areas where Europe has a competitive advantage and aims at accelerating the take up of services. It provides assistance in the critical launch phase of a service, including the preparation of a solid business plan. In *e*Government, the programme supports electronic procurement; secured access to online services; personal security; environment and tourism.

*e*Government in the *Information Society Technology (IST)* research programme focuses on multimedia systems and services addressing the specific needs of administrations and offering interactive services to citizens. Significant advances are being made to design, develop and deliver services that are based on the real needs of users. In addition, the innovative use of new technology allows increased participation of citizens in democracy-related matters–e.g., more transparent presentation of public policies, consultation/voting, and interaction with elected representatives.

The Community instruments, such as the Framework Programme or IDA, and the focused intergovernmental co-operation between EU ministers for public administration, form together what I call the "*e*Government Policy Platform," which frames and presides over the further development of the major relevant activities taking place in Europe (see graphics).

ACHIEVEMENTS

Substantial progress in *e*Government is being achieved in Europe and even greater opportunities lie ahead. New edge tools are now avail-

FIGURE 1. The eGovernment Policy Platform

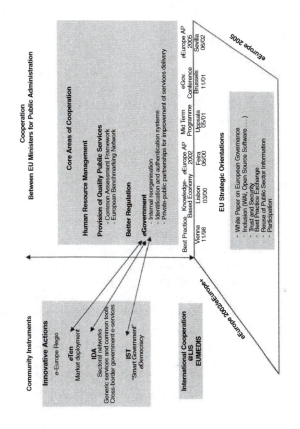

able thanks to which *e*Government applications and services are developing rapidly across Europe. Investing in the future, EU public administrations and the Commission are implementing innovative *e*Government approaches. Table 1 gives an overview of progress to date on the main *e*Europe 2002 targets for *e*Government.

The Brussels *eGovernment* Conference–Framing Key Policy Actions

How, then, is Europe concretely moving forward on *e*Government? All Member States of the EU now have policies to put public services online, and *e*Europe, using the open method of coordination, makes an important contribution to this by comparing performances through benchmarking and exchange of good practices. In this way, transparency of policies is assured, promoting mutual learning and constructive peer pressure. A key political platform for *e*Government in Europe was the ministerial *e*Government conference "From Policy to Practice," organised by the Commission in Brussels on 29-30 November 2001, with the Belgian EU Presidency.[3]

The purpose of the conference was to promote *e*Government and present the state-of-the-art of online public services applications, to show how citizens and businesses can derive concrete benefits from such services in their day-to-day needs, give a picture of where Europe currently stands in this field and stimulate uptake and dissemination of best practices. The conference turned out to be a manifestation of the commitment of Europe's political leadership to *e*Government: Some 40 ministers and deputy ministers, also from the accession candidate countries, attended the conference. This event made Europe the arena for discussions on *e*Government policy. The Ministerial Declaration lists *e*Government priorities and challenges, such as inclusion, and highlights the need for reinforced coordination to ensure trust and security, as well as to promote pan-European services in order to support cross-border mobility.

In my view, the main lessons which came out from the conference have been the following:

a. Top-level commitment is required–there is much opposition to change so senior sponsorship and leadership is critical.
b. "Think big, start small, scale fast"–governments should have a vision, identify the right customers and services, start small and be prepared to learn and adjust while going, then they should roll further services out to ever larger user groups.

c. There is a crucial need for sound business case, coupled with real-istic expectations underpinned by milestones, metrics, bench-marking and progress reporting.
d. Customer Relationship Management (CRM) should lie at the heart of the solution provided.
e. Back-office integration is in its infancy, yet progress there is es-sential to implement connections across public administrations and provide a single face to citizens and businesses.

The Brussels conference also highlighted several European actions related to *e*Government.

TABLE 1. *e*Government Targets 2001-2002

Action	Progress
Promote the use of open source software in the public sector and *e*Government best practice by exchange of experiences.	The IDA Programme is analysing what mechanisms are required to promote the sharing of Open Source solutions between public administrations.
All basic transactions with the European Commission must be available online (e.g., funding, research contracts, recruitment, procurement).	Plans developed in context of White Paper on Reform. The communication "Towards an *e*Commission" (2001). Electronic sub-mission to EU recruitment piloted. The IST programme enables electronic submission, the Publications Office online payment of publications.
Promote the use of electronic signatures within the public sector.	Pilot projects on: Secure e-mail between administrations; interoperability of public key infrastructures; bridge authority for mu-tual recognition of digital certificates (IDA). Roll-out of secure e-mail in the Commis-sion.
Essential public data online, including legal, administrative, cultural, environmental and traffic information.	Directive on the exploitation of public sector information adopted by the Commission in June 2002. IDA programme is working with Member States' portal managers on estab-lishing a portal of EU administrations.
Member States to ensure generalised elec-tronic access to main basic public services.	Most Member States have set targets. Prog-ress is benchmarked twice-yearly based on list of 20 public services (see details in Ta-ble 2). Latest results: Second measure-ment, June 2002.
Simplified online administrative procedures for business, e.g., fast track procedures to set up a company.	Simplification of procedures for businesses addressed in Action Plan to Promote Entre-preneurship and Competitiveness. Results: Red tape has been cut, but registration peri-ods remain long in many EU countries.

Sharing Best Practices

The Brussels conference clearly highlighted the fact that European countries are advancing in the implementation of *e*Government. Almost 300 running applications were received by the Commission from all EU Member States and from all levels of government. Fifty of them were selected for an exhibition organized during the conference. This way, the Commission encourages and promotes exchange and dissemination of best practices. However, best practice exchange is not about copying solutions and considering it to be the only model. It is about learning from each other. The principle of subsidiarity applies–local solutions are best developed locally. The Commission cannot–and would not want to–impose "one size fits all" solutions.

Building on the richness of the applications submitted to the conference from all over Europe, the Commission launched a competition entitled "*e*Europe awards for innovation in *e*Government." The awards are intended to draw attention to exemplary practices in government and to provide a platform for public-sector innovators behind these practices to disseminate their achievements.

Online Public Services

The objective of *e*Europe benchmarking is to measure progress in the access to and use of the Internet in Europe. It is also to allow Member States to compare their developments, identify best practice, provide insight into the factors of importance for widespread diffusion, and to enable remedial action. To ensure comparability in measuring progress in bringing public services online, a common list of 20 public services, 12 for citizens and 8 for businesses, had been adopted by Council (Table 2). The degree of online sophistication is measured using a four stage framework, going from posting government information line (stage 1) over one- and two-way interaction with government administration (stages 2 and 3) to a full online transaction, including delivery/payment (stage 4).

The first measurement, in autumn 2001, showed that overall, around 45% of the 20 services were available online. Income-generating services perform best, whereas permits and licenses, often complex and composite public services, obtain the lowest scores. A conclusion from this survey is that comprehensive and efficient *e*Government services require a reorganisation of government back offices in terms of data management, information exchange and interagency coordination. The

TABLE 2. Common List of Online Public Services

	Public Services for Citizens	Max. stage
1	Income taxes: Declaration, notification of assessment	(4)
2	Job search services by labour offices	(3)
3	Social security contributions (3 out of the 4 below): • Unemployment benefits • Family allowances • Medical costs (reimbursement or direct settlement) • Student grants	(4)
4	Personal documents (passport and driver's licence)	(3)
5	Car registration (new, used, imported cars)	(4)
6	Application for planning permission	(4)
7	Declaration to the police (e.g., in case of theft)	(3)
8	Services of public libraries	(3)
9	Certificates (birth, marriage): Request and delivery	(3)
10	Enrollment in higher education/university	(4)
11	Announcement of moving (change of address)	(3)
12	Health-related services (e.g., appointments for hospitals, availability of consultation by specialist, e-mail services doctor to patient, etc.)	(4)
	Public Services for Businesses	Max. stage
13	Social contribution for employees	(4)
14	Corporation tax: Declaration, notification	(4)
15	VAT: Declaration, notification	(4)
16	Registration of a new company	(4)
17	Submission of data to statistical offices	(3)
18	Customs declarations	(4)
19	Environment-related permits	(4)
20	Public procurement	(3)

results were encouraging but there is still a widespread lack of real interactivity. Also, the results are uneven between countries. The second measurement, in spring 2002,[4] shows a substantial progress of about 10 percentage points, with an average score of 55% of the measured services available online. Ireland and Sweden are in the lead, but there is a growing homogeneity in the performance of the surveyed countries.

Attached to the concept of quality of online public services are the concepts of trust and confidence (electronic signatures, smart cards) and the access of all to online government (*e*Inclusion), including providing services for minorities and disabled. In September 2001 the Commission adopted the communication "*e*Europe 2002: Accessibility of Public Web Sites and their Content." The aim is to make Web sites more accessible to people with disabilities and older people. This communication aims at supporting efforts to adopt and implement the guidelines on Web accessibility. Steps will be taken within the European institutions, such as the creation of an inter-institutional group to promote adoption and implementation of the accessibility guidelines and the launch of awareness-raising and training operations.

On security of electronic networks, the EU promotes a comprehensive strategy. Several initiatives have been taken: The trade of encryption technologies has been fully liberalized and legislation to ensure the lawfulness and mutual recognition of electronic signatures between EU countries has been adopted–key to securing the integrity and authentication of electronic data. The Commission has also published a communication on Network and Information Security and one on cyber-crime. Steps have furthermore been taken to protect privacy in the information society. The new electronic communications regulatory framework entered into force in 2002.

Private-Public Partnership

The Commission will continue to emphasize the advantages that public-private partnerships can bring, including in the field of *e*Government. The role of intermediaries and partnerships that can add value to *e*Government services should therefore be strengthened. Several Commission initiatives contribute to this.

In June 2002, a proposal for a Directive aiming to facilitate the reuse of public sector information throughout Europe was adopted by the Commission.[5] There is huge potential in the reuse of public sector information for added value services. The aim of the Directive is to address the barriers which Europe's content companies face as they develop a new generation of information services and products based on public sector information by creating a European legal framework.

In addition, the *e*Content programme has a strong focus on public sector information. The programme promotes the development and use of European digital content on the global networks and encourages linguistic diversity in the information society, to reflect the European context with its diversity of cultures and languages. Developing contents is primarily up to the market but the *e*Content programme can contribute to create private-public content partnerships.

At the initiative of the EU ministers of Public Administration, a "Forum for European *e*Public Services," in short e-Forum (www.eu-forum. org), is being created with the support of the IST programme. It is open to all players and stakeholders, public as well as private, and it is used on a consultative basis for the development and continuous implementation of *e*Government in Europe. The e-Forum has already attracted a large number of members, including European public administrations, companies, banks and financial organisations. The public sector can certainly learn from the experiences of the private sector, and many good practices comprise successful examples of private-public partnerships in the realisation of *e*Government applications, including those in which the private sector has an active role in delivering public services. Specific examples are placed on the e-Forum Web site.

EU Research Projects–Sowing the Seeds of Change

Financial support from the EU comes mainly from the Framework Programmes–the 6th Framework Programme covering 2002-2006 was adopted in June 2002. *e*Government applications cover Government to Business, Government to Government, and Government to Citizen. Reaching these objectives requires investments in technologies and process redesign, knowledge and organisation transformation. For *e*Government services, specific business models can be developed, helping governments to move from enablers to transformers. To produce the systems and tools necessary to meet challenges in this field, extensive research has already been carried out in areas that can contribute to future development of *e*Government. Key examples are single point of access and knowledge management.

Single point of access. EU-funded research projects have made major contributions to making government function as a single enterprise, in particular in terms of the provision of secure digital signature services and legal digital documents to citizens and governments in a pan-European environment.

Knowledge management. The inter-networked economy is placing a new premium on knowledge as the key resource of organisations. Knowledge management research explores and develops methodologies and tools to ensure that knowledge is created and reused effectively in support of organisational objectives. The research also considers new approaches to inter-organisational collaboration, and new ways to encourage and sustain self-organising networks and communities within and across organisations boundaries.

Just as the last decade of the 20th century was the decade of information and communication technologies, the first decades of the 21st century will see the maturation of what is presently called *ambient intelligence*. This refers in particular to the applications and services that are based on the convergence and intimate integration of wireless and wired systems, the next generation of embedded systems, and interactive, multicultural, multidomain content creation and management facilities. The field of *e*Government is expected to benefit from these technological advances, provided of course that the nontechnical environment does not stick at the starting point.

Providing Administrations with Trans-European Telematic Networks

Pan-European eServices (Government-to-Government)

The management of the Single Market and associated Community policies entails the exchange of various kinds of administrative data between the Member States' public administrations and with the European Institutions.

The sectoral trans-European networks implemented through IDA cover many Community policies, including agriculture and fisheries; employment and education,[6] environment,[7] civil protection and environmental emergency, enterprises,[8] health and consumer protection, and social policies. Furthermore, developers of pan-European Government-to-Government services can build today on a number of generic services and common tools. Examples of these are TESTA and CIRCA.

The private European backbone network TESTA connects governmental intranets operated by national authorities. The network also provides links to the European institutions. Data transmitted over the network includes information on job vacancies and social security, trade licenses and pharmaceutical products, road accidents and communicable diseases. In addition, the infrastructure makes available groupware tools that facilitate effective and secure sharing of resources and documents.

CIRCA (communication and information resource administrator) is a simple and effective Internet-based groupware which supports information sharing among public administrations, institutions and agencies. It enables closed workgroups such as committees or project teams to maintain a private space on the Internet. Members can work simultaneously on documents, participate in discussion forums. Password protection and optional encryption provisions prevent unauthorised access.

Pan-European eServices (Government-to-Citizens and Government-to-Business)

In the context of *e*Europe 2005 Action Plan, IDA is giving increasing attention to the provision of pan-European *e*Government services to citizens and enterprises. This is due to a concern that while providing information and services aimed at their own citizens, public administrations in Europe may neglect the needs of potential users in other Member States. This can result in barriers to mobility on the Single Market or to increased costs and administrative burdens for enterprises active across borders.

LOOKING AHEAD

The introduction of broadband *e*Government is a challenge for the public sector. This is a new frontier for all EU Member State public administrations. Presently, interactive public services have been underdeveloped–even though the applications that have been presented at the Brussels *e*Government conference arguably feed hope. Most public administrations in Europe offer passive information and "shop windows" on the Internet, but do not give their clients–citizens and businesses–the opportunity to carry out complete transactions. To move ahead, in particular towards the creation of interoperability for the availability of interactive pan-European public services for citizens and companies, broadband connections in public administrations must be developed. The *e*Europe 2005 Action Plan, which was approved at the Sevilla European Council in June 2002, sets the target for the Member States to have broadband connections for all public administrations by 2005.

Exploiting Broadband

Governments worldwide are increasingly realiSing that broadband access will be central to the economic development of their countries. At the same time, however, the upgrade of existing infrastructure, including the transition from the current Internet Protocol (IPv4) to the next-generation

Internet Protocol (IPv6), and the roll-out of new networks, require significant investment. As companies are currently facing difficult capital markets and low rates of broadband take-up, one of the main objectives of
broadband policy should be to reduce uncertainty in the market. This is
not an easy task, because broadband strategies are affected by many different policies–territorial planning, research policy, taxation and
regulation–which are carried out at all government levels (international,
European, national, regional and local). Therefore, a broadband initiative
should bring the application of such policies together, to provide a consistent and effective policy solution. The new regulatory framework, which
will be applied in all Member States beginning in July 2003, is expected
to encourage efficient investment in infrastructure and promote innovation (by new entrants and incumbent operators).

Infrastructure investment is driven by availability of content and services, and the development of new services and content depends on infrastructure deployment. Infrastructure evolves and upgrades when new
services and applications emerge and vice versa. Therefore, Europe
must implement a positive feedback between infrastructure upgrading–both broadband and multiplatform–and service developments.

Reorganising for e*Government*

Tackling back office integration requires true service integration and
a connected government. As illustrated in the eEurope benchmarking
survey of online public services, many straightforward services are being brought online. However, efficient delivery of complex public services calls for multiple integration. First, integration with the back
office, which requires connection within a department between the front
and back office functions. Second, integration of services to provide
one face to the customer, which requires connection between and across
departments. This process will be supported by further dimensions of
reorganisation, such as standardisation across platforms, sharing of data
and integration of distribution channels.

Integration along these lines is a basic pre-condition to successful
eGovernment. It poses challenging change management issues but the
benefits are compelling, not the least of which is bringing citizens closer
to government. Successful reorganisation means that staff can be rede-
ployed to more fulfilling roles, and can devote more time to customers
who require it. Redeployment of staff means education and retraining.

Governance

At the Brussels *e*Government conference, ministers emphasized that *e*Government is a useful way to implement good governance, based on the principles of openness, participation and accountability. Effective governance indeed resides at the heart of European government agendas to modernise public services. There is also a recognised need for public sector organisations to work together to counter fraud and corruption, implement effective risk management strategies and to promote high ethical standards within public services. This implies, among other things, the sharing of experience and good practice, that is, shared responsibilities as more activities will be devolved closer to the people and from the central level of government to regional and local governments. So, the possibilities for simpler, single online entry points for information and data collection are likely to grow and may well be positioned at the regional and local level where citizen and business online access and expectations are fast growing. The use by governments of the Internet is broadening and becoming more sophisticated.[9] All levels of government are increasingly turning to the Internet to conduct paperless acquisitions and provide interactive electronic services to their "clients." The number of Web portals–or online electronic front-doors to common services–is growing rapidly. The first European E-City Awards rewarding the best Internet city portals were presented in September 2002 in Vienna. This is the culmination of a long effort in Europe–yet, we still have a long way to go. In this context, close and sustained cooperation between governments, at all levels, and industry, such as the joint actions which have been developed by the Global Business Dialogue on *e*Commerce (GBDe[10]) and the Global Cities Dialogue (GCD[11]), is of utmost importance.

CONCLUSIONS

Progress towards electronic government is changing the landscape of public administration and government services in Europe and in the rest of the world. *e*Government has come to stay. It is a development that holds promises of more convenient and responsive public services for citizens and businesses, but also enhanced participation in government, improved governance and strengthened competitiveness of our societies. Realisation of these benefits will depend on:

- the *capacity of governments*, to transform themselves and provide leadership;
- a *solid legal framework*, especially for telecoms and information security;
- *state-of-the-art technology*: infrastructure; user identification, network security;
- the *demand*–encourage use of attractive and user-friendly services; and
- the *expectations of the benefits* of *e*Services by all the key stakeholders.

This development must take place in the context of a socially inclusive information society. Access to technology, learning, bandwidth must be assured for all. *e*Government will fail if it is only for those with the technology and skills.

If we master these challenges, Europe will be off to a promising start in the 21st century. The process has been launched but substantial challenges remain ahead of us. This is why we need to commit ourselves to realising the potential of *e*Government. While national *e*Government policies are carried out, often at regional or local level, the EU plays an important role. The European level is a forum for discussions on visions and policies, bringing together the players and stakeholders across Europe, and also for defining common targets and strategies. The realisation of the targets is boosted by EU-level benchmarking of progress and exchange of best practices. The EU also brings *e*Government forward by funding innovative research.

*e*Government is about facilitating the life of citizens and businesses by increasing the efficiency, quality and user-friendliness of government, as well as improving governance. That is also why Europe is engaged.

NOTES

1. The Italian Government hosted in Naples, on 15-17 March 2001, the Third Global Forum on governance, dedicated to *e*Government as an instrument of democracy and development.

2. International Conference on *e*Government for Development organised by the Italian Government and the UN Department for Social and Economic Affairs, Palermo 10-11 April 2002.

3. *http://europa.eu.int/eeurope/frompolicytopractice.*

4. *http://europa.eu.int/information_society/eeurope/benchmarking/list/source_data_pdf/2nd_measurement_final_report.pdf.*

5. European Parliament and Council Directive on the reuse and commercial exploitation of public sector information, COM(2002)207.

6. European employment network (EURES), which, used by employment offices and can be accessed by citizens through the Internet, facilitates recruitment in the single European labour market.

7. European environmental information and observation network (EIONET) connects European environmental organisations, providing access to harmonized and comparable information.

8. European telecommunication network in pharmaceuticals (EUDRANET) provides organisations and authorities in the pharmaceutical sector with a basis for one-stop market authorisation for medical products in Europe and contributes to the protection of public health.

9. See, for instance, Accenture, *Government Leadership–Realizing the Vision,* April 2002.

10. Established in January 1999, the Global Business Dialogue on Electronic Commerce (GBDe) has developed a framework through which consensus continues to be achieved between companies of different countries, cultures and sectors to provide one of the world's leading private voices on *e*Commerce policy. A special GBDe Web site is the *e*Government Database which contains information, classified by region/country, on *e*Government projects from around the world.

11. Mayors and senior representatives of twelve cities from different parts of the world launched the Global Cities Dialogue (GCD) and signed the so-called Helsinki Declaration on 23 November 1999 in the setting of the European Information Society Technologies Conference. The GCD proposes an open framework for action for all cities interested in working together to realise the potential of an information society free from social exclusion and based on sustainable development.

REFERENCES

eris@ Annual Conference, Toledo, Spain, 14-15 June 2002–Re-engineering the public administration, presentation by Jonathan Sage, PriceWaterhouseCoopers Belgium.

"From Policy to Practice," Report from the Ministerial *e*Government conference in Brussels, 29-30 November 2001.

Hearn, Paul, Bradier, Agnes, and Jubert, Anne. *Building Communities.* Organizational Knowledge Management Within the European Commission's Information Society Technologies Programme. 2002. Article forthcoming in *Collegium*, the magazine of the College of Europe.

Liikanen, Erkki. "Europe's Path Towards Innovation and Technology," Munich Economic Summit, Munich, 8 June 2002.

Liikanen, Erkki. "Exploiting the Broadband Potential," European Cable Communications Association (ECCA) Conference, European Broadband Communications 2002, Brussels, 27 May 2002.

Liikanen, Erkki. "Convergence and the Information Society," Conference on Media Convergence: Opportunities for a Closer Relationship Between Europe and the Americas, Madrid, 13 May 2002.

Liikanen, Erkki. "Status of the Information Society in the European Union and Future Challenges," Biel's 1st Communication Days, Biel-Bienne, Switzerland, 2 May 2002.

Liikanen, Erkki. "Better Regulation After Barcelona," European Policy Centre, Brussels, 22 April 2002.

Liikanen, Erkki. "Challenges and Perspectives for the Information Society: The Vision of the European Commission and Its Plan of Action," CII (Confederation of Indian Industry) Partnership Summit 2002: Local Boundaries, Global Frontiers, Bangalore, 11 January 2002.

Liikanen, Erkki. "The European Commission's Vision on *e*Government," Forum on *e*Government Issues, Antwerp Digital Mainport (ADM), Antwerp, 17 December 2001.

Litan, Robert E. and Rivlin, Alice M. (eds). "The Economic Payoff from the Internet Revolution," Brookings Task Force on the Internet.

Suurla, Riitta, Markku, Markkula, and Mustajärvi, Olli. *Developing and Implementing Knowledge Management in the Parliament of Finland*. Edita Prima Oy. Helsinki, Finland.

United States General Accounting Office (GAO). TELECOMMUNICATIONS: Characteristics and Choices of Internet Users, February 2001.

SOME IDA REFERENCES

The IDA catalogue of generic services:

http://europa.eu.int/ISPO/ida/jsps/index.jsp?fuseAction=showDocument&parent=crossreference&documentID=285

The IDA WP 2002:

http://europa.eu.int/ISPO/ida/jsps/index.jsp?fuseAction=showDocument&parent=news& documentID=543

The preliminary study for the Portal of the EU Administration:

http://europa.eu.int/ISPO/ida/jsps/index.jsp?fuseAction=showDocument&parent=highlights&documentID=321

The study into the use of Open Source Software for the public sector:

http://europa.eu.int/ISPO/ida/jsps/index.jsp?fuseAction=showDocument&parent=highlights&documentID=333

APPENDIX

Web Site Links of Member States and Other Countries

Austria

http://www.help.gv.at	Austrian government's portal
http://www.bmf.gv.at	Finance Ministry's *e*Government pages
http://www.austria.gv.at	Government's official WWW pages

Bulgaria

http://portal.government.bg	Bulgarian government portal includes public information and electronic payment

Czech Republic

http://www.uvis.cz	Access to public sector documentation
http://www.centralni-adresa.cz/cadr/index.htm	An information system on public procurement and auctions

Denmark

http://www.danmark.dk	Service pages for *citizens*
http://www.indberetning.dk	And for *business*

Estonia

http://www.riik.ee	Estonian National *e*Government site
http://www.gov.ee	Estonian National *e*Government site

Finland

http://www.vn.fi/vm/kehittaminen/tietohallinto/portaali.htm	An extensive portal for public services
http://www.opas.vn.fi	Information presented in 'life stages'

France

http://www.service-public.fr/	Public services portal (central level)
http://www.fonction-publique.gouv.fr/tic	French *e*Government pages
http://www.finances.gouv.fr	French Ministry for Economy, Finance and Industry
http://www.internet.gouv.fr/	Information society programme pages
http://www.atica.pm.gouv.fr/	Agency for ICT

Germany

http://www.bund.de	The central gateway to Web content of the German administration

Italy

http://www.paforum.net	Italian government's public administration forum

APPENDIX (continued)

Luxembourg

http://www.eluxembourg.lu	Luxembourg eGovernment Web site

The Netherlands

http://www.overheid.nl	Dutch eGovernment Web site

Poland

www.mg.gov.pl	Ministry of the Economy
www.kprm.gov.pl	The Chancellery of the Prime Minister

Portugal

http://www.infocid.pt	Portugal's public services portal

Slovenia

http://www.gov.si/mid	Ministry of the Information Society
http://www.gov.si/cvi	Government Centre for Informatics

Sweden

http://www.statskontoret.se/egov	Swedish national eGov sites

Switzerland

http://e-gov.admin.ch	'Cyberadministration' project site
http://www.admin.ch	Federal Authorities of the Swiss Confederation

Turkey

http://www.bybs.gov.tr	National eGovernment site

United Kingdom

http://www.ukonline.gov.uk/online/ukonline/home	Public access to government online information and services

Hong Kong

http://www.esd.gov.hk/eng/default.asp	Electronic services offered by the Hong Kong Government

Singapore

http://www.gov.sg	Government portal

South Africa

http://www.gov.za	South African govt' online

United States

http://www.firstgov.gov	The official United States Government Web pages

NEW ZEALAND

E-Government in New Zealand

Brendan Boyle

State Services Commission, New Zealand

David Nicholson

Wellington, New Zealand

SUMMARY. Although it has just 4 million people and an economy which is almost entirely based on agriculture, New Zealand has been nominated by the UN as the world's third most advanced in e-government.

Brendan Boyle is Director of the E-Government Unit at the State Services Commission, New Zealand. He has a Bachelor of Laws from Otago University and an MBA from the Alfred P. Sloan School of Management at the Massachusetts Institute of Technology.

David Nicholson is a Wellington-based journalist who has formerly worked for the NZ Herald, Australian Broadcasting Commission, UPI (London) and Television New Zealand. He has an MBA from the University of Auckland.

[Haworth co-indexing entry note]: "E-Government in New Zealand." Boyle, Brendan, and David Nicholson. Co-published simultaneously in *Journal of Political Marketing* (The Haworth Press, Inc.) Vol. 2, No. 3/4, 2003, pp. 89-105; and: *The World of E-Government* (ed: Gregory G. Curtin, Michael H. Sommer, and Veronika Vis-Sommer) The Haworth Press, Inc., 2003, pp. 89-105. Single or multiple copies of this article are available for a fee from The Haworth Document Delivery Service [1-800-HAWORTH, 9:00 a.m. - 5:00 p.m. (EST). E-mail address: docdelivery@haworthpress.com].

10.1300/J199v02n03_06

That might surprise foreigners but not Kiwis, who have always had a rapid uptake of new technology. Leading the country into an electronic world is the E-Government Unit, which is charged with coordinating and integrating e-services across all government agencies. Some of the solutions are original but New Zealand has not hesitated to scour the world for best-of-practices solutions and modify them to its own environment. *[Article copies available for a fee from The Haworth Document Delivery Service: 1-800-HAWORTH. E-mail address: <docdelivery@haworthpress.com> Website: <http://www.HaworthPress.com> © 2003 by The Haworth Press, Inc. All rights reserved.]*

KEYWORDS. E-government, PKI, portal, metadata, education, e-commerce, successes, budget

When a United Nations survey of e-government put New Zealand at number three in the world, few in New Zealand were surprised.[1]

This small country in the South Pacific, with a population of barely 4 million, has always been an early adopter of new ideas and technology, from open heart surgery (pioneered at Auckland's Greenlane Hospital in 1963) to the conversion to digital telephone exchanges beginning in 1981.

In June 2002, the former state-owned Telecom, which still owns the national telecommunications infrastructure, formed a partnership with the French company, Alcatel, to migrate the entire network to Internet Protocol. The first steps of the relationship will be to deliver high-speed network capabilities, optical Ethernet, Multi Protocol Label Switched IP core and advanced Digital Subscriber Line. When the project is complete, New Zealand will be among the first countries in the world to have an end-to-end IP network on which all voice and data will be carried.

Technological competitiveness is particularly important for New Zealand. Located 20,000km from its major European markets and lacking any economies of scale (its largest industry, dairying, produces only 1% of world output), the country must squeeze cost advantages from wherever it can.

That imperative is reinforced by the government's desire, urged on by the business sector, to reduce its share of GDP below the current 32%.

Although e-government is today viewed as a significant opportunity to improve the delivery quality of government services and reduce compliance costs for citizens and businesses, the transition to e-government in New Zealand began informally and without coordinated planning.

As traffic on the Internet began to rise exponentially from the mid-1990s most government agencies established a phase one Web presence (on a four-phase Gartner Research model from Web Presence to Interaction, through Transaction to Transformation), delivering basic information to the public–policy statements, press releases, contact details and the like. They were on task quickly but there was no overall government-mandated plan to either move to phase 2 (interaction), to begin coordination between state agencies, or to achieve a single point of access to government e-services. Secure communication between agencies, metadata standards, citizen authentication of external access to their personal information on agency databases and so forth had barely been thought of.

Today, all those issues are the responsibility of the E-Government Unit (EGU), a division of the State Services Commission, which is now into its third year of driving through the technical and cultural changes required to achieve a seamless electronic delivery of government services to the public.

Its responsibilities, defined by Cabinet, are:

- Strategy–develop an overarching e-government strategy and common system and data management policies, standards and guidelines;
- Leadership–facilitate the achievement of the e-government vision and strategy by the public sector;
- Coordination and collaboration–identify opportunities for beneficial collaboration across government agencies; leverage better returns from existing information management and technology investment; and provide coordination for multi-agency e-government projects;
- Policy–provide advice to Ministers on e-government; and
- Monitoring–watch progress toward achieving the e-government vision and strategy in relation to Information and Communication Technology ("ICT") investment.

The EGU was established when it was observed that in some overseas jurisdictions e-government had become a patchy process in the absence of a central organisation to coordinate advances across all sectors.

The government's objectives are nothing less than the eventual transformation of government, although it is understood that the process will be incremental, that there will be disappointments along the way, that government leaders will, from time to time, become disillusioned and that it will sometimes be expensive.

Undoubtedly, Gartner's "e-government hype cycle" will apply here as much as anywhere else.

It is also certain that, so far, few of the country's 30,000 public servants, even at quite a senior level, understand the revolutionary implications of the adoption of e-government. The traditional "silo" structure of New Zealand government agencies is under challenge. Rather than reaching for the restructuring lever to affect change, technology will provide the government with more flexibility and a different set of options as to how it organises itself to deliver services.

THE OBJECTIVES OF E-GOVERNMENT IN NEW ZEALAND

Broadly, the two key objectives of e-government are, first, the improved efficiency in the use of citizens' taxes through increased sharing and rationalization of systems, technology, delivery channels and the integration of business processes across agencies.

Second, the government aims to make dealing with government simpler and more efficient for citizens and businesses. Nobody in western society needs to be reminded of the complexities of the interface between citizens and their government. Take an 18-year-old setting out on life's journey–personal identification details have to be provided, separately, for a driver's licence, passport, university enrolment, taxes, voting, medical records, welfare entitlements, mail delivery and so forth. In an ideal e-government model that process should occur but once.

It is worse for businesses–the compliance costs of running a business are frequently identified as a major impediment to business start-ups, or expansion. Rather than spending their time on growth opportunities, the business' owners are consumed by filling out forms on occupational health and safety, compliance with labor laws, environmental protection and many more. Each area is managed by a different agency, with different reporting requirements. Their offices are scattered across town and it is frequently impossible to raise them by telephone. It is more of an art than a science for a business person to know how to navigate through the labyrinth, without even beginning to quantify the hours spent on legal obligations which do not add a single cent to the company's turnover.

This is a particular problem in a small country such as New Zealand, where the vast majority of businesses have fewer than five staff. That means the employment of dedicated specialists (in areas such as labour law, taxes, etc.) is quite impossible. The company's owners have no choice but to do as much as possible themselves (often in the evening, using a home PC on a narrowband connection) before handing over individual tasks (taxes, for example) to external specialists, who are invariably expensive. Consequently, any help they can get through the conversion of a service into an electronic format, available online and with all government services aggregated onto a single channel has the potential to generate significant efficiencies.

By July 2002, the EGU was able to chalk up a series of milestones aimed at putting in place the underlying framework for e-services by government agencies:

- Web site guidelines have been developed so there will eventually be consistency across all government Web sites. The guidelines recognize that for some years the majority of users will have standard 56k connections. The special needs of the disabled have also been taken into account. It is intended that the next version of these guidelines will become compulsory early 2003.
- A metadata standard (the NZ Government Locator Service, or NZGLS) is complete for the description of all government products and services. This means that users do not need to know which agency delivers what product, or service. Neither do they need to know that the product, or service, comes from central or local government. Instead, they can focus on finding the service.

  NZGLS is based on two similar templates, one from Australia and the second from Ohio. However, it goes further than either of those as it includes a template for services (not just information) and has "subject" and "functions" thesauri. The developers of the Ohio template are now examining the prospect of incorporating the services component into their own system.

  As NZGLS enables businesses and citizens to easily use a single point of entry to access any government service, without the need for specialised knowledge, it is the first embryonic step in the transformation of government from the current "silo" model, common to governments around the world, to a horizontal structure which clusters similar products and services—for example, driver's licence, car registration, change of address, voter registration and the like.

- The design of a New Zealand E-Government Inter-Operability Framework (NZ e-GIF) has been completed (the underlying speci- fications came from Britain), and all new EGU projects in the gov- ernment sector are now obliged to conform. This is a set of standards and business rules to guide decision-making about investment, de- velopment, design standards and the management of EGU resources across all agencies and is designed to ensure firewall-to- firewall compatibility between agencies.
- A standard database format for all addresses, road and place names in New Zealand has been developed by the emergency services agencies. Consideration is now being given to its incorporation into the NZ e-GIF.
- Government agencies are now incorporating e-services strategies in their annual plans. While the EGU does not have sign-off au- thority over individual agency plans, each agency is required to consult with the EGU so that strategies and principles are aligned across the state sector.

  Further, the EGU has mandated various detailed standards which ensure that the core components of each agency project will eventually interface seamlessly with the whole-of-government portal and with other agency Web sites and e-services. These stan- dards were developed through an extended negotiation process, with up to 60 groups involved.
- The EGU, with the support of agencies, is currently working with selected vendors, including Oracle, to pilot an e-procurement pro- gram which will put government purchasing online.

  The system will streamline the procurement process from order through to payment, and give better information to purchasing managers. It will allow agencies to work together more collabor- atively and suppliers will benefit from simplified links to govern- ment.
- A critical objective for the EGU has been the creation of a Secure Electronic Environment (S.E.E.) within and between agencies.

  S.E.E. Mail is based on a number of tested commercial products which temporarily establish a secure electronic pathway between agencies (in effect, a gateway-to-gateway Virtual Private Network but with much stronger authentication at both ends). So far, 20 agencies have installed these approved applications. A further 12 have committed to applications. Those agencies which have not yet purchased an application are waiting for the upgraded versions which will impose lower administrative overheads.

To enable one agency to securely access data from the network of a second agency, an EGU team has designed a S.E.E. Public Key Infrastructure (PKI) management framework to guide the development and deployment of inter-agency authentication.

Although S.E.E. PKI is not designed for citizen-to-government or business-to-government communication, it does recognize there are a number of external entities which interact with inter-agency applications in many situations. These include private sector agencies and individuals working on behalf of the government, State Owned Enterprizes and other public sector entities such as local government bodies.

Treasury has already used the framework to deploy S.E.E. PKI compliant digital certificates to designated individuals (financial controllers/managers) across a number of external government departments and agencies to authenticate these people as remote users of the Crown Financial Management System (CFISnet).

The originality and quality of the S.E.E. PKI project has attracted considerable attention from the Internet security community.

> . . . it's impressive . . . very pragmatic, thorough and well thought out technical and procedural policies, and looks like they've got a lot of support from vendors and government agencies. I don't know of any comparable efforts, so hopefully they'll keep publishing and developing this. (Comment from a commercial developer on an Internet security site)

- A shared workspace on a closed Internet site is being established so government agencies can work together to develop cross-agency policies.

While progress has been excellent in all sectors, there are also areas of exception.

Clearly absent from the mosaic of e-services is an e-billing application. Although that was a priority when the EGU first worked on its strategy, subsequent analysis revealed the absence of an e-billing market with critical mass. Consequently, the EGU has decided to meet this market as it emerges.

Fortunately, there will not be an urgent scramble to find a product at short notice, as New Zealand Post, owned by the government, has already developed and implemented a comprehensive and sophisticated e-billing service as part of its strategic development to compensate for its expected loss of revenue as communication by post is progressively overtaken by e-mail.

The commercial banking sector is also expected to have a role to play.

THE NEW GOVERNMENT PORTAL

So far, true e-government transaction services (level 3 in the Gartner model) are available from only a limited number of government agencies–Land Information New Zealand, the Companies Office (both described later in this article) and the new e-procurement service currently being tested. These services are narrowly focused–those who use them are specialists who have the incentive and the time to master the procedures.

For a wider audience, business and private, the EGU has built a new government portal, with a wide range of products (2,500) and services (around 1,200) and providing access to 90 agencies, many of them local government.

Designed to be a one-stop shop to access government for whatever purpose, the portal is based on the new cross-agency protocols described earlier. The most important of these is the new metadata standard, which will eliminate the perennial question faced by many citizens–which government agency does what? For example, do I go to the New Zealand Immigration Service to get a passport, or is it the Department of Internal Affairs (DIA)?

Now, keying in "passport" takes a citizen directly to pages which explain that passports are issued by DIA. They describe how the process works and offer the forms (as PDFs) to make the application.

While this is a rather simple example, access to all services from a single point of entry clearly has important implications for the delivery structure of all government agencies. In theory at least, there will eventually be no need for each agency to have its own downtown and suburban offices. The potential exists for them all to be integrated into a single location, with staff retrained to assist citizens to access any desired government service. If that ideal were to be achieved, then the vertically integrated government agency, the worldwide norm for a century, becomes obsolete.

In the long run, this is the most fundamental outcome of e-government, which, as it matures, may become the catalyst and enabler of the most sweeping transformation of government since the evolution of modern administrative structures over the past 200 years.

At this point, back office staff will find that in using the common elements of the e-government infrastructure (such as the New Zealand eGIF and the metadata standard) they will be operating, to all intents and purposes, in a virtual "all of government" environment.

Further out, by using common e-government applications, policies, standards, information technology, services and data and information resources, agencies will be using what amounts to a common platform.

At present, the new portal is owned and managed by the EGU but that might change over the next 18 months. Although no firm decisions have been made, it is possible that a team comprising the CEOs of the major government agencies will jointly own and manage the portal. This model has the advantage that as the portal is the primary public gateway to each agency, the CEOs will want to ensure its success. Additionally, it should automatically achieve coordination, as each CEO will want to ensure that their own agency ICT projects will be properly aligned to the organizational logic of the portal.

The EGU target is that, from an e-government perspective, by 2004 New Zealand's public sector will be working towards operating as a single, integrated organisation, enabled by technology, rather than driven by structure. If that target is achieved, any New Zealand citizen with online access should be able to say:

- Access to the service I want is easy;
- I can get information and services any way I choose;
- Online services are available to me any time, anywhere;
- It is easy to comment on the service I am using;
- I can contribute to the way policies are developed;
- Privacy is not a problem–I know my personal details are secure and confidential; and
- I have confidence that the authentication process ensures that the government is delivering services and products to the right people.

THE NEED FOR CULTURAL CHANGE

Before then, though, the majority of agencies must go through a demanding process of cultural change. While the technical hurdles of transactional e-government are very large indeed, the requirements and the process to get there are well understood and will be implemented by experienced project teams. The much larger challenge will be changing the mindset of public servants so they embrace the new e-government model.

A critical early step is achieving buy-in from the agency planning and policy staff responsible for new products and services. That process is working well–over the past 18 months or so staff have been enthusiastic and proactive in working to ensure that the IT systems behind new products and services have cross-agency compatibility and are outward looking so they can be accessed by other agencies and, where appropriate, by citizens.

Inevitably, there have been failures. It is only too easy for an agency to unconsciously assume that a new IT product has exclusively internal applications and that its own needs are unique, then build a product suitable only for itself. Fortunately, such errors have been rare and none have had long-term implications.

While primary responsibility for cultural change resides with agency CEOs (five of whom are on the EGU's board of management), the EGU itself has a facilitating role to play. To optimise coordination between agencies it runs a monthly forum for agency CIOs. Besides enabling them to contribute to all facets of the EGU's program, it should also ensure they are aware of what is happening in e-government across all other agencies. Second, it runs a forum of e-government champions ("agency leaders") who promote and drive e-government change within agencies. Its members are second-tier staff involved in the core business of the agency with the authority to engage their CEO in e-government proposals and to ensure that appropriate staff are engaged in consultation.

Over time, e-government criteria are also being included as part of the CEO performance assessment process with the State Services Commission.

Although the EGU itself cannot directly drive cultural change inside the agencies, it has defined the characteristics it believes agencies must have if e-government is to succeed:

- We have a culture which values collaboration with other agencies;
- Our back office is integrated with those of other agencies;
- We are moving towards the use of a common infrastructure;
- Our agency is building new capability through staff and business processes so it can work successfully in an e-government environment.

PARALLEL DEVELOPMENTS

Besides the role of the EGU in developing internal projects to bring about e-government, a number of state agencies also have responsibilities to encourage the development of Internet-enabled products and services by other sectors. Not only are these products and services important in their own right but they must also be ready to take advantage of e-government initiatives as they are launched.

This reflects the government's recognition that unless all sectors of society move into an electronic environment at much the same speed, overall success will be compromised by the absence of key components.

At the centre of that task is the Ministry of Economic Development (MED), the primary agency for driving the development of e-commerce. Its job, in conjunction with the private sector, is to lead by example through e-government and e-procurement, to provide leadership in communication, to encourage the development of broadband highways, to monitor e-commerce capacity and to establish the statutory and regulatory environment to facilitate e-commerce (for example, new legislation against electronic fraud). In meeting these responsibilities it works in partnership with local authorities, businesses and communities.

To advance its broadband objective, the Ministry has launched a number of initiatives. It has, first, funded six regional broadband pilot programs in association with local authorities, with additional input from the Ministry of Agriculture and Forestry, the Ministry of Education and Industry New Zealand. The objective is to identify and develop sufficient ongoing demand for broadband services to encourage suppliers to extend their infrastructure from the metropolitan areas to provincial communities.

Complementing that objective is a joint MED-Ministry of Education program to provide broadband access to all New Zealand schools.

The MED has also established an E-commerce Action Team (ECAT) with members drawn from central and local government, community organisations and the education sector. ECAT's task is to coordinate regional, or sector-based teams and to provide support for existing groups working on broadband and e-commerce projects.

This initiative has spawned a series of mini-ECATs, including one dedicated to the research sector and a second led by the rural NGO, Federated Farmers.

Primary responsibility for tackling the so-called "digital divide" has been assigned to the Department of Labor. Its brief is far ranging–at a macro level it is developing best-practise planning tools which would otherwise be unavailable to local communities, while at the other end of the scale it is providing training programs for workers involved in ICT projects.

A huge task faces the Ministry of Education. Besides working with MED to get broadband access to all schools it has to assist school administrators and teachers to move into the digital age. Four pilot projects have been launched in association with schools, the business sector and government to explore various approaches to ICT to enrich learning, with an emphasis on mathematics, science and information technology. A dedicated portal, LeadSpace, has been built to provide principals with online access to the materials and services they need, and an online network has been established with ex-principals to provide support, mentoring and professional discussion opportunities for working principals.

Those schools which, on their own initiative, are already well advanced in the use of ICT have been contracted (on a commercial basis) to mentor clusters of less advanced schools. Currently 50 clusters are contracted, with another 20 being added next year.

In recognition that the ground-up development of original online curriculum for the education sector is probably beyond the resources of a small country, the Ministry of Education has formed a partnership with the Australian states to develop high quality digital learning objects, as well as the standards for the development, management and delivery of digital material. This 5-year project is scheduled for completion by 2005 by which time all schools should have broadband access and teaching staff and administrators ought to have acquired the skills to take pupils into a digital learning environment.

TWO MAJOR SUCCESSES

One way or another, success for e-government comes down to reduced transactions costs–reduced time in conducting the transaction; one online location for finding services and products; or the replacement of multiple paper documents by a single online form (e.g., for a change of address).

Two outstanding examples of these efficiencies have been achieved in New Zealand.

Landonline is an information technology project which is converting millions of land title records, title instruments, plans, parcels and geodetic survey marks into an electronic format. It means that the staff of Land Information New Zealand (LINZ) and its customers (land professionals such as surveyors, conveyancers and search agents) are radically changing the way they work, moving from a traditional paper-based system to an exclusively electronic environment.

More than 100 years ago the New Zealand government began keeping survey and title records. Under the "Torrens" land administrative system these titles are absolute proof of land ownership. Until now this system was based on a vast paper archive of upwards of 30 million documents. It became so unwieldy that LINZ was adding over a kilometre of shelving every year just to cope with the volume of new records.

The vision of Landonline was to create an entirely electronic survey and title infrastructure. To achieve that objective, the Landonline project is converting into an electronic format a total of 3 million title records, 2 million title instruments, 1.2 million plans, 1.3 million parcels, 40,000 existing geodetic survey marks and a further 50,000 new geodetic marks.

During conversion, systems of data entry and quality control maintain the integrity of these records and the state guarantee of title becomes electronic rather than paper-based.

Landonline has been implemented in a phased roll-out schedule because of the sheer number of documents which needed converting. Stage One, through which land professionals can conduct remote searching of the Landonline survey and title database from their own PCs via the Internet, began rolling out in the southern provinces in April 2000. The roll-out progressed steadily northwards as titles were converted and is now complete.

By the end of 2002, Landonline Stage Two–enabling survey plan lodgement and routine title dealings to also be undertaken electronically– is scheduled to have been piloted and be ready for implementation.

It has not been a painless process for LINZ. A number of offices have been closed and staff numbers have been reduced. There were early complaints that the delivery of data from servers was excessively slow, although that was more frequently the result of land professionals with a desire for broadband speed over narrowband connections (the file sizes are often large).

Despite some disappointments along the way, Landonline is now a remarkably successful story of e-government and is attracting worldwide attention. A number of Australian states, which share the Torrens land tenure system, are investigating the purchase of Landonline modules.

Equally complex has been the conversion of tens of thousands of company records, shareholders lists, the names of banned company directors, financial securities of all descriptions, bankruptcy records, motor vehicle registrations and superannuation schemes held by the New Zealand Companies Office.

In June 2000 LINZ began the task of capturing in a digital format all of its critical historical documents. That task was completed in March 2001.

The practical benefits of this success for the business community have been substantial. In the past, companies' offices around New Zealand were a hive of activity as dozens of secretaries carried out manual searches for law firms, the police, accountants and the like. Today, there is just the hum of servers as the records are accessed online.

Instead of the service being available only during traditional office hours, the electronic registry is now available day and night, seven days a week. It is permanently up to date, as any modifications to company details–change of address, changes to directors, new securities, etc.–are made online in real time and the data processing centre has moved to a 24-hour operation.

Neither is there any longer an excuse ("I forgot") for not filing a company's annual return–clients now get a computer-generated reminder text message on their mobile phones.

Besides a vastly superior service to the business community, costs are also down–after three reductions in the past five years, companies can now be registered for just NZ$25. An online search for company directors costs NZ$3.00; tracking down a company by name costs NZ$2.00; to register a security over a motor vehicle costs NZ$4.00; to reserve a company name costs NZ$7.00.

The business community has embraced the changes with enthusiasm. Last year, 88% of company registrations were done online, up 50% on 2000. Manual registrations were down 70%. Company searches, previously a paper-based process requiring a visit to the local company office, are now conducted online by 91% of its clients. In a number of offices, the big reduction in clients requiring manual assistance has enabled the public counter to be closed and replaced by an Internet terminal.

As with LINZ, there was a downside. A number of public offices were closed as operations were consolidated. Today, all phone queries, previously handled by offices up and down the country, go to a single online call centre, which also handles e-mail questions.

These changes at the company offices have been so fundamental that its name is now probably a misnomer. Today, it has responsibility for so many legal registries–if it has the skill set to manage one electronic register, then why not the whole lot–that it has become a definitive example of how a number of similar e-services can be aggregated within one organisation and delivered through a single point of access.

That, of course, is the *raison d'etre* of e-government.

GOVERNMENT AS CHEERLEADER

None of this could be achievable unless the government itself was genuinely committed to the values, principles and purposes of e-government.

Serendipity played a certain role in New Zealand's early interest in e-government. The country's first Minister for Information Technology, Maurice Williamson, a former programmer for Air New Zealand and ICT enthusiast, was appointed in 1994, before the first Mosaic browser revolutionized the Internet. Although his was an early voice, by the mid-1990s a consensus had formed that ICT presented transformational opportunities for government.

However, although a number of agencies set off on ICT paths of their own in the mid to late 1990s (generally making good decisions and excellent progress), it was not until 1999 that a coordinated, all-of-government approach was adopted and the EGU was established.

The current Minister for State Services, Hon. Trevor Mallard, now insists that the government itself becomes a "model user" of new technology. In a presentation 2001 to a senior managers conference he described e-government as "the clearest opportunity for improving capability and performance across the public sector that you are ever likely to see and be involved in." If anyone present was still in doubt about his commitment, he added that he expected "no agency to shrink from the task."

Drawing on the experience of other jurisdictions has been important to the government's strategy–to ensure New Zealand remains current in its thinking on e-government issues, the CEO of LINZ, Dr. Russ Ballard, 2001 visited five leading e-government jurisdictions (Washington, North Carolina, Virginia, Ireland and Britain) to identify strategies, opportunities and potential pitfalls. In addition, the Minister of

State Services and the Director of the E-Government Unit have visited Asia, the United States and Europe to learn what direction other countries are moving in.

Even so, wary of the notorious budget overruns on IT projects (in the private sector, as well as the state), the government has put a fiscal fence around e-government initiatives. The majority of e-government projects are expected to be undertaken within existing budgets and must be able to demonstrate net financial gains. In the case of projects which require new funding, they must develop a business plan which demonstrates they are aligned with the government's annual budget strategy and must include a full assessment of the costs, benefits and risks for the relevant budget year and three years beyond.

While apparently daunting, those requirements have not slowed progress. Compliance with such prudent criteria has not been a problem for well constructed and managed e-government projects.

THE FUTURE

While it might be tempting for New Zealanders to ascribe the country's third place in the worldwide e-government hierarchy to local brilliance, it would be more impartial to point out that this country has a set of circumstances which provides an unusual opportunity to produce an optimised e-government environment. Besides being small (i.e., manageable) and having an advanced technology infrastructure, it has a much simpler government structure than most other advanced countries. There is a single, central government and no state governments.

The capital, Wellington, is small (just 300,000 people) so the CEOs and CIOs of most of the various agencies know each other, which makes shared knowledge and coordination so much easier.

The standard of literacy and computer skills is the much same as the United States or western Europe, and the uptake of new technology has always been high.

The business environment is also conducive to technological change and new business combinations, as the New Zealand economy is very open and is characterised by far fewer regulations and restrictions than most OECD countries.

Those factors–along with the government's enthusiastic commitment to e-government and the success of the EGU in building the underlying foundations for easy public access to online government services– suggest that New Zealand is likely to maintain its leadership position.

That is certainly the EGU's ambition–it intends that by 2004 the majority of government services accessed via the new portal will have moved to the transaction phase (Gartner level 3). Achieving that target is a major challenge but the building blocks are in place, a game plan has been agreed and the environment is encouraging.

After 2004 the next step will be the transformation of government itself. That is likely to be much more of a political issue than a technological one and will engage the country for the remainder of this decade.

NOTE

1. United Nations Division for Public Economics and Public Administration. Benchmarking E-government: A Global Perspective–Assessing the Progress of the UN Member States, 2001, *http://www.unpan.org/e-government/Benchmarking%20E-gov% 202001.pdf*

GERMANY

BundOnline 2005–
The E-Government Initiative
of the German Federal Administration

Gerd Wittkemper

Booz Allen Hamilton, Berlin, Germany

Ralf Kleindiek

Federal Ministry of the Interior, Germany

Dr. Gerd Wittkemper is Senior Vice President of Booz Allen Hamilton based in Berlin. He is the partner responsible for the firm's build-up of the Public Sector Business in Europe with consulting activities in strategy, IT, organization, change management and public-private partnerships.

Dr. Ralf Kleindiek was an officer at the Federal Ministry of the Interior at the time of writing and headed the project group BundOnline 2005 between July 2001 and September 2002. He recently assumed the position of the head of the minister's office in the Federal Ministry of Justice.

[Haworth co-indexing entry note]: "BundOnline 2005–The E-Government Initiative of the German Federal Administration." Wittkemper, Gerd, and Ralf Kleindiek. Co-published simultaneously in *Journal of Political Marketing* (The Haworth Press, Inc.) Vol. 2, No. 3/4, 2003, pp. 107-126; and: *The World of E-Government* (ed: Gregory G. Curtin, Michael H. Sommer, and Veronika Vis-Sommer) The Haworth Press, Inc., 2003, pp. 107-126. Single or multiple copies of this article are available for a fee from The Haworth Document Delivery Service [1-800-HAWORTH, 9:00 a.m. - 5:00 p.m. (EST). E-mail address: docdelivery@haworthpress.com].

http://www.haworthpress.com/store/product.asp?sku=J199
10.1300/J199v02n03_07

SUMMARY. The German e-government initiative BundOnline 2005 was launched by the German government in 2001 to ensure that citizens, enterprises and the administration itself can access the services provided by the federal administration easier, faster and at lower costs through the Internet. Euro 1.65 billion are devoted to this purpose. The German e-government initiative is characterized by central coordination, central implementation of shared components and the establishment of competence centers. Finally, the current status is presented especially with respect to the challenges applying to the German legal environment–German data protection requirements and the federal legislation. *[Article copies available for a fee from The Haworth Document Delivery Service: 1-800-HAWORTH. E-mail address: <docdelivery@haworthpress.com> Website: <http://www.HaworthPress.com> © 2003 by The Haworth Press, Inc. All rights reserved.]*

KEYWORDS. E-government, BundOnline 2005, modernization of administration, information and communication technology, information society

INTRODUCTION

E-government is considered a key element to shape Germany's future. The use of sophisticated information and communication technology creates a quantum leap on the way to an administration centered around the needs of its customers, citizens, enterprises and other authorities. Therefore, e-government is considered a pivotal element in the modernization of governmental administration. The German government has launched the e-government initiative BundOnline 2005 to ensure that citizens, businesses and the administration can access the services provided by the federal administration easier, faster and at lower costs than presently. By making services for enterprises more easily accessible, the attractiveness of business location in Germany will be improved. BundOnline 2005 acknowledges that the quality of life of citizens largely depends on their access to government services in a cost-efficient and convenient manner. Last but not least, by using the virtues of the digital age, BundOnline 2005 aims at reengineering administrative processes by making them simpler and more efficient.

This article takes a closer look at the German e-government initiative BundOnline 2005. Part 1 describes the goals of the e-government initiative in Germany. Part 2 deals with the concepts applied to implement, monitor and steer the initiative. In Part 3 two challenges for e-government that apply in particular to the German environment are described and analyzed.

PART ONE:
GOALS OF THE GERMAN E-GOVERNMENT INITIATIVE

Provision of All Services of the German Federal Administration Online

The German e-government initiative aims at delivering *all* e-government services of the federal administration online by the end of 2005. The service portfolio of the German federal administration includes not only services for enterprises and citizens but also services which are directed at other authorities, be it at the federal level or at the level of the states (Bundesländer) or municipalities. Thus, the German e-government initiative has not chosen to put in place only those services that provide the highest benefit to the administration, but to offer *all* services online focused on the needs of citizens and enterprises.

Implementation of a Customer-Focused Administration

At a first glance the German e-government initiative deals with IT technology. Its ultimate goal, however, is to refocus the way the government and its agencies approach their "customers," notably citizens, enterprises and other administrative bodies.

Previously and to the present date, the provision of services by government agencies has been structured along the constitutional and functional powers entrusted to the various agencies. This was to guarantee organizational transparency and made it easy to ensure that government authorities do not reach beyond their legitimate authorities.

A more recent approach to the way government agencies interact with their citizens requires that government agencies be more than merely an executive tool, but a service organization. This approach follows the insight that the well-being and development of a modern industrial society largely depends on the speed, efficiency and transparency with which government agencies act and interact.

A modern society characterized by multiple and highly complex interactions of its members calls for rule setting, standards and implementation processes which are at the front edge of technological and organizational developments. This means that government services should allow enterprises to benefit from the latest developments of technology to make their lives easier and give them the competitive edge to survive and excel in worldwide markets.

The introduction of online services in the government agencies will force government agencies to reorganize and refocus their internal work process to:

- ensure a more "customer-centred" rendering of services (organized by industry, social groups, state organization, citizens and so on);
- redefine, and to the extent possible simplify, the interfaces between various agencies and between ministries and their subordinate authorities;
- train the staff of each agency to deal with modern information processing technology;
- link government information services with other information services providers to improve the speed of access of citizens to relevant information.

Standardization and Synergies

At the outset of the development of online services there was almost no standardization with regard to the provision of government services. Therefore, each government authority developed its own IT environment at the cost of stable quality, efficiency and accessibility. BundOnline 2005 aims at realizing considerable synergies by using standardized approaches to the way government agencies will provide services. Further, the initiative will develop a structure which allows standardized and thereby more cost efficient IT solutions to prevail.

Government services must be compatible and interoperable. To achieve this goal, the basic organizational and technical components will be developed centrally and applied to the entire federal administration. The infrastructure will be based on uniform standards with open interfaces. The implementation of the individual applications which are the responsibility of government agencies will be centrally monitored and evaluated to guarantee that IT standards and quality standards are met. The responsibility for development of the basic components and the monitoring of the implementation lies with the Ministry for the Interior.

Providing Fully Integrated E-Government Services Throughout Germany and Europe

E-government in Germany does not stop with putting in place services of the federal administration for enterprises and citizens only. It aims at including all levels of administration. The ultimate goal is to reach fully integrated e-government services, encompassing the services of the federal administration as well as the states (Bundesländer) and the municipalities.

Today, the e-government activities of the federal administration and the states are still poorly coordinated. Due to constitutional restraints, the federal e-government initiative cannot be imposed on the states or municipalities. However, BundOnline 2005 aims at coordinating and ultimately amalgamating the e-government programs of the states with the federal initiative and seeks to generate synergies where practicable.

Finally, BundOnline 2005 seeks to be compatible with the e-government programs of the other European member states. Therefore, members of the project group BundOnline 2005 take an active role in working groups directed at harmonization and synchronization of e-government initiatives on the European level.

PART TWO: IMPLEMENTATION OF BUNDONLINE 2005

Definition of Service

The identification and description of the services is based on the view that the Federal administration can be seen as a very large service organization similar to an enterprise in the private industry. The notion of a service is further illustrated in Figure 1. A government service according to BundOnline is thus defined as the "complete processing of a task for an external user." An example of a transactional service is the application for civil service by conscientious objectors to military service and the notification of the applicant about the result. Accordingly, a government service includes all activities or steps required for delivering a service, e.g., filing of an application, processing of an application and notification of the applicant.

In a second step, the services were analyzed on the level of sub-activities required to accomplish a service and mapped against the framework of information-communication-transaction (Figure 2). The result was a classification of government services into eight different service types which require an increasing depth of interaction between the administration and the user. In the category of information services there is the service type "general and specialist information." Examples of services requiring communication between the administration and the user are "Preparing political decisions" or "Cooperation with authori-

FIGURE 1. The Definition of Service

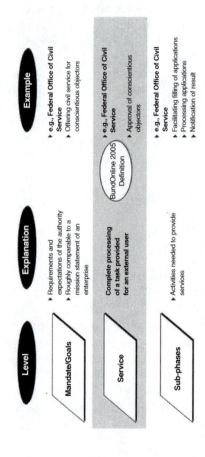

FIGURE 2. The Eight Service Types

Classification of services on the value-added chain

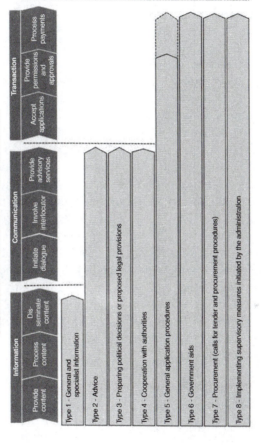

ties." Finally, there are complex transactional services such as "General application services," "Procurement" or "Government aids" which result in the issuance of a permission, an approval or a notification and may or may not result in a payment (dotted arrow in Figure 2).

Establishment of the Service Portfolio of the Federal Administration

Based on this service definition and categorization the next step in creating BundOnline 2005 was to develop a comprehensive catalogue of all services which could be offered online. This was done by performing interviews with representatives from individual authorities and by analyzing the results of a questionnaire mailing. The list of services thus obtained was then refined to keep the aggregation of the individual services at a comparable level. The result of this effort was a service portfolio consisting of 376 services, all of which can be offered at least partially online. About 40% of these services were classified as "information services" (Type 1). Roughly 25% of the services were categorized as "general application procedures" (Type 5) and another 9% as "government aids" (Type 6). Thus, roughly 75% of the services could be attributed to only three of the eight generic service types. The entire service portfolio along with the implementation strategy of the German federal administration was published in the cabinet resolution for the e-government initiative BundOnline 2005 in November 2001.

Central Coordination

While the implementation of the individual services is the responsibility of every ministry or agency, the whole undertaking is centrally coordinated. The federal cabinet commissioned the federal Ministry of the Interior with the central coordination because information and communication technology is one of the competencies of this ministry. The project group used the Booz Allen approach "Strategy-Based Transformation" which established a transformation project office for central coordination. The central coordination of the e-government initiative is to ensure that the individual activities give rise to an integrated overall architecture.

Furthermore, central coordination and provision of a series of basic components will provide major savings.

To duly perform this task, a project group consisting of members from the federal Ministry of the Interior and the management and technology consulting company Booz Allen Hamilton was formed.

Central coordination of the implementation activities in the authorities is accomplished by a group of people who work at the interface between the project group and the authorities, for which the term "catalysts" was coined. Their task is primarily to coach the project leaders of the individual implementation projects by offering support with planning, identifying synergies between individual projects and by informing them about the status of the shared components of BundOnline 2005 overall. Furthermore, through these catalysts the implementation process is tightened in accordance with the "time-to-market" principle. A supra-authority monitoring process was established to guarantee that goals and milestones are being met and critical issues and risks are made transparent and addressed as early as possible. A subgroup was established to create a knowledge management system that institutionalizes the lessons learned from the various decentralized e-government projects, identifies best practices and provides opportunities for sharing this know-how. A communication team ensures that the public and the political leaders are informed about the progress of the initiative on a regular basis. The project group is a part of the IT department of the Ministry of the Interior. The project leader of BundOnline 2005 reports to the Chief Information Officer of the federal administration, who was appointed at the beginning of 2002. The project group coordinates the implementation, monitoring and quality management and resolves critical issues with a group of nominated contact partners of each ministry in regular monthly meetings.

Standardization

The introduction of e-government solutions in the IT environment of the federal administration requires standards, guidelines and recommendations to be specified to safeguard the efficiency and effectiveness of implementation projects and to develop innovative applications aimed at end users. Because of the heterogeneity of the state of implementation of the planned or existing solutions in the federal administration, the provision of supra-standards for going forward is particularly important.

Setting IT standards for the implementation projects of the BundOnline 2005 initiative follows five basic principles:

- IT standards are vital to all elements of an IT architecture for e-government solutions. Local requirements have to be considered in the specification via suitable coordination processes;
- IT standards should ensure interoperability and portability between e-government applications and existing procedures;
- The use of IT standards is to help decentralized realization teams with respect to the development of technical specifications for e-government solutions;
- IT standards support the implementation of technical guidelines for e-government applications. Examples of this include openness, scalability, ability to support multiple back-ends, simplified system management, independence of fixed workplaces and neutrality of operating systems;
- IT standards and architectures are not provided statically, but are being continuously analyzed and adapted in line with developments and trends of the industry via change management processes.

Furthermore, by setting IT standards and architectures, investment protection of hardware and software systems that have already been introduced in the federal administration (in particular local PCs) is ensured. The coexistence of new and existing applications on existing hardware is a further requirement.

Basic Shared Components

A fundamental design hypothesis of the BundOnline 2005 initiative is that IT components that are used by a number of e-government applications must be developed centrally and provided to the authorities who will integrate them for their electronic services. These central IT components identified are data security, a payment transaction platform, a content management system, a form server and the portal of the federal administration. Furthermore, a call center is planned to offer support for the introduction of e-government in Germany. The technical basic components are currently being realized.

Data Security

E-government must be secure; otherwise citizens will not trust the system and, hence, will not use the new opportunities offered by electronic communication. The technical requirements placed on qualified electronic signatures in Germany are already available nationwide. The necessary legal framework is also already in place. It is nevertheless foreseeable that the widespread use of electronic signatures will only be achievable in the medium term.

The federal administration strives to achieve adequate security measures for electronic communication with industry, citizens and other administrations, i.e., on the state level. The requirements are confidentiality (protection against unauthorized knowledge), integrity (protection against manipulation) and authenticity of the communication (ensuring that a message actually comes from the person or institution claiming to be the sender).

To achieve this, the federal administration will electronically sign documents it sends to its partners. The addressees can test integrity and authenticity and encrypt documents to protect confidentiality if the addressee provides his/her public key. In addition, the federal administration ensures that citizens and industry are given free verification software to test the electronic signatures of the federal administration.

The communication partners of the federal administration will be provided with as secure, user-friendly, and cheap procedures as possible for communication with the federal administration. It will be up to the communication partner to decide which security level they want to use for communication with the administration.

The federal administration will provide its public keys to encode documents (protection of confidentiality, acceptance of electronic signatures from its communication partners to test integrity and authenticity).

At present, some administrative procedures require certain form regulations, for instance, the personal signature of an applicant may be required. The planned Third Act to Amend Administrative Processes requires that a written signature is to be replaced by a qualified electronic signature. Therefore, the administration and its communication partners must be equipped with qualified certificates and hardware to carry out such administrative procedures electronically. The market currently offers solutions using smartcards and readers.

Since the equipment of the administration and its communication partners with smartcards and readers is not reasonable in the short term because of the high cost to the citizen and insufficient standardization, transitional solutions that can be used for administrative procedures where writing is required are under examination now.

For communicating with electronic signatures and for encryption between heterogeneously equipped communication partners, standards are needed. They guarantee interoperability between various software and hardware products (horizontal interoperability), and interoperability between different advanced and qualified signatures (vertical interoperability).

Payment Transactions Platform

A number of services in the federal administration rely on a fee or a payment to be transmitted to the authority by the citizen or enterprise that is being serviced. Since the actual payment transaction does not depend on the individual service, an electronic payment platform can be developed centrally. Interfaces will be used to link the payment procedures of the federal administration with the external transaction processors (credit card companies, etc.) and the respective decentral application. This can be implemented via the Internet with very little effort in analogy to existing commercial payment platforms.

Content Management System

Currently, a large number of different content management systems (CMS) are being installed in the federal administration. CMS are to provide topical, relevant content for various output media. They facilitate the provision and the updating of information service offerings of authorities on the Internet. Today, in the federal administration proprietary do-it-yourself solutions coexist and compete with externally developed systems and standard products. To standardize these systems in the medium term, a CMS will be centrally provided.

In addition to the savings due to provision and maintenance of the system, further synergistic effects can be gained by providing templates that can be used by the entire federal administration. Also, a central CMS is an important basis for a customer relationship management (CRM) system.

Form Server

A form server is used to provide the forms of the federal authorities. All forms can be found easily on a central Website and provided to the user for further processing. The form server will be provided on the portal of the federal administration (www.bund.de). Forms can be completed online or offline. The latter option provides users who are not yet able to sign electronically with the possibility of submitting hand-signed forms to the authority through conventional means.

To ease the updating, the electronic forms are stored on the authorities' central Webservers. In this way, each individual authority can access its forms flexibly and make any necessary adjustments.

Internet Portal

The existing service portal of the Federation (www.bund.de) is designed as a central gateway to the services of the German federal administration. In addition to the links to the existing Websites of the individual authorities, all online services for citizens or enterprises will be integrated.

Call Center

Users will be offered support via traditional communication media, especially when a new online service has been rolled out. A call center will offer competent operator services as well as the possibility for e-government users to make inquiries or give feedback about the functioning of individual services.

Competence Centers

To integrate the basic components efficiently into individual applications, five competence centers are being set up in parallel with the development of the basic components. The competence centers are staffed with IT experts who disseminate specific know-how about the basic components in the federal administration. Furthermore their task is to advise and support the authorities and troubleshoot in case of technical problems with the basic components.

Three competence centers are designed to complement the basic components: data security, payment transaction and content management system; one competence center will share know-how about business process reengineering in the administration to transform paper-based processes to streamlined electronic processes. A fifth competence center will deal with workflow management and document management systems and advise the authorities in selecting, introducing and operating workflow management systems.

Workflow management systems enable process participants to collaborate in a reliable and secure manner in complex processes. With the help of a workflow management system, it is possible to determine the order of individual steps of a job and what staffing, material and organizational resources are needed for implementation. In addition, workflow management systems manage interrupted, stopped and resumed processes by allowing for a roll-back of uncompleted processes.

Implementation Plan

A fundamental step towards the implementation of the 376 individual services was the establishment of a master plan. The master plan sets forth which federal services are to be made available online in which year between 2002 and 2005. It further contains the technical requirements and standards needed, the basic components to be provided centrally and a top-down estimate of the funds needed over the years and by individual department.

To allocate the implementation of the 376 services over the years 2002 to 2005 several considerations were applied. First, still-existing legal constraints, especially with regard to the requirement of a written signature, were taken into account. Next, the earliest possible time of the introduction of basic components was determined and the time to implement the individual application was estimated. Finally, overriding aspects were taken into account like department-specific priorities and political requirements of the BundOnline 2005 initiative.

The proposed allocation of online services over the years is shown in Figure 3.

It is important to note that the master plan was approved by the federal cabinet and thus has the legal status of a cabinet resolution. It can therefore serve as the basis for cooperation between the Ministry of the Interior in charge of the central activities and the different ministries with their affiliated authorities.

A further step in the development was the integration of pilot projects. These are innovative applications developed by different ministries and authorities to offer a particular service over the Internet. These pilot projects have been planned and implemented independently prior to the launch of the BundOnline 2005 initiative. They cover a broad spectrum such as the electronic filing of tax declarations for citizens and enterprises (Project ELSTER), the PROFI information system for efficient management of project promotion of the Ministry of Education and Research that handles 15,000 running projects and 1,400 registered users. A total of 18 e-government solutions have been given the status of "pilot projects."

Pilot projects serve as models and create an incentive for other areas of the administration to develop e-government solutions. Furthermore,

FIGURE 3. Distribution of Services Over the Years

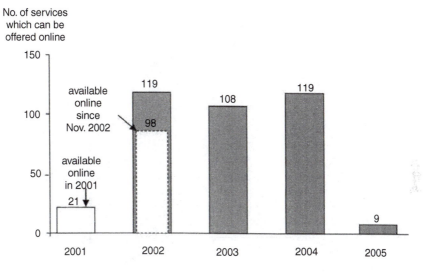

Distribution of services by earliest readiness date

they demonstrate to the broad public the benefit of e-government services. However, as they have been developed independently, they do
not rely on common standards or joint IT architectures. A key finding
from analyzing the model projects is that e-government is more than the
sum of individual applications. E-government has to be based and built
on a common integrated architecture that has to be designed and developed centrally.

A third major aspect is the implementation plan which covers a
top-down estimate of the financial requirements needed for the implementation of BundOnline 2005. According to this estimation, the complete online-provision of all services of the federal administration
requires a total of Euro 1.65 (plus/minus 0.2) billion in funding over the
years 2002 to 2005. The lion's share (48%) of this funding is to be spent
on the development of local applications in the authorities. Process and
organizational adjustments in the authorities for processing electronic
files account for another 25% of the estimated budget. The central activities, i.e., development of basic components, build-up and operation of
competence centers and the central coordination of the overall initiative
contribute roughly 9% to the overall amount (Figure 4).

FIGURE 4. Top-Down Estimate of Financial Requirements and Its Functional Break Down

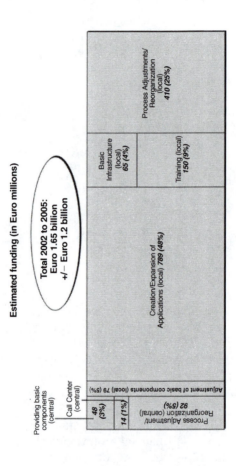

Estimated funding (in Euro millions)

Total 2002 to 2005:
Euro 1.65 billion
+/– Euro 1.2 billion

Providing basic components (central)

Call Center (central)

48 (3%)

14 (1%)

Process Adjustment/ Reorganization (central) 92 (5%)

Adjustment of basic components (local) 79 (5%)

Creation/Expansion of Applications (local) 789 (48%)

Basic Infrastructure (local) 65 (4%)

Training (local) 150 (9%)

Process Adjustments/ Reorganization (local) 410 (25%)

The greatest funding requirement occurs in 2003 (31%) and 2004 (37%), while preparatory and expansion work is primarily due in 2002 (13%), and 2005 (19%).

PART THREE: CURRENT STATUS AND CHALLENGES

Currently e-government in Germany is in a state of transition. Since the beginning of the German e-government initiative in September 2000, much progress has been made. Nearly 100 government services have been implemented online so far. However, as critical basic components for the implementation of transactional services are presently developed and are therefore not yet available, most services which were implemented in the year 2002 are information services. However, a couple of highly sophisticated transactional services have been realized as pilot projects. Most noteworthy is the fully transactional e-procurement platform which was launched in May 2002. The electronic procurement operates under the strict rules of German public procurement law which allows for authentication of bidders and clerks by means of a digital signature via a smartcard. A first fully electronic procurement process was started in May 2002.

In the first eight months of centrally coordinated implementation the following observations were made. The catalysts as delegates of the project group who support the project leaders in their planning and implementation activities have mostly been adopted by the authorities. In most cases stable and fruitful working relations have been developed. Increasingly, authorities understand the goals of the initiative and how they can contribute. Local implementation projects are being set up and are gaining impetus.

However, in line with the master plan much of the work still lies ahead in the next three years. The following chapters deal with two specific challenges of implementing e-government in the German administrative environment.

The Effect of Data Protection Requirements Under German Law

Data processing as needed in sophisticated information and communication technology becomes most effective once the user has unrestricted access to several databases, if databases are linked with each other and if data has to be entered only once and may be used by several databases. However, with the advent of increasingly advanced electronic data processing it became obvious that the unrestricted storing and use of an unlimited number of personal data may violate the individual rights of citizens. German constitutional courts therefore ruled that each individual has a right to determine which of his or her personal data be raised, stored and used, unless there are serious public interests which are paramount to the individual right.

Deriving from this constitutional principle the German Data Protection Act regulates that personal data may only be raised, stored and used in a restricted manner, i.e., personal data may only be raised for reasons which are known and have been accepted by the individual and transfer of personal data is only allowed if the individual is informed about it and agrees to the data transfer.

From these basic requirements for the use of personal data a number of restrictions are being derived which limit effective and centralized data management, in particular:

- data may not be stored any longer than absolutely necessary for the achievement of the purpose for which they have been raised;
- government agencies which have different functional tasks may not use one data pool, even if the data each of those agencies may use are identical;
- personal data have to be raised immediately for the respective individual person and may not be retrieved through indirect means (e.g., through access to joint data pools).

The principles of data protection provide a number of challenges in the effective organization of e-government projects in Germany. Since no data capital may be generated, data must be raised for each single case separately which requires more capacities and limits economies of scale.

A horizontal exchange of data between government agencies is generally prohibited and therefore limits the sourcing of government services by one person. Thereby, the implementation of a customer-based approach may not fully be achieved, since the one-stop shop approach would severely violate the principle that each government agency should remain an island that keeps personal data locked.

There are a few solutions which can ease the problems described above: Citizens may waive their rights to restrict protection of their personal data. This leaves room for a pooling of data if this is in the best interest of the individual. Second, government agencies may use a joint data pool if this use has already been determined and communicated to the individual at the moment when the data have been raised. Therefore, some thoughtful planning may help to avoid problems down the road.

Third, if the public interest outweighs the interest of the individual to have personal data protected, government agencies may share data. This solution, however, is limited to certain fields of government services, like, for example, interior security. The mere interest of the public in an effective provision of services by the government is not sufficient to outweigh the individual's right to protection of personal data.

Implementing E-Government in a Federal System

The e-government initiative of the German government is focused on the administrative services of federal government agencies. No doubt, from a user's point of view, it would be attractive to have all government services delivered online through one portal (one-stop government). However, imposition of e-government by the federal government to the states and municipalities conflicts with the German federal system.

The German federal constitution provides for three administrative levels: the federal administration, the sixteen states and the municipalities. The sixteen independent states (Bundesländer) have original constitutional rights which make them independent in a number of matters relevant to e-government. For example, the entire educational system as well as the arts are administered on the state level without involvement of the federal government. Furthermore, collection of certain taxes is the responsibility of the states. As the states have set up their own e-government initiatives, cooperation and coordination of the e-government activities between the federal administration and the states is a challenge. It is no surprise that this system puts attempts to standardize government services on a supra-stated level to a test.

A similar situation applies to the interface between the federal administration and the municipalities. The approximately 14,000 municipalities form ipso jure part of the states. However, Article 28 II of the German constitutional law provides for the right of self-administration of the municipalities in all matters concerning the local community, specifically regarding personnel, organization, finance, statutes and civil engineering. Self-administration with respect to organization means that municipalities can organize their internal administrative processes as well as the provision of administrative services by themselves. Thus, implementation of an e-government program is the responsibility of the municipalities and cannot be imposed upon them by the states. On the other hand munipalities have to contribute to certain tasks of the federal administration which are being supervised by the federation, e.g., issuance of passports, etc.

BundOnline 2005 tries to bridge this gap by offering open interfaces in its system which invite the state agencies and municipalities to join the federal e-government initiative on the same basis as applied to the agencies of the federal administration. Furthermore, BundOnline 2005 encourages the states and municipalities to integrate and use applications developed within BundOnline 2005 by communicating openly about the progress of the initiative and taking an active role in joint committees between the states and the federal government.

To increase the impetus of e-government on the level of the states and the municipalities, the German government could consider an amendment of the Administrative Procedure Act which would equate e-government processes with traditional administrative processes. The increasing demand for e-government services would increase the pressure to offer services online because municipalities are competing with each other with respect to the attractiveness as business location.

THE "BUSINESS"
OF E-GOVERNMENT

RANKING THE WORLD'S LEADING COUNTRIES

Realizing the Vision of eGovernment

Vivienne Jupp

Global eGovernment Services, Accenture

SUMMARY. This article discusses the emerging trends in eGovernment, based on the most recent results of Accenture's global study and rankings of countries' eGovernment maturity. Governments began outlining their visions for online service delivery some five years ago, and, since that time, have had varying degrees of success in turning those visions into reality. The benefits are clear–faster, cheaper, more personalized and efficient service delivery that citizens and businesses can access literally whenever they need it.

Vivienne Jupp is Managing Partner of Global eGovernment Services at Accenture and Global Head of Accenture's Service Lines within the Government Market Unit (E-mail: vivienne.jupp@accenture.com).

[Haworth co-indexing entry note]: "Realizing the Vision of eGovernment." Jupp, Vivienne. Co-published simultaneously in *Journal of Political Marketing* (The Haworth Press, Inc.) Vol. 2, No. 3/4, 2003, pp. 129-145; and: *The World of E-Government* (ed: Gregory G. Curtin, Michael H. Sommer, and Veronika Vis-Sommer) The Haworth Press, Inc., 2003, pp. 129-145. Single or multiple copies of this article are available for a fee from The Haworth Document Delivery Service [1-800-HAWORTH, 9:00 a.m. - 5:00 p.m. (EST). E-mail address: docdelivery@haworthpress.com].

10.1300/J199v02n03_08

Realizing those benefits has, however, proven somewhat elusive. The article discusses what governments will need to do to realize their eGovernment visions and highlights through example best practices in eGovernment. *[Article copies available for a fee from The Haworth Document Delivery Service: 1-800-HAWORTH. E-mail address: <docdelivery@ haworthpress.com> Website: <http://www.HaworthPress.com> © 2003 by The Haworth Press, Inc. All rights reserved.]*

KEYWORDS. eGovernment, Customer Relationship Management, CRM, CIO, portals, governance

Governments began outlining their visions for online service delivery some five years ago, and, since that time, have had varying degrees of success in turning those visions into reality. The benefits are clear–faster, cheaper, more personalized and efficient service delivery that citizens and businesses can access literally whenever they need it.

Realizing those benefits has, however, proven somewhat elusive. In moving government online, the challenges are complex–legal, administrative, regulatory, social and political forces combine to create a delicate mix of stakeholders that must be managed in the transition to online government.

In 2002 Accenture's annual study of eGovernment Leadership, *eGovernment Leadership: Realizing the Vision*, mapped the eGovernment landscape and uncovered some interesting trends. This article will provide an abstract of our findings. (For a full copy of the report, please visit *http://www.accenture.com/xd/xd.asp?it=enWeb&xd=industries\ government\gove_thought.xml*)

OUR METHODOLOGY–A BRIEF OVERVIEW

Behaving as citizens and businesses, Accenture researchers in each of 23 selected countries (Australia, Belgium, Brazil, Canada, Denmark, Finland, France, Germany, Hong Kong, Ireland, Italy, Japan, Malaysia, Mexico, the Netherlands, New Zealand, Norway, Portugal, Singapore, South Africa, Spain, the United Kingdom and the United States) utilized the Internet in an attempt to fulfill service needs that might typically be provided by a national government. They accessed and assessed the Websites of national government agencies to determine the quality and maturity of services, and the level at which business can be conducted electronically with government.

The 169 services surveyed were representative of what citizens and businesses require from their government throughout their life cycle. The services were traditionally offered over the counter, by phone or in paper format. No government surveyed offered all 169 services. In most countries, aspects of all of the services are offered at a lower tier of government–examples of which include state or province, region, municipal and county. In such instances, these services were removed from the data under consideration before the analysis was undertaken, and the government concerned was in no way penalized in our analysis for not delivering a service outside of its area of responsibility.

Two measures were used to determine the eGovernment maturity of the countries in the research: Service Maturity (the number of services for which national governments are responsible that are available online and the level of completeness with which each service is offered) and Customer Relationship Management (CRM–a measure of the sophistication of service delivery, thereby helping citizens get the best value from their online interaction with government). These were then combined to calculate each country's Overall Maturity, which allowed each country to be allocated a ranking within the 23 country sample (Overall Maturity).

In addition to the quantitative element of the research described above, we also gathered information about the eGovernment environment in each of the 23 countries surveyed, including the history, content and ownership of each country's eGovernment program, any recent political and legal developments around eGovernment in that country, and details on the processes being used to implement it.

OUR eGOVERNMENT MATURITY GLOBAL RANKINGS

In our research report, we found that governments are, albeit slowly, realizing their visions. More importantly, there is a growing recognition that eGovernment is not just about technology but about harnessing technology as just one of the tools to transform the way governments operate. Governments are learning that transformation comes not from moving services online, but from redesigning government organization and processes to put the citizen at the center, integrating across agencies to simplify interaction, reduce cost and improve service. Transformation is only possible with the right governance structure, coupled with the political will to drive change across the whole of government.

In 2002, the leaders remained unchanged from our research the year before. Despite Singapore closing the gap, Canada maintained its position in first place, and continues to advance toward its stated goal of providing Canadians with electronic access to all federal programs and services by 2004. In the top category, the Innovative Leaders, Canada and Singapore are joined by the United States–these three countries all recorded Overall Maturity scores of greater than 50 percent.

The distance between the leaders and the followers is widening; however, there is a late mover advantage emerging as a number of countries that were late starters make exponential strides and become serious challengers. The second group we call the Visionary Challengers, countries with overall eGovernment maturity scores between 40 percent and 50 percent. Among the Visionary Challengers, Germany, Ireland, Hong Kong and France all doubled or came close to doubling their 2001 score, indicating that they are starting to make significant strides in their eGovernment programs.

We call the third group the Emerging Performers; these countries have maturity scores ranging from 30 percent to 40 percent. All of the Emerging Performers were in the top 10 in terms of percentage change in their Overall Maturity score in 2002. The drivers for this result are mixed; Belgium made strides in CRM, Spain in Service Maturity depth and breadth, Japan in Service Maturity depth and New Zealand on all three measures.

Platform Builders, the countries embarking on their eGovernment programs, have also improved upon their maturity performance, by 5.8 percent on average. The bar continues to be raised and these countries have demonstrated that while they have a long distance yet to travel on their eGovernment journey, they are making steady progress (Figure 1).

In 2002, we noted several interesting patterns that are emerging in eGovernment. Governments that adopt Customer Relationship Management (CRM) principles early in their eGovernment initiatives are improving at a much faster pace. Portals are becoming far more prevalent, but their true potential continues to be unrealized because of the barriers to cross agency cooperation. The events of September 11, 2001, may yet be the catalyst for dismantling these barriers, as governments, businesses and citizens acknowledge that the benefits of common platforms and information sharing outweigh the perceived costs associated with disrupting the status quo.

The path to eGovernment is gradually becoming clearer, as early movers learn from their mistakes, as governments begin to appreciate the complexity of the eGovernment landscape and as the collective

FIGURE 1. Overall eGovernment Rankings

2002 - Overall Maturity by Country

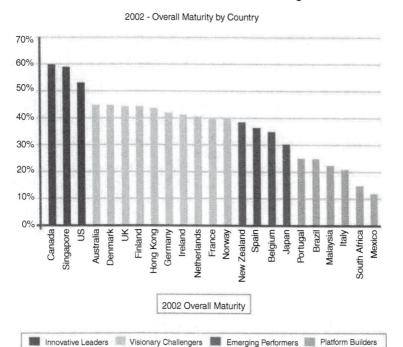

2002 Overall Maturity

■ Innovative Leaders ▦ Visionary Challengers ■ Emerging Performers ▦ Platform Builders

mindset changes toward citizen-centered service delivery. The landscape has changed dramatically. What has not changed, however, is the adherence of the governments in this survey to the implementation of eGovernment. Since we first began surveying eGovernment leadership, governments around the world have continued to pursue their eGovernment visions. Far from withdrawing from these initiatives, they have demonstrated determination to harness the power of the information economy for the benefit of their private and corporate citizens, albeit at vastly different speeds and levels of sophistication.

At the highest level, the findings show that the governments surveyed are becoming increasingly sophisticated, both in their articulation of what eGovernment is, and in how best to implement eGovernment initiatives to maximize benefits to citizens, businesses and government alike. Blanket statements exhorting all agencies to "get online" without a blueprint for what this means and how this can improve both service delivery and administrative effectiveness are disappearing. They have been replaced by detailed action plans with milestones and benchmarking that encompass all the requirements of a successful eGovernment program and address stakeholder needs.

Our first report, issued in April 2000, was entitled *Rhetoric vs Reality* to reflect the distance between where governments wanted to be in terms of online service delivery and what they had been able to achieve since their vision statements had been announced. The starting point, in the majority of countries surveyed, had been an announcement filled with rhetorical flourish, yet weak on implementation detail. The reality dawning for these countries was the complexity involved in bringing the vision to life: allocating scarce resources, and determining priorities for online service delivery while ensuring disadvantaged groups in society were not left behind by these changes. The first study found that even the leading governments had realized less than 20 percent of the journey in terms of their potential for online service delivery.

At this stage of eGovernment development, these early vision statements often had an unintended adverse effect–driving the rapid development of agency Websites limited to publishing information–in order to meet the very broad goal of "being online." Complexity in dealing with government was increased rather than diminished, and putting government online was delivering few benefits to citizens other than an electronic channel for receipt of information.

Governments typically attempted to manage this through creation of a single government Website to function as a gateway to the proliferation of agency-based sites, which for the most part were organized around the agency rather than being organized around the needs of the customer.

Since that time, eGovernment programs have made considerable strides in terms of sophistication. The rhetorical flourishes have largely been replaced with pragmatic statements about why eGovernment is critical to economic and social development, with recognition of the barriers to implementation, and clearly articulated strategies. Our 2002 study, *Realizing the Vision,* found a number of common themes in how visions for eGovernment have matured and how implementation challenges are being managed.

MAJOR eGOVERNMENT THEMES

eGovernment Is Being Viewed as Just One of the Tools that Can Be Applied to Meet the Many Challenges Faced by Governments

Governments face socioeconomic and geo-political forces that will forever change citizen expectations of government. These forces include aging populations, increased service expectations, security concerns, a talent crunch that is making it increasingly difficult to attract the right people into government, fiscal pressure that is forcing governments to find ways to do more with less, and competition, as more services are delivered by the private sector.

In its infancy, eGovernment was often portrayed as the panacea for all the perceived weaknesses in government service delivery. Technology is now being seen as a very important initiative that can contribute to reinventing government for the digital age, and facilitate the development of nimble, lean government structures for the future.

In the Netherlands, for example, the government has stated that a new "contract" between the citizen and government is needed to reflect the new relationship between citizens and government in the information society. The contract provides that each citizen must have freedom of choice regarding how he or she is connected to government and that government must be accessible and maximize participation opportunities.

eGovernment Must Deliver Real Benefits to the Citizen

There are significant costs involved in building an electronic service delivery channel and continuous operating costs that government must bear after they have installed those capabilities. Online government must be more than a duplicate channel for delivering the same services that are available elsewhere, and deliver tangible benefits in terms of operational efficiency and cost-saving. Governments are gradually learning how to measure the costs and the impact of eGovernment initiatives.

Online Services Must Be Marketed to Drive Take-Up

Many eGovernment initiatives have been based upon a "build it and they will come" mentality with little thought to what are the most appropriate services to put online. Few incentives have been built in to encourage usage. Governments have seldom incorporated marketing into their eGovernment activities, nor have they targeted specific segments of their user base to encourage them to take advantage of those services. There is emerging evidence that these skills are now being developed and marketing to citizens and businesses is assuming increasing importance.

Whole Transactions Must Be Completed Online to Drive Cost Down

Expectations that eGovernment would reduce the cost of service delivery have not been realized because of the immature nature of most online government, and critically, the lack of back office integration.

Publishing services online has little impact on cost–in most cases this is just a duplicate channel. Real cost savings are only realized when there is true integration between the Web front-end and the back office systems. Achieving this end-to-end integration requires changes to administrative structures, development of new skills, and redesign of processes. Implementing the changes necessary to truly capture the benefits of eGovernment is far more complex than simply creating an Internet presence.

The Citizen Is at the Center of the Vision, but Other Key Stakeholders Are Also Considered

Governments are acknowledging that citizens have a right to expect the same level of service from their governments that they receive from the private sector. Modern citizens want choice, convenience and control over their relationship with government. Governments increasingly see this and design with these citizen-driven guiding principles in mind. Canada, for example, has launched an online citizens panel–a virtual focus group to collect feedback and understand expectations for government online. Such feedback from citizens is becoming an increasingly important information source for selecting and evaluating the effectiveness of eGovernment initiatives.

The importance of other stakeholders is gaining currency. eGovernment statements increasingly recognize the impact of electronic government not just on citizens, but also on government employees, on private sector organizations, on government processes and on organizational structures.

For example, Singapore has developed a strategic framework that includes a "GtoE" component–Government to Employees. The government has recognized that to be successful both in service delivery and in policy implementation, there needs to be an emphasis on employees to ensure they perform at their best and meet the challenges of the new economy. Programs for eGovernment must acknowledge that there can be no eGovernment without a coordinated approach to Human Resources Management.

Connected Government Requires a Connected Vision

The leaders in eGovernment have outlined visions that are based upon the key principles of organizing according to citizen needs and taking a whole-of-government approach coordinated by strong leadership at the executive level. Canada, the leader for the second year running, outlined its eGovernment vision in 1999, stating that "by 2004, our goal is to be known around the world as the government most connected to its citizens, with Canadians able to access all government information and services online at the time and place of their choosing."

Governments are articulating key priorities for cross-agency eGovernment rather than leaving agencies to determine their own online presence. In the United States, the Office of Management and Budget announced in 2001 23 key eGovernment initiatives that would be delivered over the next two years, many of which cut across several federal agencies and involve partnerships with state and local governments. These initiatives fall into four categories–government-to-citizen, government-to-business, government-to-government and internal effectiveness and efficiency. Such an initiative is characteristic of governments increasingly realizing that delivering connected government online requires a cross-agency approach to eGovernment.

Outcomes Must Be Clearly Defined and Progress Measured

The key performance indicators that must accompany an eGovernment program are becoming clearer. Open and transparent status reporting, and the usage of and adherence to benchmarks is gaining currency across the board but needs to become further embedded.

For example, the Australian government has developed a Government Online Survey (www.govonline.gov.au/projects/strategy/GovernmentOnlineSurvey. htm) to report on its progress towards placing government information and services online. All government departments and agencies take part in the survey and provide information against five key measures (response rate, online service delivery, e-payment and e-procurement, standards and guidelines, and user confidence) contained in the Government Online Strategy.

Prior to 2001, the Canadian government relied on various International Benchmarking initiatives to measure its progress. In late 2001, the Treasury Board of Canada launched a public reporting process, which involves both departmental and government-wide reporting. In addition, the online Citizens' Panel enables the government to collect valuable information to help it to better understand current perceptions and future expectations of Government Online. Consulting with citizens and businesses is key to Canada's online initiative. The government also undertakes extensive public opinion polling to ensure that the program continues to meet client expectations.

Measurement is also gaining currency in Europe. The Benchmarking Survey (http://www.telearbeit.at/fr/bibliothek/eito/eito2002_23.html) sponsored by the European Union (EU) and published for the first time in November 2001 is being used by EU member states to assess their progress relative to other member states. This survey is due to be repeated at regular intervals and will probably change over time to focus more on service sophistication and less on service presence. In another example, Denmark's Digital Taskforce monitors progress through a variety of processes, including international benchmarking.

Collaboration with the Private Sector Is a Stated Goal

There is a growing recognition that the private sector has the capacity to invest and to innovate, and has much to gain from leaner, more efficient government. In the majority of the countries surveyed, the participation of private organizations is being actively encouraged.

New Zealand's vision, entitled "government.nz@your.service," states, "strong partnerships with the private sector are essential to the success of the eGovernment program." The eMexico program is focused on three principles–content, connectivity, and services (via portals). The connectivity goals will be achieved through a partnership with the private telecommunications companies as the scope and importance of the eGovernment project requires the involvement of all sectors in bringing the program to life.

Collaboration with the private sector is becoming more sophisticated, with government entering into new business arrangements with private sector providers where risk and rewards are shared and where the focus is on delivery of business outcomes. Far removed from the simple outsourcing models of the past, these arrangements are partnerships in every sense of the word, tackling complex projects that go beyond just information technology, and encompass all the activities necessary to provide the business service. In many cases these new transformational outsourcing projects are funded by cost savings or revenue collections generated.

Effective transformational outsourcing requires an enabling environment of good management practice, and some governments–notably the UK, Australia and New Zealand–have worked for the past decade to put these in place. The important components include "big-picture" overarching strategies and goals to guide efforts and measures of success against which to check progress.

GOVERNANCE COMES OF AGE

In previous years' research, we found a strong correlation between overall progress in implementing eGovernment and the presence of leadership, political will, commitment to deliverables, and accountability for results. These factors had the greatest influence on progress–as opposed to other social, political or economic factors.

In 2002, patterns are beginning to emerge. Governance is coming of age as political leaders and government executives recognize that eGovernment is not primarily a technology program–it is a change program that has the potential to transform the way government operates. Change programs, to be successful, must be led by pragmatic visionaries who can articulate what needs to happen, who can inspire and motivate, but who also can navigate and manage the issues that the transition to eGovernment involves. Central to governance structures is a growing recognition that the innovation necessary to transform government is beyond the scope of any single agency. They must harness the best thinking on the future of government regardless of where it resides, and make bold moves to break down barriers to success. In this section we highlight emerging patterns in governance.

Coordinating Across Multiple Tiers of Government

In taking a citizen-centric approach, eGovernment must build bridges, not only between agencies in the same tier of government, but between the different tiers of government. Little progress has been made in solving the "intergovernmental" problems. The majority of governments surveyed recognize that this issue is a significant barrier to progress but few have strategies for managing the issue.

The Italian government has outlined an ambitious vision to develop a service-oriented administration whose offices are effectively structured around the citizen's needs, but is heavily dependent upon local government and the Regioni to bring about this change. Canada's Government Online initiative will place increased emphasis on online service delivery partnerships with provinces, territories and municipalities, as well as with businesses, volunteer organizations and international partners.

Australia has made a breakthrough in cross-tier cooperation with the creation of the Business Entry Point. This initiative is part of federal government's promise to cut red tape and to make it easier for business to comply with government requirements. It does this by providing free online services and information for Australian business 24 × 7 via the

Website (www.business.gov.au). The Business Entry Point Transaction Manager allows users to locate, complete and manage online transactions with Commonwealth, State/Territory and local government agencies.

One key aspect of Ireland's eGovernment vision is to establish a Public Services Broker, which will function as a one-stop shop where the public can access and apply for a wide range of services and benefits. In order to make this cross-agency initiative work, the government has established the Reach Agency, a cross-departmental team of civil servants responsible for delivering the infrastructure to make the Public Services Broker a reality.

Deconstructing Agency Silos–Creating a Single Funding Point

In the early phases of eGovernment, progress in many countries was hindered by a governance structure that was largely powerless to overcome well entrenched bureaucratic divisions. While a whole-of-government approach is the key to success, securing cross-agency cooperation proved very difficult.

Information and communications technologies can be instrumental in breaking down these divisions. However, executives often perceive this as a threat and make investments that protect and preserve the status quo. This year's research uncovered some evidence that these barriers are now starting to break down. Governments are recognizing the opportunity cost of fragmented systems and processes that duplicate information gathering. In addition, the cost to business of multiple compliance points is a disincentive to investment and one that can be significantly reduced through cross-agency cooperation.

The United States has a stated goal of scrutinizing all federal IT investments to ensure they maximize interoperability and minimize redundancy. Cross-agency projects are key but current funding practices where appropriations are made on an agency-by-agency basis actively discourage this approach. The United States federal government has proposed overcoming this barrier by creating an eGovernment fund to support inter-agency projects to improve citizen access to federal services. While this was one of the few examples found of a specific funding initiative, it is an approach that should be considered by other countries, all of which face this barrier to varying degrees.

The Rise of the Chief Information Officer

eGovernment is about delivering improved service through dramatically improving the way governments manage information. Two of the three In-

novative Leaders (Canada and the United States) have appointed Chief Information Officers (CIOs) to manage their eGovernment programs. This
may be seen as only a title, but it conveys the crucial message that
eGovernment at its core is about how the government manages information
for the benefit of its citizens. Canada and the United States have recognized
that this is the role they need their eGovernment leaders to play. South Africa has also given its eGovernment leader the title of government CIO.
The Office of the e-Envoy in the United Kingdom is another example of a
title having been created that truly distinguishes the cross-agency
eGovernment leadership role from a more traditional agency title.

The rise of the CIO is evidence that governments recognize that a
whole-of-government approach, driven by strong leadership and sponsorship, is critical to success.

The Value of Private–Sector Experience

The United States, United Kingdom and Italy have all selected leaders for their eGovernment initiatives who have come from the private
sector. Mark Forman, the Director for Information Technology and
eGovernment in the United States, was most recently Vice President for
eBusiness at Unisys Corporation and has also worked in the public sector. Andrew Pinder, the e-Envoy in the United Kingdom, joined recently
from Citibank and his career includes 18 years in Inland Revenue. The
Minister for Innovation and Technology in the Italian government,
Lucio Stanca, has over 30 years experience in the IT sector.

The move to appoint eGovernment leaders from the private sector is
a trend to watch. The United States has a track record of making the
right moves early, and while Italy has remained a Platform Builder this
year, it recently unveiled an ambitious plan, the benefits of which it ex-
pects to reap over the coming years.

THE RISE OF CUSTOMER RELATIONSHIP MANAGEMENT–FROM CITIZEN TO CUSTOMER

A term familiar in business circles, Customer Relationship Management (CRM) is attracting increasing interest in government. CRM is a
capability that is built on reorganizing service delivery around customer
intentions. CRM allows agencies to create an integrated view of their
customers and to use this information to coordinate services across mul-

tiple channels. Governments realize that CRM is a tool that has significant potential to improve their relationships with their customers.

CRM in government is a relatively new concept and one that has gone largely unexplored. The primary drivers for implementing CRM in the private sector–customer retention and increased profit per customer–are absent in the public sector. However, the principles of CRM hold intriguing possibilities for government, given that governments are the largest service providers in the world, provide a wide variety of services and have much to gain from a better understanding of their customers.

As government looks to improve service delivery, while at the same time dealing with the pressure to do more with less, CRM has the potential to alleviate some of the most pressing service challenges governments now face. CRM can assist in, among other benefits, streamlining government processes, improving inter-agency data sharing and providing self-service options to the public.

In measuring the extent to which governments are applying the techniques of CRM in their online initiatives, our research examined the following:

1. Insight–Does government remember me or have an insight into my behavior and needs?
2. Interaction–Can I access multiple related government services through this site?
3. Organization Performance–Is this site organized around my needs? Is it intentions-based?
4. Customer Offerings–Does the site help or advise me based upon my needs or circumstances?
5. Networks–Is it possible to access other value added nongovernmental services from this site?

As Service Maturity Breadth approaches 100% and Service Maturity Depth increases as services move up the maturity curve, CRM performance is the test of whether eGovernment is realizing its promise of delivering citizen-centered services. CRM will become an increasingly important component of eGovernment leadership.

Canada has achieved its leadership position largely due to its focus on the citizen in its eGovernment programs (see Figure 2). The President of the Treasury Board, the Honorable Lucienne Robillard, who serves as the champion for the Government Online program, explained the primacy of the citizen as follows: "Too often in the past government

FIGURE 2. Evolving CRM Capabilities

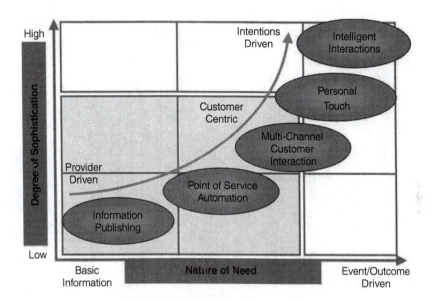

services were designed from the inside out; they reflected the structures of government organizations rather than the needs and priorities of citizens. This is changing . . . we cannot stop until all Canadians can have seamless access to all government services quickly, simply and with a minimum of fuss."

Canada scored very high on CRM, evidence it has recognized the power of CRM in realizing the eGovernment vision (Figure 3). In the United States, the eGovernment strategy specifically states the need for the government to use the best practices of industry with regard to, inter alia, Customer Relationship Management. The "citizen as customer" idea was first articulated as far back as 1993, in the words of then-Vice President Al Gore, "we are going to make the federal government customer-friendly. A lot of people don't realize that the federal government has customers. We have customers. The American people."

This approach has been continued under the present administration, which is focused on creating citizen-centered agencies that work together to consolidate similar functions around the needs of citizens and businesses. Services will be organized around citizen preferences and not agency boundaries.

FIGURE 3. CRM Rankings

2002 - CRM by Country

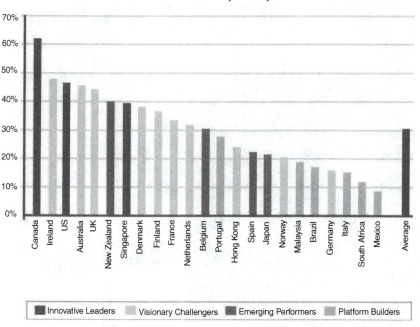

While CRM is concerned with much more than just intentions-based design of portals (a single Web-enabled point-of-access to information and services), these represent the first steps that governments are taking on the CRM journey. Intentions-based approaches are becoming the rule, rather than the exception that the research highlighted in 2001. Singapore was one of the early leaders in this area, and its central portal (www.gov.sg) continues to set the standard.

In Hong Kong, the government portal (www.esd.gov.hk) is organized around eight major user intentions during a user life cycle. France was among the leading countries on CRM measures, and its intentions-based portal (www.service-public.fr) is well placed to become a leader in the area with a new initiative (mon.service-public.fr) that will provide each French citizen with a personalized portal.

Segmentation is an emerging, albeit limited, practice that is gaining acceptance in government. Just as the citizen as customer is a relatively new concept, customer segmentation, with its connotations of seeking out "high-value" customers, may seem at odds with government's charter to serve all citizens equally. There is evidence, however, that governments are recognizing that their private and corporate citizens fall into distinct segments and that online services could be tailored accordingly. Yet, segmentation is not as straightforward as splitting services between public and private customers. Segmentation is currently very simplistic–limited to broad categories of businesses, citizens and employees. In order to use CRM effectively, a much more granular approach to segmentation is necessary. Delivering better eGovernment services requires that governments tailor services to their customers based upon a broader range of user characteristics. If governments expect citizens to use the Internet as an end-to-end self-service channel then they must provide citizens with a customized service. Over time we can expect segmentation to become more sophisticated as governments increasingly deliver differentiated services based on individual customer group requirements.

While the use of CRM techniques in eGovernment is still in its infancy, many governments are recognizing that CRM is a powerful tool for enhancing their online presence. Government agencies have a long way to go to turn the potential of CRM into a reality. The barriers to implementing CRM are the same barriers that have hindered the progress of eGovernment programs. The challenges lie in making a business case for investment, securing leadership support, and in overcoming the obstacles inherent in traditional agency structures where information resides in data silos. A strategy for CRM should be an integral part of an eGovernment strategy, because implementing eGovernment increases the number of channels for service delivery, and therefore creates greater complexity in customer interaction. Before eGovernment, citizens had very limited choice in where and how they could interact with government. With eGovernment they have in many cases an array of channels. CRM is essential to maximizing the efficiency and effectiveness of eGovernment.

In the time since our last report, the landscape has changed dramatically. What has not changed, however, is the adherence of the governments in this survey to the implementation of eGovernment. During that time, governments around the world have continued to pursue their eGovernment visions. Far from withdrawing from these initiatives, they have demonstrated determination to harness the power of the information economy for the benefit of their private and corporate citizens, albeit at vastly different speeds and levels of sophistication.

ON THE MOVE

Mobile e-Gov:
No Turning Back to the Swamp

Janet Caldow

Institute for Electronic Government, IBM Corporation

SUMMARY. The mobile/wireless evolution began with the familiar, but will expand rapidly to new frontiers. Wireless messaging emerged first as an extension of the office environment. Everyone understands e-mail and can translate that concept easily to a mobile, wireless device. But looking further down the road, the real payoff will be mobile, wireless access to and interaction with mission-critical, enterprise-wide applications. So what does this mean for e-government? The answer is twofold. On one hand it means governments will interact with citizens wirelessly. All those people out there with all those wireless devices are

Janet Caldow is Director, Institute for Electronic Government, IBM Corporation. She has a BA in Sociology from George Mason University, an MBA from Virginia Tech, and is affiliated with Harvard Policy Group, Advisory Panel, Congressional Management Foundation, and Council for Excellence in Government.

[Haworth co-indexing entry note]: "Mobile e-Gov: No Turning Back to the Swamp." Caldow, Janet. Co-published simultaneously in *Journal of Political Marketing* (The Haworth Press, Inc.) Vol. 2, No. 3/4, 2003, pp. 147-157; and: *The World of E-Government* (ed: Gregory G. Curtin, Michael H. Sommer, and Veronika Vis-Sommer) The Haworth Press, Inc., 2003, pp. 147-157. Single or multiple copies of this article are available for a fee from The Haworth Document Delivery Service [1-800-HAWORTH, 9:00 a.m. - 5:00 p.m. (EST). E-mail address: docdelivery@haworthpress.com].

http://www.haworthpress.com/store/product.asp?sku=J199
© 2003 by The Haworth Press, Inc. All rights reserved.
10.1300/J199v02n03_09

also citizens of governments. And, on the other hand, more than any other industry, public sector workforces stand to gain the most from wireless advances. *[Article copies available for a fee from The Haworth Document Delivery Service: 1-800-HAWORTH. E-mail address: <docdelivery@ haworthpress.com> Website: <http://www.HaworthPress.com> © 2003 by The Haworth Press, Inc. All rights reserved.]*

KEYWORDS. Mobile, wireless, mobile worker

Mobility is one of evolution's most enduring principles. From the time the first prehistoric creature crawled out of a swamp, to early hunter-gatherers' migration patterns, to discovery of ocean trade routes, to transportation inventions of the Industrial Revolution, to the triumph over earth's gravity in space exploration, mobility continually redefines our concepts of time, space, communications, and the nature of work.

The first few decades of computerization could be characterized as largely sedentary. Although the mobility of data through high-speed communications networks has been astounding, human access points are still largely anchored to physical infrastructures–data centers, desktop computers, wired phones and fax machines. Innovative use of mobile/wireless in public safety has been the exception. (Can you imagine a police officer without mobile data and voice communications in the cruiser?) However, evolutionary forces march relentlessly ever forward. There's no turning back. Mobile/wireless capability is beginning to permeate every governmental function.

Mobile computing means extending the availability of information technology infrastructure to mobile workers through mobile, wireless devices. It represents the continuing evolution of the nature of work. You used to "go answer the phone." No more. The phone is in your pocket. And, it won't be long before you won't have to "go to your PC" anymore either. You'll literally carry your desk around in your pocket on any one of a number of handheld devices–connected, wherever you go and whenever you need it.

But, we're getting ahead of ourselves. In the mid 1990s, a new class of small, user-centric devices began to appear. Known as Personal Digital Assistants (PDAs), these devices provided functions similar to paper diaries, address books and notebooks, popular primarily with highly computer-literate, early adopters of new technology. They were largely viewed as expensive toys. Newer PDAs are designed around open architectures with embedded TCP/IP networking support and infrared communications ports allowing simple connection to digital cellular telephones.

Sociologically speaking, these new devices emerge at a time when "work" is no longer defined as a place, but a state of being. The distinction between modern white-collar and blue-collar workers, differentiated by access to computer technology on the job, is evaporating as notions of work are redefined. Field workers, previously cut off altogether from computer systems, suddenly will be able to interact with these systems and do things that before had been impossible. This will affect how government operates to the extent that wireless workflow is not only possible, but becomes inescapable due to obvious derived cost benefits. Additionally, a whole range of mobile/wireless government information and services to citizens not previously possible will develop.

As the price of mobile components continue to fall, virtually everything you buy over $10 will have embedded wireless network access to the Internet. For example, all IBM Thinkpads manufactured before the end of 2001 were already wireless enabled. Vendors predict $20 disposable mobile phones along with disposable digital cameras. When you compare the cost of a traditional desktop PC with a handheld device to the respective total cost of ownership, the savings are significant, not to mention the impact on bridging the digital divide.

The mobile/wireless evolution began with the familiar, but will expand rapidly to new frontiers. Wireless messaging emerged first as an extension of the office environment. Everyone understands e-mail and can translate that concept easily to a mobile, wireless device. But looking further down the road, the real payoff will be mobile, wireless access to and interaction with mission-critical, enterprise-wide applications.

So what does this mean for e-government? The answer is twofold. On one hand it means governments will interact with citizens wirelessly. All those people out there with all those wireless devices are also citizens of governments. And, on the other hand, more than any other industry, public sector workforces stand to gain the most from wireless advances.

Even with casual observation, one might conclude that even before high tech, at least 30% of government workers have always been "mobile." Among those who have "no office" or spend less than half their work day in an office include police, fire fighters, parole officers, traffic enforcers, health inspectors, building inspectors, transportation inspectors, fire inspectors, facilities management employees, fleet management personnel, internal mail carriers, social services case workers, transportation officials, parks and recreation employees, maintenance employees, and the list goes on. These employees, by the nature of their job responsibilities, are immediate candidates for wireless. Throw in another 25% of office workers who are projected to become mobile and that's almost 50% of all governments' workforces! Finally, there is a mobile/wireless component to virtually every worker when he or she is out of the office–whether traveling, at home, working in the field, or just attending a meeting in another building. Even *within* the office environment, wireless LANs are becoming a venue of choice for a variety of reasons. Governments need to extend their infrastructures so that workers through their wireless devices can interact with existing backend, mission-critical systems.

A wireless workforce strategy covers a variety of government-to-employee (G2E) applications sharing common core technologies. These employees have similar requirements in their jobs–both mobile and/or wireless. Their needs range from messaging (e-mail), Internet connectivity, mobile incident or status reporting that can be uploaded or transmitted, query of backend databases, alerts, personalized workflow management, updates, scheduling, dispatch, communications with coworkers, and access to mission-critical applications. Wireless allows employees to be mobile while maintaining the ability to access core applications. This frees them of the constraint of only having critical information while they are sitting at their desks. Mobile employees can get to information when and where they need it the most with levels of security proportionate to the nature of the transaction.

The value in transforming field services employees into a mobile, wireless workforce includes exceptional improvements in productivity, effectiveness and efficiencies, reduced costs, decreased paperwork, auditability, elimination of redundant data entry, reduced cycle times, secure information available immediately–anyplace, anytime–improved employee safety, accelerated report preparation, and simplified review and approval workflow processes.

In *public safety,* silent dispatch over a private data communications network eliminates eavesdropping on police calls; reduces errors caused by voice communication; allows direct access to local, state and federal databases for motor vehicle and warrant information; reduces the number of paper forms used to report noncriminal incidents; enhances the ability to respond to calls with the closest officer location by touching an icon on a mobile computer monitor; en route look up of HAZMAT databases; and more effective monitoring movements of persons under legal supervision. The Toronto Police are saving US $2.9M each year through its use of eCops, a wireless-enabled police operational records management system. In Bullhead City, Arizona, the Police Department reduced over-the-air time for dispatchers by at least 50% and increased the accuracy of information received.

For *maintenance employees*, wireless optimizes on-call maintenance scheduling, reduces overall repair cost and time by having the immediate ability to review service history, check maintenance manuals, determine product specs, check parts inventory for availability, process orders, look-up warranties and mechanical drawings while on location, and when coupled with GPS provides more accuracy for utilities location and configuration. Improved preventive maintenance enabled by wireless communication also extends operational life of vehicles and equipment. Continual wireless monitoring of location, operation, and condition of major assets for preventive maintenance needs (fleet, heavy equipment, and costly portable/moveable assets) reduces cost of ownership by reducing incidence of major repairs.

Wireless empowers *social services case workers* with on-location information access and update reporting to backend case records. Wireless leverages integrated case management by greatly improving service delivery with ability to process and schedule instant collaboration and referral among social services agencies (such as police, public health, mental health, child welfare, alcohol and drug abuse, social services, housing, child abuse). Wireless communication saves precious time, especially in basic safety and life-threatening situations and reduces costs and time to prepare reports (otherwise having to travel back to the office and office paperwork time). Wireless alleviates overburdened case loads by allowing case workers more time with clients and improves safety of case workers themselves.

For *inspectors,* wireless boosts effectiveness of the inspection process; saves time and overall costs of inspections; and improves public health and safety with immediate reporting and action such as license revocation and notification. Inspectors can conduct on-location query of inspection histories, previous violations, fines, prepare inspection certificates, eliminate paper reports and report time lags, as well as take advantage of general office functions through wireless scheduling, communications, and alerts. New York City's successful mobile building inspection capability has prompted a citywide, cross-department mobile/wireless strategy.

Governments can no longer assume that a citizen is using a traditional computer to access data and applications from a government

Website. To meet the anticipated demand, government's challenge is to deliver data and applications efficiently across the network regardless of citizens' access devices or connectivity configurations. Virtually all information and transaction services currently developed for wired access will eventually need to be wireless-enabled. And, innovations in citizen service delivery will emerge.

Virginia's "Lobbyist in a Box" is an interactive application accessible from mobile devices for citizens, legislators, and lobbyists to track progress of bills as they move through the legislative process, including the bill number, sponsoring patron, a brief summary and last action for each bill. A number of jurisdictions have included wireless-enabling their Website information for use by citizens in their public emergency preparedness plans.

Wireless isn't just for the big governments. In fact, small and/or rural government jurisdictions stand to benefit tremendously from all kinds of wireless capabilities. Quaint Nantucket Island, Massachusetts, installed a wireless LAN for public Internet access in the town library. The entire island is classified as a historical landmark with many construction restrictions. Given the nature of the historic library structure, a wireless LAN was not only cheaper, but also prevented destruction associated with drilling and pulling cable throughout the building.

Wireless has the potential to significantly close the digital divide. Citizens who cannot afford traditional desktop computers can now opt for relatively inexpensive wireless devices and connectivity. Rural or underserved communities, lacking ground communications infrastructure, can suddenly leapfrog to wireless and eventually provide high-speed access for their citizens, governments, and businesses.

Going wireless isn't rocket science. However, it's useful to understand the process at a high level. Using a variety of modular hardware and software components, new technologies allow you to build upon your existing infrastructure to easily extend operations to wireless devices. Information exchange flows back and forth from the handheld device, through a Wireless Service Provider's network, to the enterprise network, to the application server, and to backend legacy systems and data. At each step along the way there is a technical translation of different protocols that allows all these elements to communicate with each other. It's like converting English into German, then to French, to Japanese, and then back to English.

When a request from a handheld device is initiated, an application server identifies the device type (a cell phone, PDA, etc.) and captures the content. Using several logical processes, the application server processes the data into an Extensible Markup Language (XML) document, which can then be communicated with backend systems via the Application Programming Interface (API) connection. Going back the other way, the result of the requested data will be reformatted for the handheld device that made the request initially, end to end, in a reliable and secure manner.

The process can become complex very quickly, depending on the number of the handheld devices supported and the types of services offered. New software and hardware products handle data dynamically to adapt to a handheld device, and easily integrates it with the backend system–without rewriting code for each protocol.

The technology selects the correct screen template, formats the data for the handheld device, and delivers the requested data back to fit the constraints of small screens on mobile phones and PDAs thus synchronizing handheld devices with enterprise solutions.

New wireless hardware pops up daily. Web-enabled cell phones, two-way, e-mail capable pagers, camera and telephone-equipped PDAs, thin client devices, laptops, Palm, Workpad, Ipaq, and smart phones are all examples. The operating systems of handhelds are the software programs that manage basic operations. For example, Windows CE is a Windows "light" version developed by Microsoft, installed on many PDA devices. Palm OS, developed by 3COM, is the most popular OS on the handheld due to the large market share that the Palm Pilot owns today. It supports some Java applications. Linux is very promising for growth in this area. Open source based, Java friendly, and very efficient, it can be installed on many PDA devices and smart phones. EPOC is an operating system mostly for smart phone devices used by Ericsson and Nokia. EPOC is one of the major operating systems in this market.

Each one of these handheld devices require certain ways of communicating. They require their own gateways to communicate with application servers. Various sizes of screen displays create different data and screen layouts. Different keyboards or other input methods generate different navigational options. The challenge for the application server is to sort out all these devices, recognize them, and send the data in the correct format to each handheld device. (This is called transcoding, discussed below.)

Coverage refers to a Wireless Service Provider's (WSP) geographical service range. A handheld device accesses a local cell tower from the user's provider. The cell tower is responsible for delivering local geographical coverage in a certain region. The coverage is divided into hexagonal boundaries. The cell tower sends the data to a base station.

The data is then transferred to a switching center. A mobile switching center connects all the base stations. The mobile network system will record and identify all of the user's information by Home Location Register (HLR), if the user is in the geographical network. If not, then the Visitor Location Register (VLR) will be tracking the call. This is when you pay big bucks for roaming. Once the call is initiated, the device will send its identity via its Electronic Serial Number (ESN) and Mobile Identity Number (MIN). This information is vital so the gateway can authenticate the user. This is also where the application server can prepare the data to send back to the appropriate unit to be displayed.

The *Connectivity Gateway* is the first point of entry to the network for handheld devices. The diverse nature of wireless devices means there are significantly different protocols. For example, screen size, input mechanisms (keyboard or voice, etc.), information processing capability, storage capacity, battery life, and network bandwidth vary greatly. Some devices are equipped with non-browser-based communications facilities to support occasional connected models of operation.

You can plan and control the types of handheld devices your mobile workforce uses. But you can't control what your citizens use. Therefore, to extend your infrastructure to citizens' wireless devices, the infrastructure needs to be network and device-independent, accommodating a variety of wireless connectivity gateway protocols, including Wireless Application Protocol (WAP), Global Systems for Mobile Communications (GSM), Code Division Multiple Access (CDMA), Time Division Multiple Access (TDMA), TCP/IP, and others. The industry is rallying around Wireless Application Protocol (WAP) as a standard for network and device-independent wireless Internet access. Europe and Asia have progressed much faster than the United States because they have, for several years, had mobile standards.

Next comes the application server. Remote access authentication at this level has traditionally been a one-way street. The gateway determines whether or not the client requesting a session is valid. But, the client could not authenticate the gateway. In other words, how does the client know that it is communicating with a valid gateway? If the gateway is an impostor, the client's ID and password have now been intercepted. The impostor can gain access through the gateway with the intercepted user ID and password. To prevent this, it is important to securely authenticate both parties of a remote connection using an advanced bi-directional authentication process. Authentication should be combined with authorization of what the client is allowed to do. Strong encryption can keep information secure and private. Digital signature capabilities may also be implemented for additional protection when needed.

User IDs and handheld device IDs are stored in the database at the application server level. The application server will access the database once a login request is received. The middleware database is used to prepare and format the data for the device requesting the login. The application server will also compare the registered device ID to the user ID for additional security verification. The application server communicates with the gateway server for the specific device that initiates the request. The gateway will push the information to the handheld device according to the connectivity platforms like CDPD, SMS, Mobitex, and CDMA.

With up to 80% of all data residing on mainframes, government needs quick, easy and efficient ways to extend data to users on wireless devices. New technologies let you implement wireless without modifying the host applications. They enable easy mobile access to legacy data by managing the complexity of new devices and markup languages so handheld devices, traditional PCs, and backend systems can communicate with each other and readily exchange data.

The industry is separating content (information) from presentation (how you see it on your device) using Extensible Markup Language (XML). Transcoding software dynamically adjusts data going back to the user to "fit" whatever device the employee or citizen is using–cell phones, screen phones, voice-capable browsers, PDAs, such as the Palm Pilot, IBM WorkPad, handheld Microsoft Windows CE devices, and Blackberries. For example, the transcoder converts images to links to retrieve images, converts simple tables to bulleted lists and removes features not supported by a device; reduces image size and color level to make them easier to transfer and quicker to render on each respective device; responds to the limited storage capacity of devices by subdividing content into small sections that can be viewed more effectively; and tracks network connectivity profiles so that content can be transcoded according to network constraints.

Web content is written in Hypertext Markup Language (HTML), not the specialized markup languages required by wireless devices. Transcoding dynamically also bridges the different HTML structures, tailoring the content to the specific device. "Clipping" refers to the process of adapting Web page content when delivered to cell phones. This allows cell phone users to retrieve only the relevant portion of a Web page that they need, such as a daily stock price.

Today's wireless networks are called second generation (2G) net-works—what supports cellular phones and PCS. Current mobile devices transmit bite-size text extremely well. But, they cannot yet easily handle large amounts of graphics-rich information. That's all changing. The dawn of broadband, wireless third generation (3G) networks will allow wireless users to access and conduct business at broadband speeds. 3G will be more than 35 times faster than today's fastest dial-up personal computer modems and more than 200 times the speed of most current handheld wireless data devices. That means even full-motion real-time video can be streamed literally to your fingertips.

Bluetooth is a new short-range wireless technology which can be em-bedded in mobile PCs, smart phones, and other portable devices. It pro-vides three voice and data channels via a one-to-one connection with built-in encryption and verification. A Bluetooth-enabled PDA could access your Bluetooth-enabled cell phone and use it to dial up the Internet. With Bluetooth you can synchronize contacts in your PDA with your desktop just by putting them in the same room and then sending names and telephone numbers straight to your cell phone—no docking cradle, no infrared dongles, no cables!

Location-sensing equipment is capable of providing information about a mobile phone user's physical location or the location of a vehi-cle, providing the ability to deliver location-based services. This has huge implications for emergency response as we are approaching al-most 50% of 911 calls coming from cell phones.

Put your government ahead of the curve while you still have time. By all accounts, you have about 12-18 months to prepare your infrastruc-ture, enable a wireless workforce, and meet your citizens' demands in time to scale to critical mass. The following eight steps will help you crawl out of the swamp the to meet the evolutionary challenges of mo-bile technology:

1. Get smart about wireless. Read everything you can. Consult with the many governments that have already implemented mobile and wireless solutions. Enlist the help of your IT partners to learn more. Go wireless yourself. Buy a handheld device and become familiar with what your citizens already know.
2. Build funds into budgets now for wireless devices and enabling software and include wireless in all your strategic planning. Be a leader. Challenge and stretch the thinking of your people.
3. Name a wireless lead, responsible for coordinating wireless im-plementation across agencies.

4. Pilot a mobile workforce. Select an employee group who will benefit from going wireless and pilot a wireless program. Begin your strategic planning to roll out wireless to all applicable work groups. A pilot will take your IT employees up the learning curve.
5. Pilot wireless-enabled citizen services. Select a group of e-gov services and information on your e-gov portal (Website) and enable your citizens to access them wirelessly NOW. You may not be ready, but they are. Lay the IT foundation and planning for remaining applications.
6. Liberate your office workers from their desks. Give them experience with wireless operations. Target an office group to go wireless and outfit them with handheld devices. Set parameters to monitor results.
7. The next LAN you install, make it a wireless LAN. Document the cost savings and benefits in your own environment.
8. Beware of proprietary dead-ends. Above all, you want an open, flexible infrastructure that's scalable, reliable, and secure. Pick your partners wisely.

SERVING THE STAKEHOLDERS

Customer-Oriented E-Government: Can We Ever Get There?

Robert D. Atkinson

Technology and New Economy Project, Progressive Policy Institute

Andrew Leigh

Harvard University

Robert D. Atkinson is Vice President of the Progressive Policy Institute, and Director of PPI's Technology and New Economy Project. He holds a PhD in Urban Planning from the University of North Carolina, a MUPD from the University of Oregon, and a BA from the New College of the University of South Florida.

Andrew Leigh is a PhD candidate at the John F. Kennedy School of Government, Harvard University, and a Fellow at the Malcolm Wiener Center for Social Policy. He is a former lawyer, and holds an MPA from Harvard University, and LLB(Hons) and BA(Hons) degrees from the University of Sydney.

Address correspondence to: Robert D. Atkinson, The Progressive Policy Institute, 600 Pennsylvania Ave., SE, Washington, DC 20003 (E-mail: ratkinson@dlcppi.org), or Andrew Leigh, 6 Ash Street #219A, Cambridge, MA 02138 (E-mail: andrew_leigh@ksg02.harvard.edu).

The authors wish to thank the following individuals for their comments on earlier drafts: Perri 6 (Kings College, London), Arun Baheti (formerly of the Office of the Governor of California), Randolph Court (Democratic Leadership Council), Marc Cummings (Infotech Strategies, Inc.), Shane Ham (Progressive Policy Institute), Brian Newkirk (Progressive Policy Institute), Alan Proctor (LexisNexis), Gary Robinson (Acting CIO, State of Washington), and two anonymous referees. Their review should not necessarily constitute endorsement of the findings or recommendations contained in this paper.

[Haworth co-indexing entry note]: "Customer-Oriented E-Government: Can We Ever Get There?" Atkinson, Robert D., and Andrew Leigh. Co-published simultaneously in *Journal of Political Marketing* (The Haworth Press, Inc.) Vol. 2, No. 3/4, 2003, pp. 159-181; and: *The World of E-Government* (ed: Gregory G. Curtin, Michael H. Sommer, and Veronika Vis-Sommer) The Haworth Press, Inc., 2003, pp. 159-181. Single or multiple copies of this article are available for a fee from The Haworth Document Delivery Service [1-800-HAWORTH, 9:00 a.m. - 5:00 p.m. (EST). E-mail address: docdelivery@haworthpress.com].

SUMMARY. E-government's next phase–a seamless, customer-oriented Web presence–faces more formidable barriers to development than did earlier advances. Progress toward customer-focused e-government requires fundamental organizational changes to existing bureaucracies, so that the government's Web presence can be comprehensive, efficient, and easy for citizens to use. To compel individual "stovepipe" agencies to develop a combined Web presence, chief information officers must be able to focus political and bureaucratic resources on making government websites truly customer-centric. The rewards for success in this next stage of e-government are significant–not only will it benefit citizens directly, but integrated e-government can also make offline government more efficient and effective. *[Article copies available for a fee from The Haworth Document Delivery Service: 1-800-HAWORTH. E-mail address: <docdelivery@haworthpress.com> Website: <http://www.HaworthPress.com> © 2003 by The Haworth Press, Inc. All rights reserved.]*

KEYWORDS. E-government, holistic governance, Websites, chief information officers

INTRODUCTION

It's been nine years since the U.S. government first went online.[1] Initially, e-government meant a passive presence on the Web. Government Websites provided information, but did not allow citizens[2] to interact with them. The second phase has seen a growing number of governments and agencies using the Internet to allow individuals to interact with government–from paying taxes to renewing drivers' licenses. This article focuses on what needs to be the next phase of e-government–breaking down bureaucratic barriers to create functionally oriented, citizen-centered government Web presences designed to give citizens a self-service government. Overall, however, the work of rebuilding and transforming government for the digital age is only just beginning.

But while the first two phases largely presented technological challenges (e.g., writing the software and entering information), moving to the third phase presents much more fundamental organizational, bureaucratic and political challenges that will not be easily overcome. Governments remain organized according to political and bureaucratic imperatives, not according to what citizens need. This is reflected in the fact that many governments use the Web to project their own internal self images online, organizing their Websites in ways that reflect how government personnel view their world, not how the average citizen views the world. As a result, customer-centered digital government requires a fundamental change in outlook on the part of government, with the focus being placed on the needs of citizens/customers. This requires organizing governments' web presences in ways that are intuitive; easy to use; and without jargon, program names and acronyms. It means focusing on information and transactions people want, rather than information government wants them to have (e.g., a picture of the department secretary accompanying their latest press release). It means putting people in touch with solutions to their problems, not just giving them access to the agencies' own programs or services.

More fundamentally, customer-focused digital government requires moving from separate departmental Websites and computer systems to a seamless Internet presence, organized around the citizen's needs. To make this work, integration must occur not only between agencies at the same level of government, but also between different tiers of government, and even with the private sector. Even if the solution is provided by a different tier of government, by the private sector, or by a nonprofit agency, a government Website should help the user locate it. Citizens usually don't care if they are dealing with their local, state or federal government, they just want an answer, help or to conduct a transaction.

Currently, most government agencies are stuck in phases one or two. Some are still not even online, far from the ideal of integrated digital government. Now is the time to accelerate the move into phase three. A majority of Americans have still never accessed a government Website, and only 3 in 10 Americans currently use online government services once a month or more.[3] Nonetheless, 73% of all Americans believe that e-government ought to be a high priority—including a sizeable majority of those who do not use the Internet.[4] Without doubt, government has a mandate for change. Moving to this third phase will require resources, political leadership, and hard work. But most fundamentally, it will require a fundamentally different view of government than we've had for the last 50 years. Given these challenges, it's not clear that most governments will develop satisfactory online systems, at least within the next five years or so.

THE BENEFITS OF CUSTOMER-FOCUSED E-GOVERNMENT

A slew of e-government reports have emphasized the benefits of on-line government. As an organization that primarily provides services, government is in a prime position to reap the benefits of all kinds of digital technology, not just the Web.[5] Many governmental tasks can be carried out more effectively and cheaply through the Internet. According to a report commissioned by PricewaterhouseCoopers, "electronic service delivery could change human resource deployment patterns and improve organizational performance."[6] The report found that once Websites were "bedded down," e-government freed up staff that could be used to provide better service to in-person customers, without the need to focus on routine tasks that could be handled by computers.

E-government that lets more citizens (and businesses) interact with government through self-service online applications (e.g., filling out electronic forms) should lead to a cheaper government. Many elected officials though only see the costs, as they appropriate more money for new e-government applications, and don't see the savings. But just as is occurring in the private sector, e-government can provide significant savings. For example, allowing citizens to file forms online can cost up to one-tenth of the cost of filing paper forms. The problem for government is that e-government usage is still modest, although growing, and governments have not been able to shrink offline government functions to capture savings. They are spending the same amount of money on offline functions while expanding online ones. However, once a larger share of citizens are using the Web for self-service interactions with government, more expensive paper, voice, and face-to-face transactions will shrink, allowing government, if it has the political will, to gradually downsize these functions, while retaining or even expanding the quantity and quality of services they provide.

Moving from a bricks and mortar (and paper and phone) customer service infrastructure more to an online one will take government doing several things. First it will need to more aggressively market online applications. It is commonplace for most government customer offices (e.g., places where people pay traffic tickets, renew their driver's license, pay their taxes, renew permits, etc.) to not prominently advertise that citizens can do this on the Web. Many jurisdictions still send out paper forms to citizens without clearly letting them know that they can do the transaction online. This will need to change if more citizens are to use the online option.

In addition, the savings from digital transactions should be reflected in the "price" people pay for interacting with government. Just as consumers buying airline tickets online or agreeing to pay their phone bills online get a discount, governments need to do the same. For example, Massachusetts offers a five dollar rebate on their driver's license fee for those who register online, since it saves the state much more. Providing rebates and discounts will encourage citizens to choose these lower cost forms of interaction.

Yet, most governments do not do this. For example, the Postal Service will not give discounts to users of "electronic stamps" or postal meters, even though they cost the Postal Service less than purchasing stamps at a post office.[7] Similarly, the IRS will not give a rebate for electronic tax filing. Some argue that providing discounts will only benefit the affluent since they are now more likely to be on the Internet. Yet by lowering the actual cost of Internet access, rebates and discounts for online transactions (both government and commercial) will probably do more to get low-income Americans online than any other factor.

But when governments calculate whether it makes economic sense for them to move more of government online they need to remember that their costs are not the only costs involved. If governments make their investment decisions based only on their own internal rate of return, they will misallocate resources. The reason is that a significant share of the savings from e-government accrue to the users, not just to the governments. People save time from not having to be in line and save money from not having to mail forms, etc. These savings can be considerable and should be considered in any calculus governments make as the paybacks of e-government investments.

Customer-focused e-government also makes interacting with government much more convenient. Tasks that previously required a visit to a government office or a telephone call during office hours can be performed by users whenever and wherever they please. E-government is likely to be a particular benefit to those who work long hours or shift work, the elderly, and those with mobility problems.

Yet the really significant benefits of e-government will come from reengineering government to take advantage of the Web–creating a fundamentally different sort of government that provides much more value to citizens. But customer-focused digital government can serve as a powerful solvent to bureaucracy and the "stovepipe" barriers that exist between agencies and levels of government. Creating customer-focused e-government will and should lead to pressures to create the same kind of government in the offline world–a world in which citizens (and businesses) who interact with government by mail, telephone, or face-to-face are not stuck in separate "stovepipes."

E-GOVERNMENT TODAY

Compared to almost every other nation, the United States is the leader in e-commerce. However, when it comes to e-government we are not in the lead, at least at the federal level. According to a January 2001 report by the international consulting firm Accenture, three countries are in the category of "innovative leaders" in e-government: Canada, Singapore and the United States.[8] But while Accenture's report last year ranked the U.S. first in the world, its 2001 report puts Canada and Singapore ahead, with other countries not far behind. There is much more that U.S. governments can do to embrace the Information Technology (IT) revolution.

Phase 1: Using the Internet to Share Information (1993-1998)

From its inception until the late-1990s, government's Web presence was entirely passive, and inspired by the view that the purpose was to provide information to citizens. Even today information provision functions remain one of the major function of many government Websites. Moreover, it's important to note that not all governments are even in phase one, particularly smaller jurisdictions, as they have yet to even get online. Policymakers from small cities, counties, and towns would like to take advantage of the opportunity to save money and improve constituent services that larger localities can more easily afford by offering government services online. But while the cost of buying technology and hiring people with the technical expertise to run Websites is feasible for governments with larger tax bases, until recently localities with small populations and small budgets could not afford to establish and maintain their own government Website.

One model that small communities can look to is to form digital government cooperatives. For example, working through the League of Minnesota Cities, policymakers from small localities partnered with a private company to create affordable Websites that meet their particular needs. Minnesota's model partnership first began when the League of Minnesota Cities policymakers decided to solicit a "Request for Proposal" to see if a private company could devise a mutually beneficial way to develop Websites for the League's member cities. A company called Avenet responded by creating GovOffice.com, a service now offered to government officials (working for populations up to 60,000) nationwide through the International City/County Management Association. This provides them the ability to offer services ranging from accepting utility or tax payments to issuing business permits and automatically sending notices about civic meetings to constituents who have requested such updates. Doing this jointly is relatively inexpensive. Governments do not have to purchase or install software. All they need is a computer, an Internet connection, and a Web browser. The costs for a basic Webpage can be as low as a $300 initial fee and a monthly hosting fee of $50 dollars.

Phase 2: Online Transactions and Service Provision (1998-2001)

By the late-1990s, an increasing number of government Websites had begun moving from just an information provision model to a transactional model. Initially, this took the form of allowing users to download a form, which could then only be submitted by printing it out and mailing it in to the agency. Yet governments are steadily, if too often slowly, moving towards allowing people to complete transactions online. However, because many governments still do not enable online transactions, completing, and in some cases even getting started on this phase is essential.

One survey found that the services people most want to be able to access online are:[9]

- Renewing a driver's license
- Voter registration
- Park information and reservations
- Voting
- Access to one-stop shopping (one portal for all government services)
- Ordering birth, death, and marriage certificates
- Filing taxes
- Hunting and fishing licenses
- Accessing medical information from the National Institute of Health

The above list includes services provided by all tiers of government. And in some cases, supply is keeping up with demand. Each year, students file more than two million applications for college financial aid online.[10] Nearly five million people use the Department of Health and Human Services' Healthfinder service to choose a health plan, a doctor, a course of treatment, or a long-term care facility.[11] In many states, driver's licenses can be renewed online. One of the most advanced government Websites is Washington state government's–which allows Web users to pay personal and business taxes (using digital certificate technology); apply for jobs, unemployment insurance or college; order birth, death, marriage or divorce certificates; obtain criminal history information; and even report suspected fraud.[12]

However, for local governments, progress is much slower. In 2000, the National League of Cities reported that while 89% of municipalities had Websites, only 58% allowed users to download forms and information, 31% provided for the completion of forms and applications, and just 8% permitted financial transactions to be conducted online.[13]

Perhaps the most frequent type of transactions that take place over the Internet are e-mail inquiries. Government agencies need to handle incoming e-mails in an efficient manner–with responses sent back within two or three days. This requires putting in place the right systems to handle a large number of incoming e-mails. In many cases, more staff will be needed, since new inquiries will be generated. But ultimately government resource limitations preclude adequately satisfying customer e-mail inquiries, especially if they are increasing over time. As a result, government will need to move beyond the e-mail paradigm toward a self-service model of customer service where citizens are able to get the answers and transactions they need from the Web. This, as the rest of this report stresses, will require much smarter, more intuitive, multiformatted interfaces to government Websites.

However, in many cases, government agencies should also be sending more e-mail correspondence instead of paper. In the long run, moving from paper to electronic correspondence can save mailing, printing, and handling costs, and provide a more efficient service to the public. For example, a citizen is probably more likely to renew her business license if she receives a friendly e-mail reminder, complete with a personal hyperlink. All she needs to do to renew her license is click on the hyperlink and enter her credit card details.

Finally, if government is to complete phase two and enable a much larger and more comprehensive set of transactions to take place online, it will need to ensure that citizens have the ability to authenticate themselves online so that the government can verify that when Mary F. Smith renews her professional license online, it is indeed Mary F. Smith. For example, the U.S. Patent and Trademark Office has implemented the use of digital signatures to allow more than 7,000 registered patent attorneys and 4,000 inventors to file patents. These allow the PTO to know that the person filing a patent is actually the person they claim to be and constitute legally binding electronic signatures. At the state level, Illinois has partnered with the software company Entrust to purchase digital certificates that, among other uses, enables Illinois businesses to do things such as submit vouchers for reimbursement to the Department of Aging online and enabling companies to send hazardous waste reports over the Internet. The system relies on encryption and digital signatures to verify an online user's identity and assure that a particular document has not been altered.[14]

E-GOVERNMENT TOMORROW

Phase 3: Integration (2001-?)

E-government offers the potential to deliver public services in a more efficient, more holistic, manner. As British Prime Minister Tony Blair has argued, "Joined-up problems need joined-up solutions."[15] Old divisions between agencies, between tiers of government, and even between the public and private sector, become increasingly irrelevant in the digital age.

Smart e-government should be focused on one goal: helping citizens solve problems. Most people are not interested in which government agency, or even which tier of government, is responsible. Nor should they be. Nor are they interested in bureaucratic acronyms and governmental self-promotion. Digital government should deliver services to citizens seamlessly and in a commonsense way, without requiring them to surf around to find the right Website.

Progress Towards Integration

Unfortunately, e-government today is fraught with problems. Visitors to many government sites are liable to find:

"Stovepipe" structures. Too many government Websites still require users to know which agency delivers the service that they are seeking. For example, before California revamped its Website, users wanting to get a death certificate had to know to contact the Department of Health Services.[16] Within the federal government, the Customs Service has fought against a cross-agency functionally based "International Trade Data System," in favor of its own expensive Customs-only solution. Agency-specific Websites are not only confusing to consumers, but at worst, can also exacerbate the "stovepipe problem," as departments develop their Internet strategy in isolation from others.

Sites that only list information provided by their own agency. Not only are Websites too often organized by agency, they frequently only provide links to "their" information. For example, several state government Websites have "Education" sections with links to local colleges, but no links to federal financial aid Websites. It's not uncommon for state departments to list online the programs they operate to people or businesses, but not other programs offered by local or federal governments, nonprofits, colleges, and others. Business.gov, the federal portal, only lists help for business provided by the federal government, not state government. Government needs to approach the Web with a philosophy of helping users solve problems, not merely delivering their same old services through a new medium. And this means that government needs to help direct citizens to a wide range of services–including those that they do not provide themselves.

Websites promoting government. Although an important role of government is to help citizens, too often e-government seems to be a publicity portal for programs and politicians. The worst Websites give top billing to a photograph of the Governor or Secretary, with the latest press releases from the agency highlighted. They then proceed to list their own government programs, often with indecipherable acronyms. This is equivalent to the Amazon.com home page featuring a picture of its CEO Jeff Bezos, along with press releases on how well Amazon's stock is doing, instead of immediately seeing how to buy books.

Unfriendly portals. Websites need to be designed with an intuitive interface, making them easy to navigate. Instead, too many are confusing and unfriendly–particularly once the user goes a level or two below the opening page. Too often "customer-focused" portals have mostly meant putting a myriad of links on one Webpage. It's as if government is saying "we're customer-focused, we've published an easy-to-use directory of all our individual agency-centric programs." For example:

- Business.gov, the federal government's Web portal for business is a confusing array of links that just take users to individual agency Websites (e.g., click on taxes and you go to the IRS Website).
- One state government Website purports to offer online help for dislocated workers. Yet one level deeper, users are shown a list of services for dislocated workers and asked to click on the boxes which apply to them, then print the page out and take it in to their local employment office for assistance, instead of giving the information online.

- Another state government site at first appears to allow customers to renew their licenses online. But once the user has navigated a maze of menus (one needs to click on "Online Renewals," *not* "Drivers Licenses"!), they are presented with a screen saying that online renewals are currently out of service.

Another state government portal simply takes users to a list of hyperlinks for 121 different state government agencies. Presumably, citizens who are unfamiliar with governmental structures are expected to read through the entire list, and attempt to determine from the names of the agencies the one that might be able to help them. Smart, service-oriented government can do better.

Search engines that don't work. Try searching for "job training" on the average state government Webpage and you are more likely to be presented with reports, financial statements and press releases about job training than about how to actually get information about where you can get job training. A short-term fix is to use a smarter search engine,[17] but the root problem is generally with the agency's "back-end" computer systems. In simple terms, most data on government Websites is not properly indexed into a core database system. There is a need for a better, more complete and standardized indexing/classification system that is used and applied across government. Setting up such a robust good database structure will be resource-intensive, but is ultimately essential. But sites should also code particular key sites so that they come up at or near the top of searches, so that, for example, when someone searches for job training, they go to the workforce and employment portal.

WHAT SHOULD CUSTOMER-FOCUSED E-GOVERNMENT LOOK LIKE?

E-government should function better than this. To properly integrate government online, federal, state and local agencies should do a number of things. They can start by throwing away the rule book and thinking anew. To create fully integrated government Webpages, government administrators ought to begin by assuming that the current bricks and mortar structures of government do not already exist, or they risk simply recreating them in the digital world. One report has described the distinction as designing online government from the "outside in," not from the "inside out."[18] Or in Web jargon, the goal should be to create an online environment that is "pure play" (like Amazon.com), not merely replicate the "bricks and mortar" structure. While not all "pure play" dot.coms survived, they were unique in the sense that they designed commercial applications unencumbered by the practices of the offline world. As a result the most successful "bricks and clicks" companies that have added an online presence to their physical presence have done so by designing applications specifically to take advantage of the Web. Only in this way will government be making the most of new technology to reengineer itself.

Two good ways of organizing government online are around topics and customer groups:

a. *Topics:* This may include anything from buying a house to traveling overseas. For example, a pilot program in Australia has established an online one-stop shop for recreational fishing, allowing quick access to information on fishing policy, regulations, safety and the environment, plus transactions such as license applications-integrating services across all levels of government.[19] Another, for parents whose children are starting school, contains information on term dates, immunization requirements, afterschool care and statistics to help choose the right school, as well as to enroll and pay school levies online.[20] Similarly, the UK Government has a Website with information on various "Life Episodes," including "Going Away," "Having a Baby," "Learning to Drive" and "Looking for a Job."[21] Such topic-based integration should not be confined only to the Web. For example, the government telephone "blue-pages" could be cross-referenced so that government is listed in the telephone directory by function across agencies, rather than by agency/organization structure alone.

b. *Citizen groups:* Government portals for particular groups of people recognize that individuals not only tend to be interested in varying types of information, but also that the same information sometimes needs to be presented in different ways for each group. At the federal level, citizen group portals now include *www.seniors.gov, www.students.gov, www.business.gov, www.workers.gov, www.kids.gov, www.disabilities.gov* and *lifelines2000.org* (for naval personnel).[22] These sites are still far from perfect. To improve they need to enable users to get help with a range of common issues in one place. Moreover, users should be able to complete almost all of their transactions online. Many of these user-oriented portals point to information, but provide only a limited number of transactions people can engage in.

These two ways of organizing information along more functional lines are not mutually exclusive, but are actually complementary and are best used together. In either case, these sites need to be much more than simple collections of URLs and hyperlinks. The U.S. federal government's *www.firstgov.gov* site is still a directory, rather than an integrated portal for the federal government. And it doesn't go much beyond putting categories on the front page that lead directly to agency or program Websites. For example, when firstgov.gov users search on "rural development," they get over 1,000 hits, of any Webpage that has the words in it. If they search on the topic list and click "rural development" they are taken to the homepage of the Rural Development Office at the Department of Agriculture, which at the time of writing this article showed a picture of a political appointee being sworn in.

True customer-oriented sites would employ a logical, "tree-like" structure that would enable people to drill down to find exactly what they need, somewhat like how Yahoo organizes its search engine. But even more is needed. For the goal is not to find some Website, for example, it's to find answers. For example, a customer-focused Website would have collected all the government (state and federal) programs on rural development, along with university research centers, reports, and other information that people interested in rural development might need. This will mean that government Websites need to develop common standards on database architecture and information display. In Australia and Israel, the government has established uniform standards for its Websites, but the U.S. federal government has yet to do so. In many cases it will also mean that government needs to design from the bottom up information for the Web, not just provide links to complicated and out-of-date reports, press releases and other information that gets put up online. In short, users need Websites designed around them!

As these functionally organized Websites come online, existing departmental Websites should be scaled down. Eventually, many of today's departmental Websites will either be removed, or only contain information for those interested in policy development, such as press releases, policy documents and statistics. For example, much of what now appears on the Department of Agriculture's Webpage should more logically appear on pages like the existing *www.nutrition.gov* (dealing with food safety and nutrition), and new functional Websites like *www.farmers.gov* (which could contain information about farm loan programs, crops, foreign agricultural markets, etc.).

But these citizen-centered Web portals also need to go beyond their current focus on one level of government and integrate all levels of government around the needs of the citizen. Local, state and federal governments need to put far more effort into creating integrated sites, bringing together resources from different agencies, different tiers of government and the private sector. This kind of thinking should permeate e-government from the outset. For example, federal government Websites should be built with extensible architecture that can easily incorporate other information and links, so state and local governments can be brought into the system. And likewise, state government Websites should be ready-made to integrate with local governments.

So far, most efforts to get government on the Web have been too timid. Bureaucratic culture rarely encourages inter-agency projects, let alone cooperation between different tiers of government. All too frequently, good cooperative ideas are thwarted by petty turf wars and disputes over budgets. Without a streak of boldness from our leading policymakers, integrated e-government will never achieve its full potential.

WHY HAVEN'T MORE GOVERNMENTS MADE THE TRANSITION TO THE THIRD PHASE?

In many ways, creating citizen-centered e-government should not be particularly difficult. Certainly the technology is not the barrier–after all, these applications exist in the private sector. So why is progress not faster and why do most government Web efforts remain stuck in phase two? The answer lies in the fact that moving to phase one and even phase two requires few significant organizational changes. Rather, these phases simply extend the current bureaucratic framework and put it online. All government needs to do is hire a Webmaster, and he or she can solve most of the problems. Moving to phase three is vastly harder. It involves reorienting what agencies actually do and how they do it. In particular, it necessitates a number of new behaviors and attitudes that are not necessarily in place today. It requires a fundamental change in outlook on the part of government, with the focus being placed on the needs of citizens/customers. Customer-centered e-government requires moving from separate departmental Websites to a seamless Internet presence, organized around the citizen's needs.

First, customer-centered e-government requires a customer-focused perspective. But since the development of bureaucratic government in the early 20th century, the focus has been in the opposite direction. Bureaucracy was defined by its separation from the environment and by its inward orientation. Most government agencies do not talk to their real customers when developing and refining their Web strategies. Atkinson recently gave a seminar to the CIOs and IT leaders of a large federal agency. The CIO overseeing the entire agency related how he asked his team to develop an e-government strategy for the agency and to first consult with the agency's "customers." When the team came back with its report, it turned out they had spoken with "customers," only they were all inside the agency. To his credit the CIO sent them back to the beginning and made them talk to businesses, educators, and citizens who were its true customers.

Ongoing consultation with users is a necessary condition of revamping e-government to be more citizen-centric. Layouts that seem intuitive to experienced bureaucrats may not be so user-friendly to ordinary customers. The only way to ensure that government Websites are structured the right way is for users to be involved throughout the design process. Once pages are launched, all users should be invited to rate them online, and this information used to make improvements. Private sector marketing and customer research methodologies, including quantitative and qualitative market research techniques such as interviews, polling, sampling and focus group discussions should all be used. These can also be used over time to form tracking studies that highlight government progress in improving quality and performance of government service delivery.

The next phase in e-government requires government to rethink its core mission. Clearly some parts of government focus only on enabling citizens to engage in routine transactions. But much of government sees its role as providing "its" program. This has several implications. It makes cross-agency and inter-governmental applications difficult. In addition, it reinforces governments' tendency to provide information about their own program offerings, rather than about the entire array of services and programs to help citizens solve problems. It is important to not underestimate the resistance and in some cases fear from individual agencies, including individual agency CIOs, to more functional, less agency-centric digital government. Issues of turf, power, funding, and lack of vision can all come into play in maintaining the digital status quo.

As a result, organizing Websites and computer systems around the needs of citizens, not bureaucrats, requires at minimum high-level leadership and advocates who have the authority and vision to overcome bureaucratic inertia and resistance in the move to customer-focused government. One model to bring about coordination and enterprise-wide initiatives is inter-agency groups. But such an approach suffers from several distinct limitations. First, they lack the resources to implement government-wide efforts. Second, they are largely a meeting of equals, and lack the authority to impose central direction on individual agencies. Moreover, their primary focus remains on their individual agencies, not on government-wide reinvention. Without more centralized leadership, the traditional model of agency-specific Websites is likely to predominate.

In this area, the states are well ahead of the federal government. According to an October 1998 survey by NASIRE, 14 states had a Chief Information Officer who reported directly to the Governor.[23] By August 2002, at least 34 states had such an official.[24] At the local level, it is not only major cities like Phoenix and Los Angeles that have CIOs; smaller jurisdictions such as Milpitas, CA, and Bellevue, WA, are now also realizing the value of having a single person to coordinate and provide leadership for their technology efforts.[25]

Yet although a majority of states, and many local governments, have CIOs who report to the Governor or Mayor, there is still no federal CIO, merely CIOs for various federal agencies.[26] In contrast, the Canadian Government has had a CIO since 1997.[27] In March 2000, the Progressive Policy Institute was the first to call for the U.S. Government to establish a federal CIO. In May 2001, Senator Joe Lieberman (D-CT) introduced the E-Government Act of 2001 (S.803) which would foster citizen-centric government by, among other things, creating a position of Federal CIO within the Office of Management and Budget. In the House, Congressman Jim Turner (D-TX) introduced similar legislation (H.R. 2458) in July 2001. Establishing a high-level assistant to the President on electronic governance is supported by 65% of Americans, including 71% of Internet users, 73% of Democrats, 62% of Republicans, and 59% of Independents.[28]

Unfortunately, the Bush Administration reneged on its proposal to create a federal CIO made in the 2000 Presidential Campaign, and instead appointed a mid-level official within the Office of Management and Budget (OMB) to oversee e-government efforts. In addition, because it actively opposed the Lieberman bill and in order to get the Administration's support and Republicans in the Senate, Senator Lieberman had to weaken the CIO's standing within OMB in order to get the bill passed in the Senate in 2002. Why such resistance? The simple answer is turf and power. In the Clinton Administration the Deputy Director for Management of OMB was one of the most vociferous opponents of a high-level CIO because the position would have reduced her authority. Likewise, once the Bush Administration took office, the Deputy Director for Management led the charge against a CIO. Without a real interest from the White House in creating a new kind of e-government, administrations stick with the status quo.

In contrast, Tony Blair has made e-government a more important priority, and in so doing created the UK's Office of the E-envoy, which is responsible both for getting government online and creating the best possible environment for e-commerce.[29] By creating an office with these dual functions the Blair Government has endeavored to make Britain a leader in the information age. One of the functions that gives the E-envoy some clout is that he has the power to sign off on agency IT budgets. While the E-envoy doesn't always win his fights, the fact that he is focusing on e-transformation and is in a position to lead, does help push change.[30]

For an enterprise-wide CIO to have power, he needs money. Without money he is forced to go hat-in-hand to agencies to try to convince them to fund cross-agency projects, something most agencies have little interest in doing. One way to provide the CIO with resources is for government to create a cross-agency digital government fund to provide matching finance for innovative programs that individual agencies are unwilling to fund alone. To receive funding, programs would need to help integrate different parts of government; combine public and private sector expertise; be innovative and cost-effective; and be an example of best practice e-government, which can be publicized through a Website set up to show off "model e-government initiatives."[31]

The Progressive Policy Institute has recommended the creation of a $500 million cross-agency digital government fund. When he was running for office, President Bush proposed a $100 million fund, but once in office, reduced the amount to $20 million. House appropriators then proceeded to cut this to just $5 million. If the federal government is serious about integrated government, it will need to put much more money towards cross-agency initiatives. The Lieberman and Turner e-government bills both propose a $200 million digital government fund. In a period of budget constraints, if Congress and the Bush Administration do not want to add new monies for customer-focused e-government initiatives, they could fund such initiatives by imposing a small set-aside on all federal IT budgets (e.g., half of one percent) and allocating these funds to cross-agency, innovative initiatives. In some cases, more money is not the answer. For example, the U.S. Customs Services has successfully lobbied for a $1.8 billion allocation to revamp its outdated computer system, even though an alternative and better cross-agency International Trade Data System (ITDS) would be much cheaper to develop. Proposed in 1995 as a partnership between several government agencies, continuing turf wars raise the specter that the ITDS may never be established.

But while administrations need to promote enterprise-wide e-government, so do legislative bodies. Government services are funded on an agency-by-agency basis. Congressional committee jurisdiction and OMB agency budget allocations sustain this "stovepipe" focus. Within Congress, committees and subcommittees focus on individual agencies, as does the oversight system. There are few means in Congress to take an enterprise-wide perspective. While it is unrealistic to expect that Congress and state legislatures will reorganize their appropriations processes, they can do much more to force the integration of systems.

A prime example is the current effort to develop an integrated information system to fight terrorism. After months of endeavoring to coordinate disparate agencies, the Bush Administration belatedly decided to create a new Department of Homeland Security. But while this will make it easier to coordinate databases and information systems, there will be a host of other information systems in other agencies (e.g., Treasury, State, FBI) that will not be under direct control of the Secretary for Homeland Security. The Bush Administration's efforts to create an enterprise-wide information architecture for all Homeland Security functions are likely to face significant bureaucratic resistance not only from other agencies, but perhaps also from those inside the Department of Homeland Security itself. Congress could help by adopting a simple funding rule: no funding for computer and IT systems for Homeland Security will be appropriated unless the CIO of DHS has signed off saying that the proposed system fits with the overall national information architecture plan. This simple step would go a long way in assuring that agencies can no longer just go their own way.

If inter-agency action is hard, inter-governmental coordination is even harder. While there are some efforts underway to do this, it's all many jurisdictions can do to develop their own e-government initiatives. But for many applications jurisdictional organization does not serve the needs of citizens. There is a need for both horizontal and vertical cross-governmental integration. Organizing Websites in a metropolitan area by jurisdiction means that many of the functions that people are interested in that cross jurisdictional lines (e.g., getting information on parks and recreation, cultural activities, etc.) are confined to agency-specific Websites. Organizing information by jurisdiction also means that people accessing information or transactions at multiple levels of government (e.g., a new business incorporating that must file forms with local, state and the federal government) must go to separate Websites. These issues go beyond just convenience, they go to the fundamental way in which government is organized.

While federations of jurisdictions can accomplish some of this kind of coordination, ultimately leadership needs to come from the federal government. The federal government needs to identify the applications where cross-agency, customer-centric approaches are needed, bring in the relevant government agencies to make this happen, and provide much of the funding. To take one concrete example, virtually all of the over 3,000 counties in the nation still file land and property records by paper. Digitizing these systems would result in significant efficiencies, not the least of which would be to dramatically reduce the cost of title searches. But such efforts are stalled by lack of standardization.

Such efforts require both funding (see below), but more importantly the willingness to abandon obsolete notions of federalism that suggest that states should independently control a large share of functions. The framers of the Constitution respected the rights of states to govern internal activities, but made it clear that they could not restrict interstate commerce.[32] Federalism for the New Economy is not a paean to unlimited state freedoms. Rather, it requires a new bargain between Washington and states: on the one hand giving states more flexibility and accountability; and on the other, developing national e-commerce governing frameworks. On issues such as digital signatures, privacy, SPAM, or e-commerce protectionism, state preemption is required to create a vibrant cross-border marketplace.

Finally, bringing about this kind of transformation requires investment. Government is being asked to manage paper and face-to-face government while at the same time create a new digital government, but often without additional resources to do the job. While it is true that digital government saves money, there are short-term costs for technology and project management. When funding is provided, it is usually to individual agencies. There is a conspicuous lack of funding for cross-agency applications. Agencies are not apt to use their limited funds for cross-agency applications. Yet to effectively implement many digital government functions, government must take an enterprise-wide management perspective (whether it's delivering monetary benefits to the public, organizing cross-agency or individual agency databases, or developing government portals). This unwillingness to fund cross-agency projects is a principal reason why when the Small Business Administration sought to develop a single point of entry where small businesses that interact with numerous federal agencies could enter their data just once and have it shared with the various agencies, resistance by individual agencies scuttled the initiative.

Ultimately, effective e-government requires strong political leadership. To the extent that chief executives and their top personnel see the importance of transforming government through information technology, they will push to make that happen. Unfortunately, core elements of both parties are not committed to this agenda. For many Republicans, especially anti-government supply-siders, the key task with regard to government reform is to cut "waste, fraud, and abuse," not to reinvent it to work even better. In other words, they want smaller government, not better government. Making government work in the information age implies to them that there will be increased support for government.

This orientation explains the lack of leadership in the Bush Administration for e-government. While the administration knows that it can't be seen as doing nothing on this issue, it is making at best a modest effort in this area. In fact, the President's Management Agenda is much more focused on privatization and cutting costs than it is on digital reinvention. OMB Director Mitch Daniels has stressed that there is no need for more resources for e-government, but rather to eliminate the current "waste." While it is true that some current funding is wasted and could be better managed, this is largely a smokescreen for the Administration's unwillingness to commit funding for e-government efforts. For example, the Administration's "Quicksilver" process for e-government identified over 100 possible projects, but because of funding limitations, chose to fund only 24, and most of these are proceeding slowly due to lack of funding. For all their talk, the Bush administration simply has not made a significant commitment to e-transformation.

Elected Democratic officials have a different problem. Given their traditional support for activist government, they have a stake in government that not only works, but is also perceived by the public as being effective. However, some more liberal Democrats are hesitant to embrace a new vision of governance based on technology. If the old governing system was based on top-down, managerial control exercised by large organizations, the new IT-based governing system is based more on bottom-up, networked systems that operate in chaotic and nonlinear ways. Such systems are fundamentally at odds with the big-government paradigm established from the period of the 1940s to the late 1970s and so vigorously defended by many liberals. In addition, some liberals worry that moving aggressively towards e-government transformation will leave groups behind who may not have easy access to the Internet (this is a reasonable, but not insurmountable, concern). In addition, they worry that the customization that e-government allows will enable people to be treated differently and therefore will lead to unfair outcomes. Finally, given the implications of e-government reinvention on government productivity and the possibility of layoffs, some liberals may fight such efforts to automate government.

However, there are reformist wings in both parties that see e-government transformation as progressive forces. Not all Republicans are inclined to continually move functions from government to the marketplace. To our surprise, Newt Gingrich recently wrote that the technology revolution can be used to radically reinvent government.[33] Whether Gingrich's call will be used as one more conservative justification to cut government or to truly help solve problems is unclear. But for Democrats the political threat is real. As Gingrich states, "if conservatives develop these programs first and best, they will create a new demand for change. Liberals will be left as the reactionary protectors of the bureaucrats, defending inefficiency, technological backwardness, and poor services at high costs."[34] Democrats will need to respond not with an agenda for protecting the status quo, but with an aggressive e-transformation of their own. "New Democrats" such as Senator Joe Lieberman have aggressively pushed an e-government transformation agenda. And it's likely that as the 2004 presidential campaign heats up, most Democratic primary candidates will have staked out a position and offered ideas on how to transform government through information technology.

CONCLUSION

As we come to the end of the first decade of digital government, policymakers have the chance to reshape government online so that it is centered on citizens, not bureaucracy. This will not be easy. The past few years have seen hundreds of e-government projects founder because policymakers did not appreciate the "back end" changes that are required to create good government Websites. But high-level leadership bridges the gap between bureaucrats, technology experts and politicians. Without it, more failures and unfriendly Websites are certain to occur.

At its best, integrated e-government will make life simpler for individuals and reduce the costs to government and citizens and businesses. Moreover, by showing leadership in the delivery of electronic services, government can help spur the growth of e-commerce.[35] Customer-focused digital government will even help government operate more effectively. But unlike the first two stages of e-government that required largely technical changes, the third phase is much harder, as it requires organizational changes that go against the grain of current bureaucratic and political culture of most agencies. The next few years should tell whether these institutional factors are insurmountable or whether government will be able to adapt to the new realities of the information age.

NOTES

1. <www.whitehouse.gov> was launched in 1993. In 1994, Congress went online, as did governments in a number of other countries, including Japan, the UK and New Zealand: see Zakon, R., Hobbes' Internet Timeline v5.3, <www.zakon.org/robert/ internet/timeline/>.

2. In this paper, "citizens" is used in a broad sense, to encompass all those who reside in the U.S., and form part of the American community, rather than only those who formally hold U.S. citizenship.

3. Council for Excellence in Government, *e-Government: The Next American Revolution*, 2001, p.19, <www.excelgov.org>.

4. Ibid, p. 18.

5. Tanner, L., "Connecting Government" in D. Glover and G. Patmore (eds.), *Labor Essays 2001: For the People* (Sydney: Pluto Press, 2001).

6. Cohen, S. and Eimicke, W., *The Use of the Internet in Government Service Delivery*, PricewaterhouseCoopers Endowment for the Business of Government, 2001 <endowment.pwcglobal.com>.

7. Similarly, while the Postal Service gives discounts to businesses who bar code mail, they do not give it to consumers who mail bar coded envelopes (e.g., return envelopes of bills).

8. Accenture, *eGovernment Leadership: Rhetoric vs Reality–Closing the Gap*, 2001, <www.accenture.com>, pp. 7, 10.

9. Cook, M., *What Citizens Want from E-Government*, Center for Technology in Government, University at Albany/SUNY. <www.ctg.albany.edu/resources/htmlrpt/ e-government/what_citizens_want.html>.

10. <www.students.gov>.

11. <www.healthfinder.gov>.

12. <access.wa.gov>.

13. Sander, T., "E-Government Risks." Presentation delivered at the 2000 NLC Congress of Cities, December 8, 2000, in Boston, Massachusetts, based on data from the National League of Cities. <pti.nw.dc.us/links/e_government.html>

14. Marc Strassman and Robert Atkinson, *Jump-Starting the Digital Economy (with Department of Motor Vehicles-Issued Digital Certificates)*, PPI, Washington, DC, 2001. <http://www.ndol.org/ndol_ci.cfm?contentid'1369&kaid'140&subid'290>.

15. Blair, T., *The Observer*, May 31, 1998 (untitled article).

16. Salladay, R., "Gateway to Golden State Now Just a Click Away," *San Francisco Chronicle*, 8/1/01, <www.sfgate.com>.

17. For example, <www.google.com>, <dmoz.org>, <www.directhit.com> and <www.teoma. com> are all search engines that rank Webpages by popularity or by the number of pages that are linked to that page. Within government, two search tools that are particularly effective are Washington state's "Ask George" <http://access.wa.gov/> and California's "How Do I?" Knowledge Base <http://www.ca.gov/state/portal/myca_homepage.jsp>.

18. Cappe, M., *Seventh Annual Report to the Prime Minister on the Public Service of Canada*, Privy Council Office, Ottawa. <www.pco-bcp.gc.ca/7rept2000/cover_e.htm>.

19. "TIGERS Goes Fishing." February 28, 2001. <www.govonline.gov.au/projects/services&innovation/tigers.htm>.

20. "TIGERS–Roaring into school." April 9, 2001. <www.govonline.gov.au/projects/services&innovation/tigers.htm>.

21. <http://www.ukonline.gov.uk/online/ukonline/leHome>.

22. A full list of federal government Websites organized around user groups can be found at <http://www.firstgov.gov/topics/interests.html>.

23. NASIRE, *The Chief Information Officer*, NASIRE, Lexington, KY, 1998. <https://www.nascio.org/publications/cio.pdf>. Twenty states responded.

24. NASIRE, *The Role of the State Chief Information Officer*, NASIRE, Lexington, KY, 2000. <https://www.nascio.org/publications/index.cfm>. Forty-five states responded.

25. Byerly, T., "The Rise of the Local CIO," *Government Technology*, Jan 1999. <http://www.govtech.net/publications/local.us/jan99/localcio/localcio.phtml>.

26. Sarkar, D., "E-Gov a Low Priority for Bush," *civic.com*, 5/10/01. <http://www.fcw.com/civic/articles/2001/0507/web-bush-05-10-01.asp>.

27. See <http://www.tbs-sct.gc.ca/news97/0210_e.html>.

28. Council for Excellence in Government, *e-Government: The Next American Revolution*, 2001, p. 18 <www.excelgov.org>.

29. <www.e-envoy.gov.uk>.

30. The UK government's e-envoy reports are available at <www.e-envoy.gov.uk/ukonline/progress/montprog.htm>.

31. Others have also proposed boosting matching funds for e-government initiatives. See Dawes, S., Bloniarz, P., Kelly, K. and Fletcher, P., *Some Assembly Required: Building a Digital Government for the 21st Century*, Center for Technology in Government, National Science Foundation, Washington, DC, 1999, p. 31. <www.ctg.albany.edu/research/workshop/dgfinalreport.pdf>.

32. James Madison wrote, "Such a use of the power by Cong accords with the intention and expectation of the States in transferring the power over trade from themselves to the Govt. of the U.S." [sic]: Letter from James Madison to Joseph C. Cabell, 18 Sept. 1828: Gaillard Hunt (ed.), *The Writings of James Madison*. Vol 2. New York: G. P. Putnam's Sons, 1910. Available at <http://press-pubs.uchicago.edu/founders/documents/a1_8_3_commerces18.html>.

33. Gingrich, Speech at American Enterprise Institute, May 14, 2001. Available at <http://www.aei.org/past%5Fevent/conf010514b.htm>.

34. Ibid.

35. On e-commerce, see Rob Atkinson, *The Failure of Cyber-Libertarianism: The Case for a National E-Commerce Strategy*, Progressive Policy Institute, Washington, DC, 2001. <http://www.ndol.org/ndol_ci.cfm?contentid=3439&kaid=140&subid=292>.

RESEARCHING
E-GOVERNMENT

NEW ZEALAND

An Evaluation of Local Government Websites in New Zealand

Rowena Cullen

Victoria University of Wellington, New Zealand

Deborah O'Connor

New Zealand Institute of Economic Research

Anna Veritt

National Library of New Zealand

Rowena Cullen, MA, MLitt, PhD, is Senior Lecturer in the School of Information Management, Victoria University of Wellington.

Deborah O'Connor, MA, MLIS, is an information specialist at the Institute for Economic Research, Wellington.

Anna Veritt, MSc, MLIS, is a librarian at the National Library of New Zealand.

Address correspondence to: Rowena Cullen, School of Information Management, Victoria University of Wellington, P.O. Box 600, Wellington, New Zealand (E-mail: Rowena.cullen@vuw.ac.nz).

The research was funded by the Trustees of the National Library of New Zealand.

[Haworth co-indexing entry note]: "An Evaluation of Local Government Websites in New Zealand." Cullen, Rowena, Deborah O'Connor, and Anna Veritt. Co-published simultaneously in *Journal of Political Marketing* (The Haworth Press, Inc.) Vol. 2, No. 3/4, 2003, pp. 185-211; and: *The World of E-Government* (ed: Gregory G. Curtin, Michael H. Sommer, and Veronika Vis-Sommer) The Haworth Press, Inc., 2003, pp. 185-211. Single or multiple copies of this article are available for a fee from The Haworth Document Delivery Service [1-800-HAWORTH, 9:00 a.m. - 5:00 p.m. (EST). E-mail address: docdelivery@haworthpress.com].

SUMMARY. The study assesses the effectiveness of New Zealand local government Websites in providing equitable and appropriate access to government information. All local government Websites that could be identified were evaluated using 37 criteria, and visitors to approximately half of these sites were surveyed to determine their perceptions of the effectiveness of the sites. Results show that although there is a good range of information provided on the better sites, some smaller regional or district councils sites provide little in the way of basic information to their citizens. The study also found a limited range of transactional services available on New Zealand local government Websites, and a widespread lack of disabled-enabled access to sites, along with poor provision for user privacy and security. User comments focused on the need for more information and more up-to-date information to be provided, and better search facilities on sites. Although over 90% of users approached a particular site seeking specific information, less than half were able to find the information they sought. Significant indigenous and ethnic minority groups were underrepresented among users. The study concludes that there is room for considerable improvement in the use of the Web as a primary communication and transaction channel within the context of the government's vision for extending e-government in New Zealand to local government and other agencies. *[Article copies available for a fee from The Haworth Document Delivery Service: 1-800-HAWORTH. E-mail address: <docdelivery@haworthpress.com> Website: <http://www.HaworthPress. com> © 2003 by The Haworth Press, Inc. All rights reserved.]*

KEYWORDS. Government information, Internet, WWW, local government

INTRODUCTION

The Policy Framework for Government-held Information which was adopted by the New Zealand Cabinet in 1997 (State Services Commission 1997) articulates two key principles concerning the dissemination of government information in New Zealand. These have since been built on by a series of more detailed policy statements issued by subsequent governments (Ministry of Commerce 1999; State Services Commission 2000). The core principles remain unchallenged:

1. Government departments should make information available easily, widely and equitably to the people of New Zealand, except where reasons preclude such availability as specified in legislation.

2. Government departments should make the following information increasingly available on an electronic basis:

- all published material or material already in the public domain;
- all policies that could be released publicly;
- all information created or collected on a statutory basis (subject to commercial sensitivity and privacy considerations);
- all documents that the public may be required to complete;
- corporate documentation in which the public would be interested (State Services Commission 1997).

This policy, along with legislation such as the Official Information Act (1982) reflects the underlying principle that ready access to official and government information can empower individuals and groups in society and promote effective democracy. However, this principle can find itself in conflict with other legislation originating in the so-called state sector reforms of 1984, which were cemented in place by the introduction of the State-Owned Enterprises Act (1986), the State Sector Act (1988), and the Public Finance Act (1989). These acts brought substantial change to the public sector, encouraging agencies to regard information as an economic asset subject to Crown Copyright and discouraging the free exchange of information between government agencies or between agencies and citizens.

Since the establishment of the Electronic Government Unit in the State Services Commission, many more policy documents, vision statements, and guidelines have emerged to provide guidance to government agencies on accessibility to government information, secure exchange of data, cooperation and interoperability between agencies. These policies include the promotion of joint online purchasing of supplies, or 'e-procurement,' to achieve efficiencies in the state sector, and the use of information and communications technologies to support online or 'e-commerce' transactions between citizens and state agencies. The breadth of this activity is summarised in the E-Government Unit's operational vision for e-government in New Zealand, and their stated intention to make 'New Zealand . . . a world leader in e-government.' The Unit's mission reads:

By 2004 the Internet will be the dominant means of enabling ready access to government information and services.

The New Zealand government aims, under its e-government strategy, to create a public sector (including the public service, Crown entities, State-Owned Enterprises and local government) that is: structured, resourced and managed to perform in a manner which meets the needs of New Zealanders in the information age and which increasingly delivers information and services using on-line capacity. (State Services Commission 2001a)

This vision will be manifested in a newly designed New Zealand government Web portal to be launched in October 2002, which is intended to provide seamless access to government information and services. While the vision encompasses local government (which includes city, district and regional councils with separate rating or revenue gathering powers from central government), the State Services Commission has no direct authority in this sector, and must achieve its objectives by persuasion, identifying and modelling best practice, and offering expert advice.

Emergent Issues in the Provision of Government Information on the World Wide Web

The E-Government Unit has taken on board some of the issues emerging from previous research in New Zealand and elsewhere, and consulted extensively in its development of guidelines and standards to assist Web developers in the government sector. An evaluation of central government Websites by Cullen and Houghton had shown that while central government Websites were, in the main, technically competen, and some were excellently designed, there were several shortcomings across all sites that needed to be addressed. These included:

- Lack of a clear purpose, and a failure to communicate this purpose to users;
- Lack of good metadata;[1]
- Lack of good contacts for feedback and update of information;
- Statements about (and adequate provision for) confidentiality and privacy of personal data, statements of liability and copyright;
- Access for disabled users;
- Availability of publications in both electronic and print formats (Cullen and Houghton 2000, 246).

Key issues to emerge from a user survey carried out in conjunction with the evaluation included: the need for better search engines, indexes, site maps to help people find out quickly if the information they are wanting is likely to be there, and to locate it; assistance in identifying where it is available; and assurance that the information on government Websites is accurate and up-to-date (Cullen and Houghton 2000, 256).

An evaluation carried out by a research team at Brown University in North America revealed similar shortcomings in US government Websites, especially security and privacy issues, and disabled-enabled access (West 2000). An evaluation a year later, by the same research team, of the same state and federal sites, found some improvement in the extent of electronic services offered on sites, but continuing problems with security, privacy and disabled-enabled access. The same team's evaluation of city government Websites found considerable variation across cities in the amount of material on city Websites, and that a large number of cities also needed to address problems in the areas of privacy, security, and special needs populations such as the handicapped (West 2001). The team also found that:

- 7 percent of sites were multilingual, meaning that they offer two or more languages;
- 25 percent of Websites featured a one-stop services "portal" or have links to a government portal;
- 13 percent offered services that were fully executable online;
- the most frequent services are paying parking tickets online and filing complaints about street lights, rodent control, and potholes;
- 64 percent of Websites provided access to publications and 38 percent had links to databases;
- 14 percent showed privacy policies, while 8 percent had security policies only;
- 11 percent of the Websites had some form of disability access.

A separate review by the Civic Resource Group of major US city Websites concluded that 'limited information' and 'limited interactivity' were offered by these sites, and that 'most cities used their Websites as an electronic brochure' rather than as a medium through which to interact with citizens (Curtin et al. 2002). Opportunities for publishing budget information were used by only 65% of cities overall, and other forms of business information and records by far fewer. The team noted severe limitations with regard to privacy issues (less than 10% of cities included any readily identifiable privacy statement), and that most of the nearly 50% of cities which used 'cookies' to identify previous site visitors, or to track a visitor's progress through the site, did not acknowledge this: 'it was inferred that the use of the cookies was not perceived by cities as a privacy concern.' The study also found that basic navigation tools to help visitors find information were lacking in many sites, and that transaction services were offered overall by less than 10% of cities. Disabled-enabled access was referred to by only 5% of cities, although the number whose Web design permitted uninhibited disabled access may well have been higher than this.

A recent survey commissioned by the NZ Ministry of Economic Development found that although there had been 'a huge surge in business use of the Internet over the past 21 months since a previous survey in August 2001,' with one-third of firms claiming to be engaged in e-commerce with other firms, only 11% could take payments online (Ministry of Economic Development 2002). It might therefore be unrealistic to expect government sites, especially local government sites, to offer services at a higher rate than this, and US figures bear this out. Where financial reporting is concerned, New Zealand does not lag overly far behind the US. A local study by Laswad, Oyelere and Fisher (2001) which investigated the use of New Zealand local body Websites for financial reporting, found that one-half of the 61 local authorities who maintained Websites at that time (this represented 71% of all local authorities in New Zealand) provided financial reports of any kind online. Laswad, Oyelere and Fisher commented on the opportunities missed for disseminating such crucial information across the wide geographical areas served by district and regional councils.

The success of e-government initiatives depends considerably on the extent to which citizens are connected to, and use the Internet. Figures from the most recent New Zealand Census (Statistics New Zealand 2002) indicate that in 2001 37% of households had access to the Internet (this rises to over 70% for households with an annual income of more than NZ$100,000). Surveys of actual Internet use, as reported on the NUA Website, suggest that actual individual access is higher than this, and that 51.29% is comparable to Australia (54.38%), the United Kingdom (56.88%), and the United States (59.1%) and significantly higher than France (28.39%) or Germany (36.37%) (NUA Internet Surveys 2002). However, access is still denied to groups such as the lowest socioeconomic groups (which in New Zealand contains a disproportionate number of Maori and Pacific Island people), the elderly, and those living in remote rural area. Government policy to address these issues is ongoing (Doczi 2000).

New Zealand Policy Modified

In light of these findings, one of the most significant E-Government Unit policy documents to emerge in the past two years is the document entitled 'Guidelines for the Management and Design of New Zealand Public Sector Websites,' the latest version of which, dated June 2001, also bears the short title 'Web Guidelines' (State Services Commission 2001b). The document states clearly that it is intended to be applied only to public service agencies in the first instance, 'but we encourage the use of the guidelines by state sector agencies, local authorities and other entities that intersect with central government agencies.' The document is extensively based on the guidelines developed for government organisations in the United Kingdom (Office of the E-envoy 2001), which have since been revised.[2] The New Zealand guidelines were amended from the 1st UK version through a consultation process with GOVIS[3] and in the light of some of the recent research cited above (Cullen and Houghton 2000). They therefore already address a number of points that are reflected in the criteria used to evaluate Websites in Cullen and Houghton (2000), and the current study.

The Study

Access to government information is as fundamental to good local authority government as it is to central government. It facilitates the accountability of members of local authorities by opening their dealings and affairs to the public. It enables the public to participate in local government by keeping themselves informed, and provides support and a sense of identity in a community by bringing community services to the attention of the public. The research reported here therefore set out to extend the recently completed study, 'Democracy On-Line' (Cullen and Houghton 2000), to the local government sector. The study proposed to evaluate local government Websites by applying the same evaluative criteria as were used in the central government study, and to collect data on users' view of, and use of, local government Websites in New Zealand. In addition, focus groups already being conducted were used to cover local as well as central government information issues. (This data has not yet been reported.)

The research objectives of the project were to:

- assess the effectiveness of Websites of New Zealand local authorities in providing information about local government services and activities;
- ascertain whether there is equitable and appropriate access to local government official information for all citizens.

To ensure consistency, the study employed the same method used for the evaluation of the Websites of central government agencies. As with the first study it proceeded in three stages. In the first stage a range of local authority Websites were examined for their effectiveness in providing access to information and services using the same criteria as were applied in the first study, with two minor additions where criteria were subdivided for greater clarity. In the second stage, data on Website visitors' perceptions of the effectiveness of the local authority Websites was gathered by means of an electronic self-administered survey linked from the home page of the local authority Website. These criteria, and the subcriteria on which evaluative judgements were made, are listed in the Appendix.

The evaluative criteria applied to Websites do not include any direct assessment of content, but emphasise the need for a clear statement of the scope and purpose of the site and its contents, and the inclusion of a range of content suitable to any discernible purpose of the site, and the organisation. This approach was necessary in the evaluation of central government Websites because of the wide range of types of agency included. While it might have been considered more appropriate to develop a standard list of content items for local government sites which represent organisations that are more uniform than central government departments, the benefit of using of a standard set of criteria for the two studies overrode this consideration. (The 'Web Guidelines' of the E-Government Unit do include a brief list of essential Website items, and a list of 'minimum homepage requirements' but leave other matters of content to the individual agency, depending on its function.)

Selection of Sites

Because of the smaller number of sites involved, all city, district or regional council sites that could be identified were evaluated. Since the focus in this study was on access to local government information, any Website hosted by a local government agency that was focused solely on tourism/promotion was excluded. In many such cases there was a parallel site displaying government information, the two being frequently linked. Of the 86 councils in existence, 61 Websites were initially identified. This grew during the study and by the end of the review process in Oct/Nov 2001, a total of 73 council Websites (i.e., Websites providing local government information and so selected for review) had been identified and were evaluated. While most of the Websites were stand-alone sites using the domain ".govt.nz," some were not, e.g., *www.CityOfDunedin.com* and *www.franklindistrict.co.nz* are stand-alone local government sites using a business domain. Others appeared to be stand-alone sites but were actually council sections within broader Websites (e.g., *www. ashburton.co.nz/adc/* and *www.waimate.org.nz/localgovt/*). Of the remaining 13 councils 6 appeared to have no Web presence, did not permit unauthorised entry, or had a single Web page containing no significant information, or an exclusively regional promotion/tourism focus.

The list of councils and addresses for Web pages was obtained from the Website of New Zealand Local Government Online Ltd, a joint initiative of the Society of Local Government Managers (SOLGM) and the Association of Local Government Information Management (ALGIM),[4] from other databases such as Te Puna Web,[5] search engines such as Google, and direct enquiry to councils. Some Websites were redesigned and changed significantly during the study. Where this was noticed before the evaluation was completed (or in some cases was notified to us by the Webmaster), the later site was evaluated. Sites were not reevaluated, however, and some, like Carterton District Council, were significantly improved by the time the research project was completed.

Evaluation of Sites

Sites were evaluated using Internet Explorer 5 as the dominant Web browser in the home and business markets, and the software most users could be expected to have available to them. Criteria for evaluation of the sites were derived from those developed by Kristin R. Eschenfelder et al. (1997), adapted to meet New Zealand legislation and context, and used in the evaluation of central government Websites (Cullen and Houghton 2000).

The criteria were grouped in two broad categories, information content and ease of use, and then subcategories, which assessed:

Information Content

- Orientation to Website;
- Currency;

- Bibliographic control (metadata, etc.);
- Services;
- Privacy.

Ease of Use

- Quality of links;
- Feedback mechanisms;
- Accessibility;
- Design;
- Navigability.

Specific aspects of site quality under each heading and the criteria used to assess the sites on each of these aspects are given in the Appendix. Sites were then assessed in terms of these criteria and rated on each aspect on a six-point scale: 5 = meets all criteria in exemplary manner; 4 = meets all criteria in a basic manner; 3 = meets most criteria (some extremely well); 2 = meets some criteria in a basic form; 1 = meets a few of the criteria; 0 = meets none of the criteria. An extensive database of comments on each site evaluated, under each aspect and set of criteria, was also developed during the exercise.

FINDINGS OF STAGE I

Overview of the Evaluation

All of the predefined aspects of the Websites being evaluated were rated using the six-point scale. Means for each site over all 37 aspects used in the evaluation, and means for each aspect over all 73 sites were also calculated giving a picture of which sites were rated most and least effective, and which aspects of Web quality were most effectively, and/or least well handled by New Zealand local government Websites. Tables 1-4 show overall scores for the ten sites receiving the highest and lowest ratings, and the criteria which were best and least well fulfilled.

The top sites in general scored 4 or a maximum of 5 on most criteria. However, even top scoring sites were varied in their achievement, and scores were very uneven across the criteria. For example, the Dunedin City site scored 20 '5s' out of the 37 criteria evaluated, but fell down on criteria 22 and 23 (22: The degree to which site provides users with information about whether site use information is made available [to other

TABLE 1. Means of Top-Scoring Local Government Websites

Site	Mean score
Dunedin City Council	4.22
Hutt City Council	4.05
Marlborough District Council	3.78
Palmerston North City Council	3.65
Environment BOP (Bay of Plenty)	3.59
Wanganui District Council	3.59
Tauranga District Council	3.57
Waikato Regional Council	3.57
Grey District Council	3.51
Northland Regional Council	3.51*

*The next mean score was 3.49, followed by 3.43.

parties]; and 23: Can the user exchange encrypted information) as nearly all sites did. Marlborough District Council was one of only four councils to meet criterion 22. No other site in the top ten met either 22 or 23.

The research team noted the particular strengths of the Dunedin site as being: its excellent instructions and viewing tips, including help for children using the site; copyright statements on all pages (although the even more important privacy statements were sometimes lacking); comprehensive and relevant content, including bylaws, annual reports, policies, minutes and agendas; clear language, and good use of head-ings, etc.; organization of content around user needs (not the organisa-tion's); and suggestions where to find information not present. By contrast, the Hutt City Council, another top scoring site, had a much clearer and more prominent statement of its purpose, privacy and copy-right statements, but less helpful instructions about site use, although it has a search facility always available, and scored full marks for this. Both met the requirements of disabled-enabled access (Q33) which was evaluated for each site using the Bobby software (Center for Applied Special Technology 2002). Bobby reports on any problems on a site, such as lack of headings and title, use of frames, excessive use of multi-media or moving graphics, or graphics without underlying explanatory text, that prevent users with disabilities who require simple HTML for-mats to 'read' a site, for example to translate it into Braille, to do so.

In addition to scoring particularly well on its statement about site-use data not being passed on, the third-rated Marlborough District Council site scored very well on purpose, instructional facilities, and the provision of legal information (copyright and privacy issued were well handled), excellent organization of site content based on user needs, relevant and extensive content (including annual reports and environmental reports). It scored less well on account of its use of excessively 'official' language, pages which are not easily scanned by the reader, and rated poorly on the Bobby test for basic HTML accessible by disabled users (HTML is the short name for hyper-text mark-up language, the most commonly used programming language used to create Websites). None of its printed council material supplied the URL of the Website even though it was not instinctive or easy to work out. The site did not offer any online services, unlike both Dunedin and Hutt City sites which offered a range of services such as looking up personal information held by the city in its directory (Dunedin), or payment of bills (Hutt City).

In Table 2 the lowest scoring sites are indicated, although in fairness, it should be noted that many of these organizations are very small and poorly resourced, and their place at the bottom of a 'league' table of Websites is not unexpected.

However, lack of resources does not excuse sites from good information practice–stating their purpose and scope, the use of clear language and user-friendly site organisation, or the need to include copyright, liability and privacy statements. Nor does it excuse lack of metadata and navigation aids, aspects which were very poorly performed criteria for these sites, even if a search facility is too expensive. These poorly rated sites had low scores on Bobby overall, and Opotiki was one of only two sites to score zero on its Bobby rating.

Criteria Which Were Well or Badly Performed Over All Sites

The range of means for all evaluative aspects was 0.04 to 4.30 compared with a range of 1.14-4.81 in the central government study, sug-

TABLE 2. Means of Lowest Scoring Sites

Site	Mean score
Otorohanga District Council	2.22
Waitomo District Council	2.22
Central Otago District Council	2.16
Carterton District Council	1.86
Opotiki District Council	1.70

gesting that sites performed less well overall. This impression is slightly misleading for the following reasons: it was difficult to keep judgements completely consistent between the two projects, and there is some evidence that in the second study the criteria were applied a little more rigorously; the second study covers more very poorly scored sites from smaller organisations; scores for criteria which had not been scored in the first study are included in this range.

Mean scores for the criteria that were best fulfilled over all sites are given in Table 3.

The means of 7 of the evaluative aspects were less than 2, indicating that overall these criteria were very poorly fulfilled overall, or by very few sites (see Table 3); however, in the central government study these had also been so poorly fulfilled that they were not scored, and were not the subject of much comment. They have now become far more important criteria, the expectation in the E-Government Unit's Web policy being that that they are essential elements in the enactment of e-government (State Services Commission 2001).

Table 4 therefore compares scores on these aspects in both the central government and local government studies. The number of sites which attempt to meet the relevant criterion, as well as the mean score over all sites, is given in column 2; the number of sites which attempted to meet it in the central government Website study is noted in column 3, along with the median score, where the criterion was scored.

Performance on some of these 'interactive' criteria is very uneven. One of the lowest scoring sites, Mackenzie District Council, was rated

TABLE 3. Means for Criteria That Were Best Fulfilled Over All Sites

Criteria that were best performed overall	Mean score
29. URL clear and memorable	4.30
31. The site design is consistent with the way that the organisation is represented in other media	4.10
26. Pages download with sufficient speed	4.05
5. Content is written in a clear and consistent language style that matches the expected audience	3.93
28A. Site can be found through search engines and directories	3.88
4. Content suitable and relevant to the scope and aim of the site	3.84
30. Format consistent and thoughtful throughout site	3.81
16. Meaningful headings and titles are provided	3.81
6. Content is arranged/laid-out in a form that recognises how people use the WWW	3.81
17. Descriptive information is consistent throughout the site	3.73

TABLE 4. Comparison of Local Government Site Scores on Poorly Fulfilled Criteria Compared with the Earlier Evaluation of Central Government Sites

Aspects on which local government sites scored most poorly	Local govt score	Central govt score
23. Can the user exchange encrypted information with the site?	0.04 (1 site)	Not scored (3 sites)
22. Degree to which site provides users with information about making site-use information public, or about repackaging or selling such information to others	0.27 (4 sites)	Not scored (2 sites)
21. Degree to which site provides users with explicit policy on how user's privacy rights are protected	0.75 (15 sites)	Not scored (5 sites)
18. Services are provided on the site (as distinct from information)	0.99 (22 sites)	2.71
19. All services on the site are open to everyone (do not require fees)	1.22 (22 sites)	Not scored*
20. Services are fully operational	1.25 (22 sites)	3.77
28B. The site URL occurs on printed material as part of a coherent communications strategy	1.74 (39 sites)	3.10**

*Twenty sites required fees for some services.
**Q28 in the central govt survey was divided into two parts in the local govt survey: 'There is an awareness of the Website through search engines or other publicity,' and 'URL appears on printed material as part of a coherent communications strategy.' The full central government report commented: 'A surprising number of sites were not picked up by search engines and the organisation also did not publish their URL on their published material.'

just two places above the bottom five sites, and met very few of the other criteria. However, it did offer services online, and did not list any charges for these to either local residents or outsiders, the expectation appearing to be that only residents would want to carry out an activity such as register their dogs and thus become liable for a dog-license fee. Fees such as this, however, which would be charged for a routine Council service across the counter were not counted as a fee for 'online' services.

Services, however minimal, are still only offered by 30% of sites, in comparison with 63% (n = 33) of sites in the central government survey, of which 20 required fees. It was not recorded whether these could be transacted online, but if, as is likely, they could, this is a higher percentage of actual transactions than the figure recorded in other surveys, such as Curtin et al. (2002) or the recent Ministry of Economic Development (2002) survey.

On the criteria on which the central government sites were considred to be performing poorly in the earlier study, and on which extensive comment was made, local government sites show some improvement (see Table 5). Significant improvement is made in areas such as statement of purpose, assistance to site users, and metadata.

Given that there is some evidence that in this second study, criteria were applied more strictly and scores are on balance slightly lower than in the central government study (apart from online services), the higher scores in 6 out of these 7 categories point to a significant improvement in basic Web design, and information management. Poor performance on the provision of a version of each page or site in basic HTML is a concern. Not only do Web pages that do not meet these criteria disadvantage persons with disabilities and exclude them from full use of the Web and access to government information on the Web, they also inhibit the effective application of cutting edge technologies such as the use of mobile phones to access information on the Internet.

As with the central government study, sites generally performed well on criteria related to currency and good basic Web design, clear, consistent language and layout. However, criteria relating to information access, such as navigation aids and on-site search/information retrieval facilities, have not been as well mastered, and fall well below the median score. Other aspects on which sites scored poorly, as indicated in Table 4 focus on services and privacy.

STAGE II: USER EVALUATIONS OF SITES

The Webmaster or Chief Information Officer responsible for each of the sites was asked to place an active button on the site which invited

TABLE 5. Comparison of Local Government Site Scores on Criteria Poorly Fulfilled in the Earlier Evaluation of Central Government Sites

Aspects on which local government sites scored better than central govt sites	Local govt score	Central govt score
1. Clear statement of scope and aim of Website was provided	3.1	1.38
2. Help and instructional facilities were provided	2.4	1.14
15. Metadata tags were provided	2.36	1.35
27. Address of contact person and fast update of information	3.4	2.29
3. Necessary legal statements (on confidentiality, liability) shown	2.59	2.40
21. Privacy rights stated	0.75	Not scored
33. Website written in standard HTML language	2.42	3.43

site visitors to activate a link to a questionnaire hosted on the School of Information Management site.[6] The questionnaire used was the same as in the central government study, in order to make it possible to compare results although some minor wording was changed to fit the context (e.g., 'government department' was changed to 'local body,' and 'piece of legislation' to 'by-law'). In all, 35 site managers (out of 58 approached) put a link to the survey in place. A total of 589 usable responses were recorded from visitors to these 35 sites over a period of approximately five months. The number of user responses recorded in this study was in most cases less than 20 per site. The largest number of visitors to any one site who responded to the survey was Christchurch City Council (139), followed by Waitakere City (51), and Wellington City (34). At the lower end some sites generated only 2, 3 or 4 survey responses. These were generally very small district council sites with little information on them. The user survey data, therefore, cannot be regarded as representative of all site visitors. However, it is, in many cases, the only formal feedback some sites have had, and may be more representative of those site visitors who have a definite purpose in visiting it than those who find it accidentally through a search engine and leave once they have identified the site. Because of the low number of responses from individual sites, most of the data will be reported in aggregate form.

Demographics of Site Users

Users came from a wide range of backgrounds and span all age groups; 236 respondents were male, compared with 154 female. Ages ranged from 10 to over 70 years of age (see Figure 1).

Ethnic mix was predominantly European: 329 respondents described themselves as NZ European and a further 40 as being from the United Kingdom, Canada, United States, Australia or South Africa, a total of 369 (which is 92.25% of those giving ethnicity). Only 18 (.045% of those responding to this question) described themselves as Maori (the indigenous people of New Zealand), and 2 as of Pacific Island origin; 11 described themselves as Asian. Rates of these groups in the population of New Zealand are: European 79.6%; New Zealand Maori 14.5%; Pacific Islands 5.6%; Chinese and Indian 3.4%.

A total of 85 selected 'student' as their occupational group from those offered; judging by the range of ages of respondents, many of them were at school. A further 158 selected the category 'professional,' 52 'civil servant.' Smaller numbers were from other occupations: 13

FIGURE 1

Age range of respondents

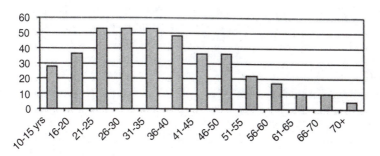

nominated 'teacher,' 15 nominated 'tradesperson,' 13 'beneficiary,' and 12 'retired.' Another 20 persons described themselves as being from the agricultural sector–not surprising given the large number of regional and district council sites included. (These demographic questions had a lower rate of response than questions about access or satisfaction.)

Users were accessing sites primarily from a home computer (326) compared with 207 from a computer in an office, or 48 at a public site. Twenty-seven were information professionals accessing information on behalf of another. Eighty-four point eighty-eight percent of all respondents described themselves as experienced computer users (n = 500), compared with 13.24% (n = 78) who did not.

Site Use

Responses for all sites indicate that more than half of the respondents reached the site in question by using the URL: 54.83% (n = 323) already knew the site address; 24.6% (n = 145) were taken to the site by a search engine; and 19.86% (n = 117) by a link from another site; 4 listed other means. This suggests that it is of some importance that the site has an easily remembered or reconstructed address, a criterion which scored highly in the formal evaluation.

A total of 92.19% (n = 543) of respondents overall approached a site with a specific purpose in mind. This compares with 93.83% in the central government study, but as in the earlier study, less than half were able to fulfil their purpose. Only 48% (n = 283) were able to fulfil their purpose, compared with 47.22 in the central government study.

Reasons for visiting the site are summarised in Table 6. Most users signalled 'Other' as well as nominating a reason from the list given, and were invited to indicate their reasons. Table 7 therefore provides a summary of the top ten reasons given by users (users could also use this dialogue box to expand on the problem they were trying to resolve).

Other reasons (not listed in Table 7) included looking for council documents or making a submission. The 13 people who gave these as reasons should probably be added to the 68 who were looking for a policy document or paper, and the 42 wanting a regulation or by-law (see Table 6). This would make a total of 123–making policy issues the second major reason overall for visiting a site, after finding out about a service. Additional reasons for visiting the site (respondents could nominate more than one) were: looking for information on public libraries or swimming pools, local government contacts, local institutions or

TABLE 6. Reasons for Visiting a Specific Site

Reasons for visiting the site (selected from 8 options)	Responses
To find out more about a service offered by the local body	154
Looking for information to solve a problem	114
To find out more about the local body	87
To obtain a policy document	68
To get the name and address of an official	51
To get the text of a regulation or by-law	42
To carry out a transaction–order a document, register information, etc.	28
Other	352

TABLE 7. Users' Own Reasons for Visiting a Specific Site

Main reasons for visiting the site (users' own responses)	Responses
Planning to visit area, events	54
To find information on utilities–rubbish collection, water, roads, cemeteries, etc.	32
Job information	30
Information on specific regional projects	27
Research for school/university work	27
Information on local body elections	22
Property valuations, consents, rents, etc.	21
Looking for maps	19

history, and 13 people who indicated they were looking for ideas about Web design.

More than half of the respondents, 56.8% (n = 335), had visited the site in question before; 41.77% (n = 246) indicated that they had not. Of the regular visitors 11.94% (n = 40) visited several times a week; 25.67% (n = 86) several times a month; 50.45% (n = 169) had visited only a few times before, and 13.73% (n = 46) only once before.

Satisfaction with Sites Visited

Respondents were asked to rate the site on a scale of 1 (Strongly agree) to 5 (Strongly disagree) against a set of criteria that matched some of those used in the 'expert' evaluation. (The criteria were worded differently from the 'expert' evaluation in order to be more comprehensible to users unfamiliar with commonly used Web evaluation terms.) Average scores on each criterion are shown in Table 8.

These scores (the lower the better, since 1 is a perfect rating) do not show much variation between individual criteria, and do not seem to reflect overall the pattern of scoring used in the formal evaluation. However, how various items rate against each other can be compared with the rank order of averages obtained from the formal evaluation, and there is some correlation between these rankings, in that users rate clear headings, instructions, navigation, and useful content well–points also picked up in the formal evaluation. User ratings of individual sites have not been reported in detail since there are insufficient responses to draw any firm conclusions, but the sites which received exceptionally high user ratings are listed in Table 9.

Users in general show an awareness of pragmatic issues, and an appreciation of content, and simple effective Web design. They are more critical of currency and technical problems encountered than our own evaluation–perhaps with their more varied needs they test these aspects more rigorously. Their overall scoring of the effectiveness of the sites (at 2.63) is below the median mark (2.50).

Of more value are users' comments. Users were invited to insert in a textbox any issues that had not been covered by the rating criteria. They were then asked to indicate which aspects of the site they found most pleasing, and which most displeasing, or least useful, and to make suggestions for improvement. Many put their comments, both negative and positive, in all four dialogue boxes, and many responses overlap.

Comments made in each of these dialogue boxes are given in Table 10.

TABLE 8. Users' Evaluations of How Well Sites Performed

Criterion	Mean
Pages on the site load quickly	2.36
Headings and text or links describe content well	2.40
Content of the site is useful	2.41
Services offered on the site are useful	2.42
Explanation of services and information provided on this site is clear and helpful	2.43
Instructions for use of the site are clear and helpful	2.45
It is easy to negotiate your way around the site	2.50
Pages on the site are well designed	2.52
Site content is accurate and up-to-date	2.55
Services offered on the site are reliable	2.56
Links to other sites are working	2.56
Links to other sites are useful	2.58
Overall the site is very effective	2.61
It is easy to download documents	2.63

TABLE 9. Sites Rated Most Highly by Users

Site	Number of responses	Median score for overall effectiveness
Wellington Regional Council	5	1.55
Manawatu District Council	12	1.88
Whangarei District Council	26	2.0
Christchurch City Council	139	2.13

In all the user comments there are three dominant expectations evident:

- technical robustness–sites are expected to load well, perform well and links to be working;
- navigation–users expect to access information on the site through good design and search aids; and
- up-to-date, relevant information.

The users' comments suggest that they are capable of making stronger judgements on these issues than the overall user scores of sites suggest, indicating that free text comments are a more reliable source of information about user opinions than set questions attached to a scoring system.

TABLE 10. Free Text Comments of Users About Sites

General comments:

Comment	Number
General positive	57
General negative	38
Difficulties in navigation	27
Technical problems/corrupt page	19
Poorly designed site	15
Information out of date	13
Lack of a search engine	11

Most pleasing aspects of the site:

Comment	Number
General positive	31
General negative	46
Well designed sites, good graphics, easy to load	58
Well-ordered, easy to navigate	46
Sites with useful links to other sites or documents	30
Sites with photos or maps	33

Negative aspects of sites (things least pleasing) were:

Comment	Number
Lack of needed information, or depth of information	53
Poor design, colour, graphics	46
Poor navigation–hard to find information that was there	47
Technical problems	35

Suggestions for improving sites:

Comment	Number
Better navigation	35
More detailed information	61
More consideration given to technical problems users have	30
Need for up-to-date and accurate information	20
Sites with useful links to other sites or documents	30
Need for e-mail contact with council officials	23

CONCLUSION

Although initially there appeared to be some conflict in local body Websites between the necessary exchange of information with citizens, and ratepayers, etc., that supports good government, and the need to promote the city or region to a national and international audience, this has not emerged as a major issue in the evaluation. This is not only because there is a clear distinction made in the parent organisation between sites which are used for promotional purpose and sites which fulfil a 'civic' role,[7] but also because of the use made by site visitors. Site visitors are purposeful in approaching sites, and serious in their requests for information. Judging by the number who stated they had not found the information they were looking for, it seems that too often they are disappointed. The issues they raise concerning search capabilities of sites and up-to-date relevant information are the same issues as were raised by users responding to the survey in the first, central government Website study.

In addition to these issues, the formal evaluation found similar deficiencies as were identified in the US studies–a lack of concern with ethnic diversity in population, and acknowledgement of the needs of persons with disabilities. The lack of use of the sites by Maori and Pacific Island populations remains a major concern, as it was in the central government study, and evidence of our failure to seriously address the digital divide in New Zealand. Furthermore, the opportunities pointed out by Laswad, Oyelere and Fisher to use the WWW as a means of reaching a dispersed population in rural areas, and to provide essential services to the growing number of agricultural workers seeking contact through the Web with their local council, need to be addressed and fulfilled.

Overall, too many sites lack the depth of information users are seeking, the financial information, and the minutes and agendas that would allow them to follow and participate in civic or regional council matters. Too few show any commitment to developing the services that could be offered via their Websites. Far too many local government Websites in New Zealand, as Curtin et al. noted of city sites in the United States, take the form of an electronic brochure. The vision of e-government, delivered seamlessly through central and local government Websites in New Zealand, seems as yet a long way off.

And yet there are things to celebrate, not least among them the expectations of constituents and site visitors who will drive the needed changes. In addition there are some very fine sites which should be promoted as examples of best practice by organisations such as SOLGM and ALGIM, and New Zealand Local Government On-line. Without the leadership of these organizations, serious flaws will continue to inhibit the use of the Web for good government. These flaws include:

- the widespread lack of disabled-enabled access, and lack of attention paid to issues of culture and ethnicity;
- neglect of vital issues of privacy and security necessary to fully develop the interactive service aspect of the sites;
- widespread lack of understanding of how the WWW can be used effectively to promote good communication between local bodies and their constituents to promote good government.

The Web has become an indispensable form of communication in local government in New Zealand. Along with the expansion of content and services that will inevitably happen over time, these are the next issues to be addressed by the sector.

NOTES

1. Metadata, in the context of the World Wide Web, is the use of data in the HTML or hypertext mark-up language source code that defines the name and ownership of the Web page. In a well-designed Web page it will include the use of keywords and indexing terms which help search engines find the page.
2. Version 2 of the UK guidelines is now available on the Website of the Office of the E-envoy (http://www.e-envoy.gov.uk/publications/guidelines/webguidelines/handbook/handbookindex.htm) and a version for local government websites is also being drafted.
3. Government Information System Managers Forum (http://www.govis.org.nz/).
4. Local Government On-line. (http://www.localgovt.co.nz).
5. Te Puna Web Directory is the National Library of New Zealand Te Puna Mataurangao Aotearoa's listing of New Zealand and Pacific Island Websites at: (http://web directory.natlib.govt.nz/).
6. Individual site managers have had user data for their site passed to them, along with the independent evaluation of their site.
7. Marlborough District Council is a good example: Its civic site at (www.marlborough.govt.nz) is an excellent one, rich in civic information. Its tourism site is held elsewhere, at: (www.destination.co.nz/marlborough), with no link between them.

REFERENCES

Center for Applied Special Technology. 2002. Bobby (http://www.cast.org/Bobby/. Accessed 5/04/02)

Cullen, Rowena and Caroline Houghton. 2000. Democracy online: An assessment of New Zealand government websites. *Government Information Quarterly,* 17(3): 243-267.

Curtin, Gregory, Robert McConnachie, Michael Sommer, and Veronika Vis-Sommer. 2002. American e-government at the crossroads: A national study of major city uses. *Journal of Political Marketing,* 1(1): 149-191.

Doczi, Marianne. Information and communication technologies and social and economic inclusion. Wellington: Ministry of Economic Development. 2000. (http://www.med.govt.nz/pbt/infotech/ictinclusion/index.html. Accessed 26/07/02).

Eschenfelder, Kristin R., John C. Beachbord, Charles R. McClure, and Steve K. Wyman. 1997. Assessing federal U.S. government websites. *Government Information Quarterly,* 14: 173-189.

Laswad, Fawzi, Peter Oyelere, and Richard Fisher. 2001. Local authorities and financial reporting on the Internet. *Chartered Accountants Journal,* March: 58-61.

Meehan, Helen. 1996. The development of government information management policies in New Zealand through a period of reform. *Government Information Quarterly,* 13(3): 231-242.

New Zealand. Ministry of Commerce. 1999. Electronic government in New Zealand. Vision statement issued by the Minister of Telecommunications, Hon Maurice Williamson, October 1999.

New Zealand. Ministry of Economic Development. 2002. E-business survey–preliminary results 20 May 2002. (http://www.med.govt.nz/irdev/elcom/ebussurvey/index.html. Accessed 24/06/02).

New Zealand. State Services Commission. 1997. Policy framework for government held information. (http://www.ssc.govt.nz/Documents/policy_framework_for_Government_.htm. Accessed 24/06/02).

New Zealand. State Services Commission. 2000. E-government–a vision for New Zealanders, issued 1 May 2000. (http://www.ssc.govt.nz/Documents/evision. Accessed 24/06/02).

New Zealand. State Services Commission. 2001a. *Government.nz@your.service.* Wellington: State Services Commission.

New Zealand. State Services Commission. 2001b. Web guidelines. Version 1.0 30 June 2001: Guidelines for the management and design of New Zealand public sector websites. (http://www.e-government.govt.nz/web-guidelines/index.asp. Accessed 5/04/02).

New Zealand. Statistics New Zealand. 2002. 2001 census of populations and dwellings. 2001 Census Snapshot 2 (Who Has Access to the Internet?)–Media Release. Wellington: Statistics New Zealand. (http://www.stats.govt.nz/domino/external/pasfull/pasfull.nsf/web/4C2567EF00247C6ACC256B7500141AB1. Accessed 15/08/02).

NUA Internet Surveys. 2002. How many online? (http://www.nua.ie/surveys/how_many_online/index.html. Accessed 15/08/02).

United Kingdom. Office of the E-envoy. 2001. Guidelines for UK government websites v 1.0. (http://www.e-envoy.gov.uk/publications/guidelines/webguidelines/guidelinesforwebsitesv1-archived/index.htm. Accessed 24/06/02).

West, Darrell M. 2000. Assessing e-government: The Internet, democracy, and service delivery by state and federal governments. (http://www.insidepolitics.org/egovtreport00.html. Accessed 9/04/02).

West, Darrell. 2001. Urban e-government: An assessment of city government websites (http://www.InsidePolitics.org/egovt01city.html. Accessed 9/04/02).

APPENDIX

Aspects/Criteria Used for Evaluation of Sites

INFORMATION CONTENT CRITERIA

Q1. Orientation to Website (Clear statement of scope and aim of the site is provided).

Additional criteria: Overview of site provided; scope clearly stated; purpose/ mission appropriate to target audience.

Q2. Help and instructional facilities provided.

Additional criteria: Services and information provided at the Website are described; instructions on use of the Website are provided.

Q3. Necessary legal information is clearly provided.

Additional criteria: A liability statement warning the user about information that may be provided through links is given (e.g., material unsuited to children); copyright statements are provided if necessary.

Q4. Content suitable and relevant to the scope and aim of the site.

Additional criteria: The content of the homepage should match the purpose/mission; the content and links match the needs of the expected audience; the Website includes only necessary and useful information.

Q5. Content is written in a clear and consistent language that matches the expected audience.

Additional criteria: Content avoids jargon, humour, condescension, accusation and chitchat; content uses a positive and professional tone; language does not show bias.

Q6. Content is arranged/laid out in a form that recognises how people use the World Wide Web.

Additional criteria: Content is available in printed form; content is scannable (users can scan text for words or phrases, they do not have to read all documents).

Q7. Content organised around user needs (not organisational structure).

Additional criteria: Content is organized logically throughout the site by anticipated user needs; user is directed to related sites for specific information.

Q8A. How extensive is the content provided?

Q8B. What percentage of documents published by the organisation in the past three years are available online? (The information is not only published and available on the WWW.)

Q9. Content is easily accessible in alternative formats.

Additional criteria: Does content require special software; are users invited to download software; if content isn't available online other methods of access are mentioned.

CURRENCY

Q10. Address of contact person and fast update information appear at the bottom of pages with substantive content.

Q11. Content is complete (no "under construction" notices).

Q12. References to sources of information cited are accurate.

Q13. Typing spelling and grammar errors and other inconsistencies are absent.

Q14. Content is reliably up-to-date.

Additional criteria: Pages have been documented as updated at appropriate intervals; content provided is up-to-date.

Q15. Metadata provided.

Additional criteria: Metadata exists on substantive pages (description and keywords).

Q16. Meaningful headings and titles provided for content.

Additional criteria: Headings are clearly phrased, descriptive and understandable; each screen is titled clearly; if the headings cannot be completely descriptive, coherent and concise descriptions follow.

Q17. Descriptive information is consistent throughout the site.

Additional criteria: The information that is provided through links matches the headings and descriptions; terminology and layout are consistent with the headings throughout the Website.

SERVICES

Q18. Provision of services (as distinct from provision of information on the site, e.g., leaving a question to be responded to is a service).

Q19. Are the services open to anyone on the Internet or do portions require fees?

Q20. Services are fully operational.

Additional criteria: Services can be purchase online; clients can be provided with necessary information online.

Q21. Degree to which the site provides users with explicit policy on how user's privacy rights are protected.

Q22. Degree to which the site provides users with information about making site-use information public, or repackaging or reselling such information to others.

Q23. Can the user exchange encrypted information with the site?

Additional criteria: Interactions which involve private information are secure.

EASE OF USE CRITERIA

Q24. Links are robust.

Additional criteria: There are no dead-end links; temporary forwarding addresses do not qualify as good links; a 'what's new' section is provided for new links; shortcut links are possible for frequent users.

Q25. Relevant information about nature of links provided.

Additional criteria: Warning statements are provided if link will take you to a large document or image; indication of restricted access for a link is provided; essential instructions appear before links requiring user interaction (e.g., e-mail).

Q26. Pages download with sufficient speed.

Additional criteria: Links are provided to mentioned documents; speed is adequate.

Q27. Feedback mechanisms exist, and work.

Q28A. There is an awareness of the Website through search engines or other publicity.

Q28B. URL appears on printed material as part of a coherent communications strategy.

Q29. URL not likely to be confused or mistyped.

Q30. Format is consistent and thoughtful throughout site.

Additional criteria: Graphics and colour lead the user through the information; large graphical elements are used sensibly; use of bold, italics, blinking and other attention-getting devises is limited; format is appropriate to subject matter and functionality; a good design directs users towards information rather than away from it; screens are uncluttered.

Q31. Site design is consistent with the way the organisation is represented in other media.

Q32. Homepage is short and simple.

Q33. Website is written in standard HTML language.

Additional criteria: Site is accessible from different browsers (tested for disabled-enabled access using Bobby software).

Q34. Navigation options are distinct, appear at top of pages and are spelled out.

Additional criteria: Links are provided to assist navigation (e.g., 'return to top' or 'return to previous page').

Q35. A search facility for the site exists and is always available.

AUSTRALIA

What Lies Beyond Service Delivery–
An Australian Perspective

Karin Geiselhart

National Office for the Information Economy, Australia

Mary Griffiths

Monash University, Australia

Bronwen FitzGerald

University of Melbourne, Australia

Karin Geiselhart has a PhD in Communications from the University of Canberra. She has been a public affairs officer in the Australian Commonwealth, and has completed a post-doctoral research fellowship in electronic commerce at RMIT University. She is a member of the community organization Computing Assistance Support and Education and is a member of the ACT Government's Advisory Panel on Information Technology (E-mail: karin.geiselhart@noie.gov.au).

Dr. Mary Griffiths is affiliated with Research Unit in Work & Communications Futures, Monash University, Gippsland.

Bronwen FitzGerald is a honours student, University of Melbourne.

[Haworth co-indexing entry note]: "What Lies Beyond Service Delivery–An Australian Perspective." Geiselhart, Karin, Mary Griffiths, and Bronwen FitzGerald. Co-published simultaneously in *Journal of Political Marketing* (The Haworth Press, Inc.) Vol. 2, No. 3/4, 2003, pp. 213-233; and: *The World of E-Government* (ed: Gregory G. Curtin, Michael H. Sommer, and Veronika Vis-Sommer) The Haworth Press, Inc., 2003, pp. 213-233. Single or multiple copies of this article are available for a fee from The Haworth Document Delivery Service [1-800-HAWORTH, 9:00 a.m. - 5:00 p.m. (EST). E-mail address: docdelivery@haworthpress.com].

SUMMARY. As government uses of information technology mature, awareness is growing of the need to effectively engage citizens in all stages of the policy process. E-democracy is often what lies beyond electronic service delivery, through a gradual process of learning and user feedback.

This article describes the national framework for e-government in Australia, levels of technology literacy in elected officials, and current electronic democracy initiatives in several Australian state and territory governments. These illustrate the potential for e-government to transform democracy, but they also highlight the need to reinforce democratic values and develop new literacies of citizenship. *[Article copies available for a fee from The Haworth Document Delivery Service: 1-800-HAWORTH. E-mail address: <docdelivery@haworthpress.com> Website: <http://www.HaworthPress.com> © 2003 by The Haworth Press, Inc. All rights reserved.]*

KEYWORDS. Internet, e-government, citizen literacies, participation

Good government is expensive, bad government is unaffordable.

–Future Retro Hits (http://mp3.com/futureretro)

INTRODUCTION

In Australia, as in other developed countries, Internet usage continues to grow. In 2000, 37% of all households were online (Australian Bureau of Statistics, 2000). It was estimated then that by the end of 2001 half of all Australian households would have Internet access at home. As of mid-2002, a report entitled *Current State of Play* released by the Australian Government's central e-government agency, the National Office for the Information Economy (NOIE), showed that the percentage of households online had, as anticipated, grown to 52% of the total population. Furthermore, in recognition that many people use alternative environments to access the Internet–their place of employment, public kiosks and Internet cafes, for instance–the report registers that 64% of people aged 16 and over in Australia use the Net. The level of public uptake in Internet usage indicates that many Australians are now in a position to engage in political interaction online, be it by patronizing online government services or exercising their rights to political comment and input.

A number of Australian governments and parliaments have recognised the potential of these developments. A survey conducted in 2002 of Australian elected representatives from all levels of government found that 85% of these representatives access the Internet, with most browsing on a weekly or daily basis (Chen, 2002). The most common use of these new media was for electronic mail, but representatives with higher technological skill levels and higher confidence in the Internet tended to explore more sophisticated applications such as chat. This indicates that an increase in information technology (IT) skill levels among elected representatives can only increase their innovative use of the Internet in service delivery and public participation practices. State, Territory and Federal Parliamentarians use the Internet more and are more comfortable with it than their local government equivalents. With regard to online consultation, the likelihood of parliamentarians using the Internet for this purpose is double that of representatives in local government, with Victoria leading both the Commonwealth and the remainder of the states in online consultative engagement. Political parties are also using the Internet as a pivotal tool in their activities. All major parties have Websites, and many politicians have their own personal sites.

Sometimes in the headlong rush to wire, there are conceptual difficulties over exactly what constitutes, and enhances, democratic practice, and what more properly belongs in the realm of e-commerce or e-government. Briefly,

> *e-commerce:* refers to relations of exchange any-sized commercial transaction online, frequently linked to social regeneration in the new economy;

> *e-government:* refers to relations of top/down power–governing populations through use of online information and services, often thought to be apolitical or more 'uninvolved' than;

> *e-democracy:* refers to relations of two-way and horizontal power–using technologies to enhance democratic practice.

The section that follows addresses the different ways some Australian governments and parliaments have utilised the Internet from the micro to the macro. It begins by setting out the varied examples of

e-government from around the country. Following this is a demonstra-
tion of how in some cases governments are endeavouring to take e-government to a higher level of sophistication, designed to make the
often-confusing area of interaction between citizens and government
service easier to navigate.

The coincidence of Internet use and a democratic polity does not necessarily lead to the presence of e-democracy (Griffiths, 2002). The third
section will thus detail what progress has been made towards e-democracy, a related yet separate use of the Internet by governments, parliaments and citizens. In addition, we outline briefly a collation of nongovernment initiatives that impact on conventional political activity.
The aim of this examination is ultimately to provide a well-rounded portrait of the current and projected approach to Australian e-democracy.
We conclude with a discussion of the interaction between new media
literacy and the renovation of democratic values.

STAGES OF E-GOVERNMENT

In a June 2000 feature article for *The Economist*, Mathew Symonds
posits four stages of e-government. The first is simple information, the
equivalent of an electronic brochure. This is based on a standard view of
government as a source of information. The second stage starts to use
the potential of the new technology, and allows citizens (or business
seeking to deal with government) to enter information, make requests,
perhaps even update their details. This is a weak form of interactivity,
but has no input from citizens as to the shaping of the services being delivered. The third stage, according to Symonds, allows online transactions and purchases, or the electronic sending of tender information.
This comes closer to an electronic commerce model, and is not unique
to government. Stage four is an integrated portal of all government services and information, via a sophisticated search engine and metadata.
This also builds on electronic commerce models, because it takes a
more customer-oriented perspective. For true usefulness, e-government
needs to transcend the bureaucratic structures that inhibit understanding
and access. An additional stage not covered by Symonds is the truly
user-driven interactive democratic model that offers multiple modes for
feedback, civic dialogue and participation. This stage is difficult for
nongovernment organizations as well as elected governments (Geiselhart,
2002).

All these stages are based on centralised electronic service delivery concepts which offer little possibility of policy engagement. A study of OECD countries (Gualtieri, 1998) found that governments had not really begun to explore the use of new technologies in the activities more particular to democratic governance: consultation, policy determination and accountability. He found reluctance came from both public servants and citizens; a combination of risk aversion and apathy. Some movement in this direction has occurred since then, as will be described in the Canadian context. However, a more recent survey of 270 municipal government Websites in California found that they were more likely to support an entrepreneurial rather than a participatory model (Musso, Weare and Hale, 2000). One of the most comprehensive reviews of current uses of electronic government in America (Curtin et al., 2002) also found a narrow view of service delivery dominated. Opportunities for interactivity or participation in actual decision making were much rarer than a transaction-based approach to e-government.

The breakthrough is the recognition that government is not and never will be just another business. Mintzberg (1996) gave a good analysis of why some activities can only be dealt with in the public sphere, and why a 'one size fits all' application of business principles to all domains of social activity is dysfunctional.

World Bank studies have shown the link between good governance and economic development (Kaufman et al., 1999, 2000). New media can deliver a democratic dividend along with cost savings and greater efficiency in service delivery. Democracy aims to achieve a significantly different set of relations between people than that constructed in either e-commerce or e-government. High expectations flourish in governing circles, and also among the governed, when governments talk about new technologies as providing the means to ensure greater transparency and accountability, more direct engagement with constituents, better consultation practices and so on. Excellence in service delivery may be a precondition for online democracy. Seeing the citizen as more than a customer implies at least that:

- services from government are offered online;
- details of citizen obligations and rights are readily available;
- citizen advice is provided about services;
- legislation is published and circulated.

At the more complex and dynamic level of policy, the fragmentation and overlap between administrative areas makes diversity of inputs and the coordination of interest group networks increasingly important for good governance. The ability of new media to reach out in unpredictable ways is part of their promise and their power.

E-GOVERNMENT THRIVES

In developed countries such as Australia, e-government presents a win-win situation. For services and transactions, it can raise efficiency for providers and citizens and businesses by lowering transaction time and costs. Australia has on occasion been singled out as an example of best practice (NOIE, 2000a; Accenture, 2002; Gibbons, 2002). The most cited example is Australia's 2001 achievement of 75% online tax lodgement, through the Australian Tax Office (ATO) Website. This provides not just tax forms, but online assistance explaining data entry requirements and identifying potential errors to citizens before they lodge their forms. Another example is the Victorian State Government's May 1998 development of one of the first government entry portals in the world, demonstrating the ability of the portal layout to present the diverse range of government services through one site (Holmes, 2001). To achieve this level of sophistication, e-government policy in Australia has been in development for a number of years. Early documents on the Australian government's approach to information technology are outlined in Geiselhart (1999).

In December of 1997, Prime Minister John Howard delivered a policy speech entitled *Investing for Growth* that can be marked as 'the catalyst' for further, more sophisticated strategic goals for the development of Australian e-government (NOIE, 2000b). This speech, after detailing a number of economic goals and incentives proposed by the government, set up an objective that was later carried out by not only all Commonwealth government agencies but all state and territory governments in cooperation with the Commonwealth. It states:

> We will establish a one-stop shop for all business regulatory needs so that all appropriate services are deliverable on the Internet by 2001.

Although this statement was directed towards the business community, it has since been considered the expected standard for the delivery of all government services rather than being confined to those at the interface between business and government.

A more comprehensive e-government strategy, *Government On-line–The Commonwealth Government's Strategy,* was released some years later in April 2000 to coordinate the varied initiatives that both Commonwealth and State departments had been developing in an attempt to meet this goal for online service delivery. The specific targets identified by the strategy included the commitment to:

> Deliver all appropriate services online via the Internet by December 2001, complementing . . . existing . . . services; ensure core minimum standards in important areas such as privacy, security and accessibility were met; and encourage government business operations to go online. (NOIE, 2002a)

At the time it was estimated that the target set in 1997 would be met by 82% of Commonwealth agencies, and by early 2002 the goals were considered accomplished (NOIE, 2002b). As a result, all State, Federal and local governments are online, as are State and Federal Parliaments and all State and Federal agencies. Some examples of the varied uses to which these agencies have applied Internet services are set out below.

The Commonwealth social services organisation, Centrelink, has for some time now run an Internet job-seeking network that is accessible both from job-seekers' home PCs and customised terminals in every Centrelink branch that also print 'receipts' for job-seekers to carry with them. The network provides the career information, training, labour market and wage conditions as well as details for available positions across the country, not just in the seeker's local area. It also allows applicants to send their applications over the Net, making the job-searching experience a relatively less expensive and time-consuming experience.

Outside the realm of government agencies, the Federal Court of Australia is an example of a site that provides a range of different information and services directed at a number of different user profiles, as well as challenging its current technological parameters. For those in the legal profession, it is possible to file documents, access court lists and download or search Federal Court judgments, a service that is also useful for students studying law at a higher level. For other students, there are explanations of the Court's history, personnel and its role in the Australian Constitutional system. Those interested in viewing the Court can embark on a virtual tour through one of the courtrooms and the media can access breaking judgments and media releases through the Court's media pages. However, of most interest is the new eCourt, a pilot which aims to improve the traditional operations of the court, as well as improving citizens' interaction with and access to the justice system. The first initiative run in the eCourt is an online forum, where 'via eCourt, the Court, in interlocutory matters, may receive submissions and affidavit evidence and make orders as if the parties were in a normal courtroom' (Federal Court of Australia, 2002).

These two examples show that Australian e-government is already moving beyond efficiency of existing services to explore new forms of engagement and the demystification of institutions such as the Federal Court. There is now widespread acceptance of parallel services online.

As part of the strategic commitment to continued best practice, NOIE's *eGovernment Benefits Study* marks the beginning of a second phase of e-government in Australia. It will analyse the current success of the Commonwealth's online program, assessing demand, benefits obtained and cost efficiency. The study emphasises quality of online service and increased levels of integration within and between agencies and an increased focus on expectations, utility and efficiency of government services.

A trial project coordinated by government Online is an example of the second phase of Australian e-government. The 'Trials of Innovative Government in Electronic Regional Services' (TIGERS) Project indicates Australian e-government can transcend electronic form filling and document searching. The TIGERS project, designed and carried out as a collaborative project between NOIE and the Tasmanian State Government, aims to provide a seamless coordinated interface to government information.

The project features a site devoted to recreational fishing, *www.fishonline. gov.au*, designed to provide the full breadth of information for any person in Tasmania wishing to fish. The most commendable feature of the site is what is happening behind the scenes. It presents information from a range of different sources: the Tasmanian Inland Fisheries Service; Tasmanian Department of Primary Industry, Water and Environment; Marine and Safety Tasmania; and the Commonwealth Bureau of Meteorology. However, despite the diversity of origins of the information, it is presented on the site in a cohesive fashion that does not hint at the complexity of the communication channels coordinating it. All that a recreational fisher could possibly need is located on the site–sorted by location–licenses, daily weather forecasts, fishing restrictions, marine safety requirements and the best location for the type of fish sought after. Similar sites have followed through the TIGERS program, one being *www.startingschool.gov.au*, a site designed as a guide to parents of primary school children who need advice. The site–again, ordered by location–contains information about schools, but also support facilities such as childcare and medical facilities in the surrounding area. Other sites in the program are aimed at home buyers, expectant parents, aquaculture exporters, land developers and people living in remote areas in need of videoconferencing with Centrelink, Legal Aid, and the Department of Veteran's Affairs. Such sites fall into the portalised fourth stage of e-government, but do not yet offer opportunities for a public conversation or participation in the policies underlying these services.

This is evidence that the Federal Government, in cooperation with the States, is pursuing its ultimate goal of developing 'more and better online, integrated services that break down the government structure and jurisdiction, and meet the real needs of individuals and business' (Accenture, 2002).

These examples from the Commonwealth Government, in concert with the vast number of services provided online by all State and Territory governments, show that in accordance with the uptake and usage of the Internet by businesses and citizens, the level of sophistication of Australian e-government is worthy of international recognition. In addition, the rise in the complexity of the information delivered through the one source and the focus on 'soft' government in the TIGERS scheme show that e-government is developing in response to the needs of the population, not just the push for governments to raise efficiency and lower operational costs. These developments in e-government lead us to query whether these advancements are mirrored in the domain of citizen participation in decision-making: e-democracy.

E-DEMOCRACY IN INFANCY

In contrast, e-democracy in Australia is still in the earliest stages of development. Although there is not a total lack of activity, there is a significant gap when compared with e-government initiatives. Additionally, because of a lack of central coordination, such as that provided by NOIE and the federal Department of Communications, Information Technology and the Arts with regards to e-government, awareness and action on e-democracy varies from jurisdiction to jurisdiction.

A national Online Council provides a venue for senior Ministers from State, Territory and local governments to meet annually to discuss policy issues related to the information economy. In 2002 this group acknowledged e-democracy as a significant emerging issue for governments in Australia and agreed to work collaboratively to further explore and develop the use of the Internet to engage Australian citizens. The Commonwealth is now developing a coordinated strategy for online citizen engagement in the federal sphere. The following is an overview of the current Australian e-democracy projects.

Federal Parliament now Webcasts its Parliamentary sessions over the Internet, allowing citizens a view into the workings of Parliament. This is arguably a broader and more accurate source of information than the argumentative 'Question Time' footage that feeds news and current affairs programs. One of the aims of the Webcasting is to make available to the public a rounded and positive portrait of politicians' work. It is hoped that this will impact positively on citizen opinion of politicians and the political system. Andrew Monaghan, a Senior Policy Adviser to the Victorian Parliamentary Committee investigating e-democracy options, says with regard to the consideration of the Webcasting of Victorian Parliamentary sittings:

> Traditional media . . . only pick the argumentative ten minutes of question time, and they leave aside all the good work that parliaments do. . . . Part of the disenchantment and disillusionment about politics and politicians is fed by only getting negative stereotypes through the media . . . politicians are genuinely concerned.

Nevertheless, other than this one-way, noninteractive method of allowing citizens a view of the Federal Parliamentary process, there is a notable lack of activity on e-democracy at the Commonwealth level. NOIE has led the way with its consultations for its national strategy in 1999, by not just accepting submissions electronically but also placing these on their Website. They then summarised the comments, and modified their strategy to take these into account. The NOIE site also has a 'currently consulting on' section.

NOIE also promotes best practice in online consultation. For example, the Australian Defence Force used the Internet to widely disseminate information prior to their nationwide consultations on the future of the defence force. This consultation process was described as 'the most successful program of public consultation initiated by any Australian government.' Over nine weeks, more than 2,000 people attended the 28 public meetings, more than 1,150 submissions were received, more than 18,000 copies of the Discussion Paper were distributed, and there were 6,453 downloads of the Discussion Paper from the Website. This is significant by Australian standards.

In 2001, the Australian Capital Territory (ACT) held 'e-voting' trials. This experiment generated a great deal of interest, and remains the first and only initiative of its type in Australia. However, it must be noted that although progressive, and a positive development in many ways, it was not e-voting as it is understood to be elsewhere. The voting public of the ACT still attended physical polling booths in the same manner as in previous elections. The only difference was that instead of registering a vote by posting a slip of paper into a ballot box, voters used touchscreens and the data was transferred and counted electronically. The public were not as yet voting over the Internet. Although progressive in terms of data management and security, the pilot was not a fully fledged manifestation of e-voting. Nevertheless, the trial had important benefits. One person with a disability reported after voting in that election that it was the first time she had ever been able to vote unassisted, and thus e-voting enabled her to exercise her constitutional right to a secret ballot (FitzGerald, 2002). While public perception often confuses e-voting with e-democracy, in terms of the definitions given above, e-voting is fundamentally a service. A nongovernment experiment in 1998 provided the first online debate between candidates in an Australian State or Territory election (Geiselhart, 1999). While this achieved good attention at the time, no similar pilots have been observed, either in the ACT or elsewhere in Australia.

The Queensland State Government is demonstrating a commitment to investigate and enact e-democracy within its jurisdiction. It has set up an 'E-Democracy Unit' that is undertaking three initiatives. The first is to broadcast the proceedings of Queensland Parliament over the Internet, the intention of the government being that it will soon be operative. The second is to set up a process by which e-petitions can be registered, signed and lodged online, and the third is to set up 'community consultations' online.

Victorian policy, at the moment, appears focussed on bridging the digital divide by building IT skills in the community, providing access, and on outreach such as helping the development of community and business Websites through:

- *Skills.net*–more than 50,000 Victorians receiving Internet training and access,
- *VEEM*–funding 39 councils to develop e-commerce projects among local businesses,
- *access@schools*–146 schools in rural areas to provide after hours community Internet access,

- *Regional Connectivity Project*–six centres in western Victoria providing Internet training and access with an emphasis on e-commerce,
- *My Connected Community*–funding for community groups to develop their own Websites,
- *Libraries Online*–provides Internet access at more than 900 work
  stations in public libraries across the state (GO Vic Media release,
  5 April 2001).

The Victorian State Parliament is also examining the prospect of
e-democracy, specifically through one of its bipartisan Parliamentary
Committees, the Scrutiny of Acts and Regulations Committee (SARC).
Over the course of this year, the Committee is undertaking an in-depth
investigation into the viability of different manifestations of e-democracy in Victoria (SARC, 2002). Over the course of its inquiry, it too will
examine the 'netcasting of Parliamentary proceedings; online interactive and collaborative approaches to policy discussion, including citizen
e-mail and online forums; and other technology solutions to promote
access and participation.' The Committee aims to examine e-democracy in order to improve current democratic processes to the benefit of
Victorian citizens. In addition to this inquiry, as a link from the Victorian government's e-government site run by Multimedia Victoria, the
agency given the task of coordinating e-government policy and practice, a Webpage is solely devoted to local, national and international
news related to e-government and e-democracy. This site includes
breaking news, lengthy academic texts and opinion pieces.

In July 2001, the Western Australian (WA) Government, through the
Department of Premier and Cabinet, established its Citizens and Civics
Unit, designed to enhance civic participation. The Unit directs the policy that supports the new 'Citizenscape' site that promotes community
involvement and consultation. Unlike the other States that focus on using the Internet as a forum for democratic engagement and consultation,
the WA Government has chosen to use the Internet site primarily as a
resource for citizens who want to get involved using traditional methods. The site exhaustively lists the varied ways citizens can increase
their involvement offline, and also provides indicators for governments
by which they can assess the quality of their consultation process. Advice for improving the public consultation process is adapted from an
Organisation for Economic Cooperation and Development (OECD) report (Caddy and Vergez, 2001). This demands that four essential conditions be met for the process to be valuable: citizens' access to objective

reliable and relevant information; presentation of clear goals; sufficient time, resources and flexibility for citizens to actively participate; and commitment from government. The display of this and a number of other graduated criteria indicating levels of interaction are in themselves a public declaration of the WA Government's long-term commitment to genuine civic participation. This offers an important attempt to set standards for public engagement.

The South Australian Government has an online debate site called 'talking point' proposed, but as of this writing it is nonoperational and no indication is given as to the future status of this initiative. The parliamentary libraries across the country have also provided a number of papers that examine the advent of e-democracy overseas and discuss it in the Australian context (Sampford, 2001; Verspaandonk, 2001).

Although these developments are promising, the most advanced activity emanates from local governments. In Victoria, a large number of local governments have embraced different methods to enhance community involvement. At the base level, almost all now display basic information on services, agendas for impending council meetings, minutes of previous meetings and contact information for councillors and mayor (Kowalski, 2002). Beyond this, councils have employed different methods for engaging and consulting their community. The Victorian Local Governance Association has been active in promoting the benefits of e-democracy.

For general engagement, some have noticeboards or other space on their Websites devoted to citizen feedback and ideas, while others give instructions for participating in council meetings. Moreland City Council, in Melbourne's inner northern suburbs, has a Webpage linked from its site titled 'Moreland Chat' where citizens can participate in live discussions with the mayor or councillors and take part in online ward meetings. Also, the council is about to begin its Community E-Discussion Forum, where citizens can discuss ideas, share opinions, ask advice and make community announcements. Wellington Shire Council in the State's Southwest Webcasts its monthly council meetings live and archives them so citizens can access them after the event.

A 2002 report on Victorian Local Governments found that 44% of local governments had elements of the consultation process occurring online, while 13% had a full consultation available online (Kowalski, 2002). This consultation varies from announcements of and documentation for public meetings, to providing the option to e-mail submissions rather than posting them or presenting them in person, and online surveys asking the community what concerned them in their area.

Typically, the most sophisticated of these consultative efforts are at the moment still less interactive than the leading engagement-orientated projects mentioned above.

ONLINE SOCIAL ENTREPRENEURSHIP

The slow growth of government-led projects has not prevented the rise of a small number of Internet sites that have a focus on e-democracy. Most do not enunciate the democratic elements of their discussion and noticeboard pages, unlike their more sophisticated counterparts in the United States (such as DNet, Minnesota E-Democracy and e-the-people), but even the most unrefined of these offer an increased personal level of political involvement. In addition to these privately run nonprofit or commercial sites, the Australian Broadcasting Corporation (ABC) sets an example for single issue discussion, with their sporadic online forums which follow a topical broadcast, most often the current affairs programme, *Four Corners*. These forums give viewers the opportunity to both express their opinion and glean information from the experts and actors within the debate, thus enhancing their political awareness and experience.

It is only possible in this overview to provide a brief list of several nongovernment e-democracy projects. Some have been initiated by successful business leaders, others by academics. Some hope to return a profit eventually. Not all would consciously badge themselves as promoting electronic democracy. They are, however, significant because they are already demonstrating their potential to influence traditional political processes, as was found with the Minnesota e-democracy project.

Onlineopinion.com.au offers thoughtful articles archived by topic. They ran an online discussion, via e-mail list, in parallel with a formal review of the Australian Labor Party. The participation was robust and varied, and may well have been the first national online discussion with federal Parliamentarians. It is not clear whether the formal review took the outcomes and data generated by this project into account.

Crikey.com.au and *www.notgoodenough.org* are overtly entrepreneurial, and both offer the opportunity to air problem areas, either in politics, business, sport, media or consumer services. Crikey in particular has broken several high profile political stories and is now widely read by politicians and their minders. On consumer issues, the Australian Consumers' Association (*www.choice.com.au*) works to stimulate policy input via its Website forums.

The Australian Policy Research Network (*www.apprn.org*) has run several online discussions on public policy issues. Founder Richard Curtain has managed these carefully, ensuring quality background reading and good stakeholder representation. Although the participants have been mainly policy developers, bureaucrats and academics, the discussions have led to better understanding and new avenues for offline relationships and information sharing.

Civic Chat (*humansciences.com.au/forums/civicchat*) based in WA aims to provide an online public space to discuss local issues. It aims to be free for citizens, but hopes councils will pay an annual access fee.

PRACTICING NEW DEMOCRATIC LITERACIES

Citizen disinterest is a recognised feature of many established democracies. The various body politics in Western democracies, and particularly the young, are growing disenchanted with the way politics is conducted, and with politicians. Sometimes the cynicism extends to the country's political institutions and to democracy itself. This is recognised as a dangerous state of affairs, given the rise of fundamentalism and populism globally. It was reported in *The Australian* newspaper that, when participating in a civics study of 28 countries,

> [t]he Australian Council for Educational Research found half of Australian students had no grasp of democracy, which ranked them behind countries like Poland, Cyprus and the Slovak Republic. (Milligan, 3)

Democratic literacies grow from and contribute to civic engagement, especially when power is shared. These include the skills and competencies needed to understand policy issues and processes, the rights and responsibilities available to citizens and the ability to communicate effectively within and across social groups. Citizens and officials are gradually becoming familiar with public virtual spaces, such as *onlineopinion.com.au* and civic chat. A range of other options are possible (see Griffiths, 2002; Griffiths and Cooper, 2002), and both successful and failed experiments need to be shared to increase community knowledge. Raising knowledge about democracy could take place more purposefully, for example, by holding e-democracy weeks in which live online chat could take place with local historians or political studies teachers, or representatives of local political parties. In real or offline committee meetings, democratic literacies are being demonstrated everyday–waiting one's turn to speak, speaking to the point, summarising argument, using reason not invective, listening to one's fellow citizen and the chair, voting, living with decisions one doesn't like, still greeting the people with whom one disagrees, and accepting the committee's decision. Online democratic literacies need to be even more carefully practised. Being succinct, addressing substantive issues directly, not flaming or wasting the time of other citizens, not personalising issues, asking for accountability in a courteous manner–these are all a 'civic' version of the 'netiquette' familiar to many of us.

Educating ourselves about these new modes of interaction is a task for both civil society and e-government planners. Well-constructed feedback forms, useful as they are in planning and in giving citizens a chance to air their views, are just a first step. Voluntary virtual commons are the next step and they can be developed from civil, reflective discussion groups. If the horizontal fellowship on which the civil contract depends is to be successful online, people need potentially powerful places to practice their literacies.

MOVING TOWARDS DISTRIBUTED GOVERNANCE

Implementation of these new opportunities for engagement suggests a networked view of government. The analysis in this section is based on Canadian research (Richard, 2000). It suggests that governments can achieve a democratic dividend from new media if they start to see their roles more as partner, broker, and facilitator. The process of policy development becomes a two-way learning process, more like action research. Nonprofits assume even greater importance (as is seen in the above Australian examples) because the worth of their input increases. The trust developed by openness becomes a valuable asset to government, because the openness of the process is more important than (broad) participation. Part of this trust comes from the transparency of the process: as a design element, transparency in the form of accurate documentation and information provision is very inexpensive online. A key feature is that the forms of transparency must be the ones participants request.

When implemented in this way, with great clarity about what is needed, consensus can be swifter than expected. The load of responsibility and accountability is actually spread out, or distributed, among the stakeholders, and this strengthens and speeds up the response. The alternative of top-down policy imposition and dealing with objections and inadequacies afterwards is inefficient by comparison. However, this networked process does not lead to final and perfect outcomes. Rather, it opens the door to a more iterative way of doing policy. The process is less expensive and less political, so it is also more mutable. This flexibility allows a learn as you go approach, because the bureaucrats no longer have to assume full responsibility. Therefore, they do not lose face when the policy needs adjusting. This builds in responsiveness, but also resilience. The underlying values and goals remain clear, so the changes in implementation needed to get there are no longer major obstacles. Government is repositioned as catalyst, more like a helpful consultant. They also manage the money, but also with an open and transparent way. These lessons from the networked model have much in common with lessons from the open software movement. Targeted consultations for particular policy outcomes is just one aspect of networked governance, the acute phase of policy diagnostics.

CONCLUSIONS

Richard's analysis of the Canadian experience with online engagement indicates that applications of information technology in government are just starting to mature. As this happens, the changing perspectives on governance mean that other players, including the media and nonprofits, as well as corporations, are likely to take stronger roles in harnessing public opinion and activity. There are many opportunities to explore what lies beyond electronic service delivery. The Canadians are not alone in realising that there are deeper efficiencies to be gained than just providing services online. Almost everywhere, government officials have much to contribute to allow this vision to be realized. There is also a need, however, for dedicated people and lobby groups outside of government to work with and in some case compliment the work of government. All these possibilities can be harnessed for e-government to realize a democratic dividend. None of this will be achieved without vision and focussing of resources.

From a theoretical perspective, there is growing awareness that political models developed in the eighteenth century are giving way to a new paradigm. The old models are based on Newtonian mechanics and linear, hierarchical structures, along with assumptions of stability as not just desirable, but possible. The new models recognise and harness diversity and pluralism as micro-drivers of democracy, and rely more on the unexpected outcomes that self-organised activity brings to the political front (Becker and Slayton, 2000; Kiel, 1994). Some authors also identify fractal patterns, or 'attractors' in human behaviour and political action (Geiselhart, 1999; Biggs, 2001). The Canadian networked model described above is part of this nonlinear paradigm shift. It is likely that the mathematical application of complexity theory to public administration (for example, Kiel, 1994) will be extended to modelling governance and developing protocols for participation, using generic democracy indicators and values to generate the rules of interaction. In ten years, government Websites that do not offer citizen engagement, and consultation programs that do not make use of advanced computerized and interactive technology, may well become relics of the past.

REFERENCES

Accenture. (2002) *e-Government Leadership: Realising the Vision*, located at *www.accenture.com/xd/xd.asp?it=enWeb&xd=industries\government\gove_thought.xml*.

Australian Bureau of Statistics (2000) AusStats 8147.0, *Use of the Internet by Householders, Australia*, at *www.abs.gov.au/austats*.

Australian Capital Territory Electoral Commission. (2002) *The 2001 ACT Legislative Assembly Election Electronic Voting and Counting System Review*, Executive Summary, located at *www.elections.act.gov.au/CompExecSumm.htm*.

Australian Perspectives on Defence: The Report of the Community Consultation Team (2000), located at *http://www.defence.gov.au/consultation2/index.htm*.

Becker, Ted, and Slayton, Christa Daryl. (2000) *The Future of Teledemocracy*. Praeger: Westport.

Biggs, Michael. (2001) 'Fractal Waves: Strikes as Forest Fires.' Presented to the Annual Meeting of the American Sociological Association, located at *http://users.ox.ac.uk/~sfos0005/fractalwaves.pdf*.

Brumby, John. (1999) *Connecting Victoria*, Multimedia Victoria, located at *www.mmv.vic.gov.au*.

Caddy, Joanne, and Vergez, Christian. (2001) *Citizens as Partners: Information, Consultation and Public Participation in Policy-Making*, Organisation for Economic Co-operation and Development, located at *http://www1.oecd.org/publications/e-book/4201131e.pdf*.

Campbell, Ian. (2000) *Government Online: A Strategy for the Future*, Parliamentary Secretary for Communications, Information Technology and the Arts, Media Release, 6 April 2000, located at *www.dcita.gov.au*.

Chen, Peter. (2002) *Australian Elected Representatives' Use of New Technologies 2002*, Centre for Public Policy, University of Melbourne, located at *http://www.webprophets.net.au/websites/chen/elected/*.

Curtin, Gregory, McConnachie, Robert, Sommer, Michael, and Vis-Sommer, Veronika. (2002) American E-Government at the Crossroads: A National Study of Major City Uses, *Journal of Political Marketing*, 1(1).

FitzGerald, Bronwen. (2002) *Australian E-Democracy: Characterizing the Use of Internet Technology in Democratic Communication*, Honours Thesis, Political Science, University of Melbourne (forthcoming).

Geiselhart, Karin. (1999) Does Democracy Scale? A Fractal Model for the Role of Interactive Technologies in Democratic Policy Processes PhD Thesis, University of Canberra, located at *http://www.bf.rmit.edu.au/kgeiselhart*.

Geiselhart, Karin. (2002) Net Value: The Use of the Internet by Non-Profit Organisations. RMIT School of Business Information Technology Working Paper, located at *http://www.bf.rmit.edu.au/kgeiselhart*.

Griffiths, Mary. (2002) Australian e-Democracy?: Its Potential for Citizens and Governments, Presentation to *Innovative e-Government for Victoria* Conference, 26 March 2002, located at *www.egov.vic.gov.au/Victoria/Conference2002/daytwo.htm*.

Griffiths, Mary. (2002) Forming Audiences for E-democracy: Government Policies, Portals, Pilots–and Citizen Literacies. Proceedings. 2nd European Conference on E-Government, Oxford, UK.

Griffiths, Mary, and Cooper, Simon. (2001) Virtual Democracy in the Latrobe Region. *Southern Review: Communication, Politics and Culture,* 34(1): 45-59.

Gualtieri, Robert. (1998) *Impact of the Emerging Information Society on the Policy Development Process and Democratic Quality.* OECD Public Management Service [cited 4/3/1999], located at *http://www.oecd.org/puma/gvrnance/it/itreform.htm*.

Hacker, Kenneth, and van Dijk, Jan. (eds.) (2001) *Digital Democracy: Issues of Theory and Practice*, Sage, Thousand Oaks.

Holmes, Douglas. (2001) *E-Gov: E-Business Strategies for Government*, Nicholas Brealey, London.

Howard, John. *Investing for Growth*, speech delivered to the National Press Club, Canberra, 8 December 1997, located at *www.isr.gov.au/growth/html/speech.html*.

Kaufman, Daniel, Kraay, Aart, and Zoido-Lobaton, Pablo. (1999, 2000) World Bank Policy Research Working Papers: "Aggregating Governance Indicators" (no. 2195), and "Governance Matters" (no. 2196), located at *www.worldbank.org/wbi/gac*.

Kiel, L. Douglas. (1994). *Managing Chaos and Complexity in Government.* Jossey-Bass: San Francisco.

Kowalski, Jane. (2002) *Use of the Internet as a Consultation Tool for Victorian Local Governments*, Report for the Victorian Local Government Association, located at *http://www.vlga.org.au/library/contents/issues/consultation_engagement_Useofthe InternetasaConsultationToolbyVictorianLocalGovernments0.doc*.

Martin, Fiona. (1999) Pulling Together the ABC: The Role of the ABC Online. *Media International Australia*, 93: 103-117.

McAllister, Ian. (2000) Keeping them Honest: Public and Elite Perceptions of Ethical Conduct Among Australian Legislators, *Political Studies*, 48(1) March 2000, pp. 22-37.

McQuail, Dennis. (2000) (rev. ed.) *Mass Communication Theory*, Sage, London.

Milligan, Louise. Students Take Apathetic View of Democracy, *The Australian*. 6 Mar.

Mintzberg, Henry. (May-June 1996) Managing Government–Governing Management. *Harvard Business Review*, 75-83.

Musso, Juliet, Weare, Christopher, and Hale, Matt. (2000) Designing Web Technologies for Local Governance Reform: Good Management or Good Democracy? *Political Communication*, 17: 1-19.

National Office for the Information Economy (2000a) *Current State of Play–November 2000*, located at *www.noie.gov.au/Projects/information_economy/research& analysis/ie_stats/index.htm*.

National Office for the Information Economy. (2000b) *Government Online: A Strategy for the Future*, located at *www.govonline.gov.au/projects/strategy/GovOnlineStrategy.htm*.

National Office for the Information Economy. (2002a) *Current State of Play: April 2002* (5th Edition), located at *www.noie.gov.au/Projects/information_economy/ research&analysis/ie_stats/CSOP_April2002*.

National Office for the Information Economy, (2002b) Government Online, *E-Benefits Study*, April 2002, located at *www.govonline.gov.au/projects/strategy/egovt_benefits_ study.htm*.

Nielson-Netratings. *Global Internet Usage,* located at *www.nielsen-netratings.com/ hot_off_ the_net_i.jsp#australia*.

Norris, Pippa. (2001) *Digital Divide: Civic Engagement, Information Poverty and the Internet Worldwide*, Cambridge University Press, New York.

Queensland Government, Department of Premier and Cabinet. (2001) *E-Democracy Policy Framework*, located at *www.premiers.qld.gov.au/about/community/democracy. htm*.

Richard, Elizabeth. (2000) Lessons from the Network Model of Online Engagement of Citizens. Paper presented to LENTIC colloquium, Brussels. Also available online from the Canadian Policy Research Networks, located at *www.cprn.org*.

Ronaghan, Stephen A. (2002) *Benchmarking E-Government: A Global Perspective*, United Nations' Department for Public Economics and Public Administration, located at *http://www.unpan.org/e-government/benchmarking%20E-gov%202001.pdf*.

Sampford, Karen. (2001) *E-Democracy and Election Campaigns: Recent Case Studies from USA and Developments in Australia*, Queensland Parliamentary Library Research Brief, located at *www.parliament.qld.gov.au/parlib/research/index.htm*.

Scope Communications/NUA, *How Many Online,* located at *www.nua.com/surveys/ how_many_online/asia.html*.

Scrutiny of Acts and Regulations Committee. (2002) *Inquiry into Electronic Democracy*, prepared for Victorian State Parliament, located at *www.parliament.vic.gov.au/ sarc/default.htm*.

Symonds, Mark. (2000) Government and the Internet–The Next Revolution, *The Economist*, June 24.

Taylor, Jill. (2002) *TIGERS Project Report* Issue 8, located at *http://www.govonline. gov.au/projects/services&innovation/TIGERSnewsletter8.htm*.

Verspaandonk, Rose. (2001) *Shaping Relations Between Government and Citizens: Australian Future Directions*, Research Paper, Australian Parliamentary Library, Politics and Public Administration Group, Vol. 5, located at *http://www.aph. gov.au/library/pubs/rp/index.htm*.

INTERNET SITES

Australian Broadcasting Corporation, Four Corners Online Forums: *http://abc.net.au/4corners/.*

Australian Capital Territory Government: *www.act.gov.au*

Australian Consumers' Association: *www.choice.com.au*

Australian Democrats: *www.democrats.org.au*

Australian Federal Court: *www.fedcourt.gov.au.*

Australian Labour Party (ALP): *www.alp.org.au.*

Australian Liberal Party: *www.liberal.org.au*

Australian National Party: *www.nationalparty.org,*

Australian Taxation Office: *www.ato.gov.au.*

Ballarat City Council: *www.ballarat.vic.gov.au*

Banyule City Council: *www.banyule.vic.gov.au.*

Cardinia Shire Council: *www.cardinia.vic.gov.au.*

Centrelink Job Search: *www.jobsearch.gov.au.*

Crikey Media: *www.crikey.com.au*

E-government Victoria: *www.egov.vic.gov.au,*

Federal Parliament Webcasting: *www.aph.gov.au/live/webcast2.asp.*

Human Sciences/CivicChat: *www.humansciences.com.au.*

Latrobe City Council: *www.latrobe.vic.gov.au.*

Mildura Rural City Council: *www.mildura.vic.gov.au.*

More Than Just Talk: *www.morethanjusttalk.com.*

Moreland City Council: *www.moreland.vic.gov.au.*

Multimedia Victoria: *www.mmv.vic.gov.au.*

New South Wales State Government: *www.nsw.gov.au*

Northern Territory Government: *www.nt.gov.au*

One Nation: *www.onenation.com.au.*

Parliament of Victoria, Scrutiny of Acts and Regulations Committee: *www.parliament.vic.gov.au/sarc/default.htm.*

Political Lobby: *www.political-lobby.com.au.*

Queensland State Government: *www.qld.gov.au*

South Australian Government's Talking Point: *www.talkingpoint.sa.gov.au.*

South Australian State Government: *www.sa.gov.au*

Tasmanian State Government: *www.tas.gov.au*

The AustralianGreens: *www.greens.org.au*

TIGERS Fish Online: *www.fishonline.gov.au*

TIGERS Starting School: *www.startingschool.gov.au*

Victorian State Government: *www.vic.gov.au*

Victorian State Parliament *www.parliament.vic.gov.au.*

Wellington City Council: *www.wellington.vic.gov.au.*

Western Australia Government, Citizens and Civics Unit: *www.ccu.dpc.wa.gov.au.*

Western Australian Government's Citizenscape: *www.citizenscape.wa.gov.au.*

Western Australian State Government: *www.wa.gov.au*

Western Australian State Parliament: *www.parliament.wa.gov.au*

Wyndham City Council: *www.wyndham.vic.gov.au*

The U.S. Congress Responds
to Online Communication Needs

Dennis W. Johnson

George Washington University

SUMMARY. The U.S. Congress, after a relatively slow start in the 1990s, is now making some progress in meeting the demands of online communications. Fueled by the growing use of e-mail by constituents and the development of online grassroots efforts, Congress has been in-

Dennis W. Johnson is Associate Dean of the Graduate School of Political Management of the George Washington University. From 2000-2002, he was the principal investigator of the Congress Online Project (www.congressonlineproject.org), a joint research project of the George Washington University and the Congressional Management Foundation, sponsored by the Pew Charitable Trusts. He is the author of *Clogged Circuits: Congress, the Internet, and Online Communications* (forthcoming) and editor of *Congress and the Challenges of Electronic Democracy* (forthcoming). He is also the author of *No Place for Amateurs: How Political Consultants Are Reshaping American Democracy* (Routledge, 2001).

[Haworth co-indexing entry note]: "The U.S. Congress Responds to Online Communication Needs." Johnson, Dennis W. Co-published simultaneously in *Journal of Political Marketing* (The Haworth Press, Inc.) Vol. 2, No. 3/4, 2003, pp. 235-254; and: *The World of E-Government* (ed: Gregory G. Curtin, Michael H. Sommer, and Veronika Vis-Sommer) The Haworth Press, Inc., 2003, pp. 235-254. Single or multiple copies of this article are available for a fee from The Haworth Document Delivery Service [1-800-HAWORTH, 9:00 a.m. - 5:00 p.m. (EST). E-mail address: docdelivery@haworthpress.com].

10.1300/J199v02n03_13

undated with e-mail. By using filtering systems, better software and hardware, and, most of all, better management techniques, many offices are now equipped to handle the great increase in electronic mail. While several steps behind the private sector, through fits and starts, Congress is attempting to catch up and meet the rising demand and volume of electronic communication. In some offices, there has been considerable progress in developing effective, interactive Web sites. These exceptional Web sites should serve as models of dynamic online communications, but for most congressional Web sites, there is a long way to go. Much depends on the attitudes and priorities set by lawmakers and their senior staff. *[Article copies available for a fee from The Haworth Document Delivery Service: 1-800-HAWORTH. E-mail address: <docdelivery@haworthpress. com> Website: <http://www.HaworthPress.com> © 2003 by The Haworth Press, Inc. All rights reserved.]*

KEYWORDS. Congress, e-mail, Web sites, communication, online, best practices

The United States Congress is not an institution that quickly embraces technological change. When congressional leaders were approached in 1869 by the young Thomas A. Edison who had just invented an automatic voting machine, they summarily brushed him off. The invention, a marvelous, time-saving device was indeed efficient: in just minutes, all of the lawmakers could cast their vote electronically on the floor of the House, saving countless hours. However, this promised efficiency transgressed the folkways and rhythms of the congressional deliberative process (Josephson, 65-66). Forty-five years later, a congressman, who had been an electrical engineer, introduced legislation to consider electronic voting, but the House of Representatives in 1914 ignored him (Griffith and Oleszek). Finally, in 1973, electronic voting became effective in the House of Representatives, with some forty voting stations plus electronic equipment at the floor managers' tables so that they could monitor progress of the voting, and computers at the rear of the chamber connected to the voting system. Despite the thirty years of successful use in the House, the U.S. Senate still does not permit electronic voting.

Congress was also slow in permitting radio or television coverage. As early as 1922, there were legislative proposals to permit radio coverage in both the House and the Senate; however, they were ignored or simply allowed to die in committee. Television first came to Congress in 1947 for the opening of the 80th Congress and returned to provide coverage of important committee hearings and investigations, such as the investigation of Alger Hiss in 1948, the Kefauver investigation into organized crime in 1951, and the thirty-six days of the Army-McCarthy hearings in 1954 (Frantzich and Sullivan, 30). In 1973, television networks devoted 319 hours of live coverage to the Watergate hearings. Then in 1979, the House agreed to have the new cable system enterprise, C-SPAN, provide gavel-to-gavel coverage of its floor deliberations; the Senate, which saw its first resolution to televise proceedings in 1944, finally agreed to have C-SPAN II provide gavel-to-gavel coverage in 1986 (Table 1).

CONGRESS ADAPTS TO ONLINE TECHNOLOGY

Congress likewise has moved slowly into the computer age. Before the 104th Congress (1995-96), the House of Representatives was characterized as "intrinsically a paper-based institution." Most documents were available only in hard copy, there was no common architecture, language or format so that documents could be shared, viewed or distributed electronically, or integrated with others (CyberCongress, 1). There were nine separate e-mail systems in the House; communications between them were haphazard and problematic; there was no directory of e-mail addresses, and the primitive mainframe computer software had been written in about 1980 and was showing its age. In 1993, both the House and Senate went online with Internet sites, but they were nothing more than rudimentary text-only configurations. Senator Edward M. Kennedy (D-Massachusetts) was the first federal lawmaker to venture online with a graphics-based Web site that year (Casey, 1996; Frantzich, 1982). While slow to create its own online communications systems, Congress did enact in 1993 an important piece of legislation, Public Law 103-40, which directed the Government Printing Office (GPO) to make legislative and executive branch information available online, beginning with the *Congressional Record* and the *Federal Register*.

The November 1994 congressional elections swept the Republican into the majority in the House of Representatives for the first time in forty years. Republicans were in charge, pushing to enact their Contract with America and eager to update and reshape the institution of Congress itself. Republicans, chafing from their long years of minority status, were determined to rearrange committees, cut staff, and streamline the lawmaking process. As the new Speaker of the House, Newt Gingrich of Georgia, championed the Internet and saw it as a vehicle to cut through what he considered the entrenched, liberal-dominated interests in Washington and in Congress. The new Speaker wanted more transparency and openness in the deliberations of Congress and saw online communications as the key element. Gingrich wanted the rules of the House changed so that congressional information would be available to "any citizen in the country at the same time that it is available to the highest paid Washington lobbyist" (Ruskin). Gingrich saw the Internet as an electronic town hall and championed the building of online support structures for conservative causes. He called for "information empowerment zones" in rural and urban areas that did not yet have access to the Internet and talked expansively about a plan to give each family in America access to computers.

Gingrich asked the Committee on House Oversight, through its Computer and Information Services Working Group, to investigate and evaluate the state of computing in the House. Quickly known as the "CyberCongress" project, the effort would be concentrated on improving communication, networking and computing technologies. Its goal was to ensure that important, time-sensitive materials, such as amendments, rules, and reports that accompanied legislation would be available online; that there would be better communications among lawmakers and their staffs with universal e-mail, fax, and voice mail connections; and there would be electronic decision support systems for Members, committees, and staff, such as having Whip counts made possible by pagers and messaging-based groupware.

Part of the CyberCongress plans were formalized at the beginning of the 105th Congress (1997), when the House adopted Rule XI, clause 2e, stating that "each committee shall, to the maximum extent feasible, make its publications available in electronic form." Witnesses were encouraged to have their official statements and accompanying documentation available in electronic format; and several House committees began providing access to transcripts, and some committees made available audio and video transcripts of hearings over their committee Web sites (Griffith, 11-12).

Just before the beginning of the 104th Congress, in December 1994, Gingrich and Representative William M. (Bill) Thomas (R-California) directed the Library of Congress to develop an online legislative retrieval system that would be available to the public. Congress had already developed the Legislative Information System (LIS) for internal use by lawmakers and congressional staff, and it became the foundation upon which the public site was built. The Library of Congress site was christened THOMAS, named after Thomas Jefferson, and quickly became available in January 1995. THOMAS was not without its difficulties: at times it trailed by hours, even days, the flow of legislative business, making information available, but not in a timely manner. THOMAS now includes bill summaries and status information from the 93rd Congress (1973-74); *Congressional Record* text, reports of the Congressional Budget Office (CBO) and General Accounting Office (GAO). Recorded votes, selected hearings and committee reports, and other materials became available beginning in the 101st Congress (1989-90). While THOMAS contains a wealth of information, it is cumbersome to use, and visitors without much prior knowledge of Congress or legislation would have difficulty in navigating through the site.

In the Senate, there was similar activity to upgrade technology, but without the flourish and press activity found in the House. In 1991, the Senate had installed its first version of e-mail and by October 1995, every Senator had some presence on the Senate Internet server, although most Senate sites were simply one-page billboards that were created by the Senate Computer Center (Safir).

PROBLEMS AND OPPORTUNITIES

Despite early successes in creating a CyberCongress, there were serious internal problems in supporting the needed technology. The old House Information System (HIS) was renamed and reconfigured in 1995 to be the House Information Resources (HIR). Office of Inspector General in the House of Representatives conducted a series of internal audits in the 104th (1995-96) and 105th Congresses (1997-98) and found many serious flaws. The House lacked a strategic plan, suffered from ineffective day-to-day leadership, too frequent security problems, and serious internal control problems. Although millions of dollars were spent on infrastructure, security systems, hardware and software, and training, the needs of House Members, their staffs, and House operations still were inadequately met. In one searing report, the Inspector General found that HIR was "only minimally prepared to meet the information technology challenges and demands in the short term and is not adequately preparing the House information systems program to move into the 21st century" (OIG, 1997). Systems improved in the following years, particularly with the creation of a new position, Chief Administrative Officer; later, that office was lauded for making significant changes in the management and operation of the technology systems in the House (OIG, 1998).

Many Members of Congress found themselves confronting a steep learning curve to master technology issues and to become familiar with the simplest of electronic tools. In 1996, Representatives Richard (Rick) White (R-Washington) and Frederick (Rick) Boucher (D-Virginia) observed that there was a lack of even rudimentary knowledge among their House colleagues about computers and online communication; for many, the Internet was a mystery. Senator Patrick Leahy (D-Vermont) caustically noted in 1997, "we have a lot of people who have strong positions on the Internet and computers . . . in the Congress who wouldn't even know how to turn on a computer if they had to" (McAllester). Representatives White and Boucher joined Senators Leahy and Conrad Burns (R-Montana) in forming the bi-partisan Congressional Internet Caucus, whose main purpose was to educate lawmakers about the promise and potential of the Internet. While the task was indeed huge, Representative White acknowledged that in just a year there had been a "real sea change" in lawmakers' understanding and support for the Internet (Stepanek).

In 1995, the first significant e-mail petition was generated and sent to the Senate. On the floor of the Senate, Patrick Leahy brandished a printout of the petition, a six-inch thick petition, with 1,500 pages and 112,000 signatures of individuals who were opposed to the passage of a proposed Internet censorship provision (Browning, 46-48). Some lawmakers began to take advantage of the benefits of online communication. Senator John Ashcroft (R-Missouri), one of the few Senators whose office would answer e-mail with e-mail rather than postal mail, noted that his office in the late 1990s had saved over 250,000 pieces of paper, had reduced staff time in processing correspondence, and most importantly, had opened up communicated with whole new sets of individuals who had never corresponded with his office before. Ashcroft was the first Senator to launch an online petition; in less than two weeks, he had gathered some 7,100 signatures in support of term limits (Safir; Browning, 8).

E-MAIL ADVOCACY CAMPAIGNS

The House of Representatives began keeping statistics on e-mail traffic in 1998, and during that year, the number of e-mails received was

TABLE 1. Milestones in Online Communications in the Congress

1979	C-SPAN: Television coverage of House of Representatives.
1986	C-SPAN II: Television coverage of Senate.
1991	Senate installs first generation of e-mail.
1993	Sen. Edward M. Kennedy first to post a Congressional Web site. Seven House members have e-mail. Public Law 103-40, making legislative and executive branch materials available online.
1995	Gingrich as Speaker emphasized CyberCongress. Forty House offices and 20 Senate offices had Internet connections in February. Library of Congress THOMAS site created. House Web site, www.house.gov, debuted. First online petition seen on floor of the Senate.
1996	Congressional Internet Caucus created. Over 222 Member offices, 27 full committees and 11 other House offices have established Web sites; all 100 Senators nominally have Web sites.
1997	Library of Congress and Congressional Research Service bring online the Legislative Information Retrieval System (LIS) for internal Congressional use. C-SPAN viewers could watch live C-SPAN coverage on their computers. Sen. John Ashcroft was first Senator to launch an online petition.
1998	First Webcast of a congressional hearing. AOL's VoteNote was launched. Last Member of Congress whose office only used typewriters retired. Impeachment hearings and MoveOn.org inundated Congress with e-mails.
1999	Internet Tax Hoax and the phantom Bill 602-P.
2001	Rep. Joel Hefley became the last Member of Congress to have e-mail. Anthrax hits Congress; postal mail ground to a halt; e-mail soared.
2002	Still 120 House offices not rapidly adapting to new technologies. All personal offices in the House and Senate have Web sites, along with committees, leadership, caucus, and administrative sites. Total of over 600 Congressional Web sites. Senate replaced antiquated and no longer supported cc:Mail e-mail system.

greater than the number of pieces of postal mail. That year, e-mails overwhelmed the House, with 108 million coming in to Congressional offices, while only 10.6 million letters and postcards were received (CMF).

Part of that wave came from popular commercial sites that in the late 1990s added information on elections, voting and legislation. America Online's (AOL) VoteNote, launched during the coverage of the 1998 elections, was the platform for more than 50,000 citizen e-mails a day to

Congress. Other popular private portals followed suit with their own links to congressional Web sites. The impeachment of President Bill Clinton also generated considerable e-mail traffic. Entrepreneurs Joan Blades and Wes Boyd created a Web site called MoveOn.org, which rallied like-minded citizens who sent over two million e-mails to Congress protesting the impeachment of Clinton. They called this a "flash campaign": activists, nearly all of them unknown to one another but rallied by a common issue, who in a matter of days flooded the electronic in-boxes of lawmakers.

At the peak of the impeachment proceedings in January 1999, House offices weekly were receiving 1,000 e-mails and some Senate offices were receiving up to 10,000 e-mails. After the impeachment deliberations ended, the e-mails continued to come into Congress at an increasing rate. In December 2000, just after the contested presidential election, the House of Representatives alone received seven million messages. The short, bitter fight over the confirmation of John Ashcroft for attorney general saw congressional e-mail peak again and following the September 11, 2001, terrorist attacks and the anthrax contamination of Congress, e-mail shot up once more. By the end of 2001, a million e-mail messages a day were routinely received in Congress, on top of the hundreds of thousands of letters, postcards, faxes, telegrams and telephone calls.

In trying to understand the new media of e-mail and the Internet, Congress and the public became victims of a policy hoax. Sometime in early 1999, a report filtered through the Internet, e-mail and discussion groups that Congress was about to enact legislation to tax the use of global computer systems. The purported bill, entitled 602-P, would permit the federal government to charge a five cent surcharge on every e-mail delivered; further, a Congressman Tony Schnell was reported to have suggested a twenty to forty dollar per month surcharge on all Internet service. Citizens were urged to flood Congress with e-mails protesting the taxation of electronic mail. To anyone who would check, this was simply a hoax. No bill in the U.S. House of Representatives or Senate was ever numbered as "602-P," and there is not now, nor has there ever been, a Congressman Tony Schnell.

A Canadian version of this e-mail had bounced around cyberspace earlier and now with a few words changed, it was ready to stir up trouble in the United States. Thousands of e-mail poured in to Congress, even after considerable publicity that the whole scheme had been a fabrication. It simply would not die. The House ultimately passed legislation in 2000 prohibiting such an Internet tax from being enacted, thanks in large part to the hoax itself, and during the 2000 Senatorial debates in New York between Representative Rick Lazio and Hillary Rodham Clinton, both opposed the nonexistent legislation. The Internet hoax had altered political reality, and to this day, some Members of Congress have felt it necessary to post notices on their official Web sites that the Internet tax is a phony issue and that there is no such thing as bill 602-P.

CONGRESSIONAL E-MAIL

By 2001, all Members of Congress had e-mail and Web sites, and in 2002, there were 605 Congressional Web sites, personal office, committee, leadership, and administrative Web sites. In fits and starts, Congress had moved into the online information age. Systems have been integrated, old hardware and software replaced, infrastructure improved, staff training programs established, and administrative hurdles by and large overcome. At the staff level, there has been widespread acceptance–indeed reliance–on online technology. Legislative business simply could not be done without it: thousands of internal e-mails flow daily among and between staffs, reports are downloaded, schedules checked, messages sent between Washington and the district offices, indeed, staffers can even order lunch over a special Internet site through the House food system (Crabtree).

The House of Representatives, with its great number of Members, committees, and staff has taken better advantage of technological changes than the Senate, which often is two or three steps behind in implementing such changes. The Senate, for example, in 2002 was just replacing a creaking, trouble-prone e-mail system that was installed in 1991. The House, on the other hand, has poured $1.5 billion into infrastructure improvements from 1995-2001, and training of staff has dramatically improved (Dreier). Yet, according to estimate of a senior technology staffer in the House of Representatives, around 120 Member offices still had much to learn about how to manage e-mail and develop informative, user-friendly Web sites (McCarthy).

The House and Senate combined are receiving over a million e-mails a day. Much of that e-mail is generated by interest groups who have discovered and now use online grassroots communications. A new industry has been born of grassroots lobbyists and activists who use e-mail to communicate with lawmakers. For many well-funded organizations who already have sophisticated communication tools at their disposal, e-mail and Web sites have become welcome additions to their advocacy arsenals. For many other groups, especially those with low budgets but big policy ambitions, online communication has become vital in getting their message across.

For example, longtime conservative activist Richard A. Viguerie developed the Conservative HQ.com, a Web site dedicated to generating support for conservative causes. Part of the site is called the "Sixty-Second Activist": each day, conservatives who sign up are sent an e-mail issue brief, asking them to "defeat a liberal proposal or pass a conservative bill." Since its inception, this site has generated over a million faxes, 260,000 petition signatures, and 350,000 e-mails to Congress, the President, and other officials. Other ideological and single-issue based organizations have set up sites to keep members and allies informed of policy issues and to bombard Congress with electronic messages. Nearly a thousand organizations, ranging from the U.S. Chamber of Commerce to the Disabled American Veterans use software packages prepared by Capitol Advantage, the leading provider of such services. The software, CapWiz, tailors the issues, message, and actions needed for each client and helps them create efficient and quick grassroots lobbying efforts. In 2001 alone, Capitol Advantage clients sent a total of 7.5 million messages to Congress, the President and other elected officials. Thousands of organizations, activist groups and causes now are capable of flooding Congress with messages, resulting in the million messages a day that are sent in.

When lawmakers first began using e-mail to communicate, in the mid-1990s, many used public e-mail addresses, such as "congressman. smith@mail.house.gov," and accepted e-mails from anyone who sent them. Lawmakers were quickly inundated with e-mails, many of which had no identifiable postal address or ZIP code. Enthusiastic e-mail senders quickly learned that it was just as easy to send an e-mail to 535 lawmakers as it was to send it to one. Congressional offices found it imperative to separate the electronic wheat from the electronic chaff. The familiar term "spam"–unwanted, junk e-mail–developed a new meaning in Congress: e-mail that came from outside the Congressional district or outside of the state for a Senate office. Given staff limitations and a crush of mail–electronic and regular–offices would much rather spent five hours on those 50 letters sent from constituents in the district than five hours answering the 2,000 postcards generated by a mail firm and all postmarked from out of state. The same policy applied, with greater force, in winnowing out e-mail. The vast majority–perhaps 80 percent–of all e-mail to Congress comes from outside the districts of the lawmakers who received the mail (Congressional Management Foundation, 285).

The resulting increase in e-mail communications means that some House offices are receiving 8,000 e-mails a month and some Senate offices are receiving up to 55,000 e-mails a month (Congress Online, 2001a). One of the critical factors, and perhaps weaknesses, of the congressional system of online communications is that each office is responsible for its own communication efforts: that means that each House and Senate office, acting as autonomous, publicly financed small businesses, must decide on communications staffing, equipment, software, and training for itself. Although there has been a boost of funding in the House in late 2001, the amount of funds available for technology and staff in both the House and Senate falls short of handling the crush of communications. Both the House and the Senate provide technical and training support, but one of the major problems found by the Congress Online Project is that software is not well-utilized by staffers: nearly half of all Member offices use e-mail software that can automatically sort messages and enter e-mailers' names, addresses, and other information into the office database, but less than 10 percent of the offices were aware that their software could do these things, and frankly lacked the technical expertise to figure out how to use the software (Congress Online, 2001a).

To cope with the flow of e-mail, congressional offices have resorted to using e-mail filtering devices, such as Write Your Representative, which are placed in the lawmaker's Web sites, and require the sender to supply name, street address, and ZIP code before sending the message. Some 66 Senators and 226 House members have stopped using a public, unfiltered e-mail address and have gone to filtered systems like Write Your Representative (Congress Online, 2002c).

Some Senate offices are using another form of filtering device, EchoMail, which not only recognizes key words such as the name of the state and ZIP codes, but also words in the text of the messages. EchoMail can automate the sorting process: it recognizes preprogrammed key words and their synonyms, even looks for and recognizes anger in e-mails (by recognizing exclamation points). This recognition software is used in the corporate world, and its main value is cutting in half the cost of processing and answering e-mail, even including the cost of having humans go over the e-mail that the software could not figure out. For Senate offices, EchoMail can plug in the appropriate response (written by a Senate staffer) and reply to the e-mail automatically. Some offices, however, may be nervous about doing this, worried that the software may miss the nuances of a message and send back an embarrassing wrong reply. Senator William Frist (R-Tennessee), an enthusiastic supporter of technological improvements, has argued that EchoMail is good enough to categorize most e-mail and send the appropriate responses without having to go through an extra step of having staffers check it for accuracy (Bulkeley).

Electronic mail is the dominant form of communication to Congressional offices. Following the anthrax attack in October 2001, e-mail has become even more important. Yet, there is reluctance in some offices to fully embrace it. The biggest hurdle is the attitude of Members and some staffers that e-mail has less importance and less gravitas than conventional postal letters. There is some evidence, however, that constituents do not share that sentiment. In a study in 1999 conducted by Juno Online Services, Inc. and e-Advocates, a Washington-based electronic advocacy firm, 93 percent of the citizens who use the Internet stated that they believed e-mail should be treated with the same seriousness as telephone calls or letters (Congress Online, 2001a).

Another hurdle is that many Members want to answer e-mail with regular mail, using their official Congressional letterhead stationery. Congressional e-mail answers to e-mail questions, however, would cut down enormously on postage, paper, printing costs, and staff costs; further answering e-mail with e-mail could produce answers far more quickly, reducing the turn-around time in communications dramatically. In 2001, only 10 percent of House offices answered e-mail with e-mail; a year later, that percentage had climbed to 25 percent, as 60 offices adopted new procedures to handle e-mail (Congress Online, 2002a).

A third concern in some congressional offices is that an e-mail message, sent by a Member of Congress might be tampered with by the recipient, words changed or sentences added, and then the e-mail would be forwarded to persons who were never intended to receive it. From anecdotal evidence and conversations with offices that do aggressively answer e-mail correspondence with e-mail, there is no evidence that such e-mail tampering has occurred (Congress Online, 2001a).

E-mail holds extraordinary communication advantages, particularly for offices that want to tailor their message and target their audiences. Many congressional offices are now asking constituents and others to sign up for policy alerts or issue updates on a wide variety of topics on their official Web sites. Citizens can receive, for example, updated policy briefings prepared by a Senator's communications staff, on environmental issues, or education, military, response to terrorism, and a variety of other topics. The House Republican Caucus, using their impressive Web site, GOP.gov, had 1.7 million visitors in 2001, and sent out 75,000 topical e-mail newsletters under the name of individual Republican lawmakers to visitors who had requested them (Congress Online, 2002a, 45).

CONGRESSIONAL WEB SITES

Each of the 605 congressional Web sites has its own look, feel, design and colors. The House and Senate have established certain restrictions on content, such as the prohibition of links to the lawmaker's campaign Web site and links to political party sites. Yet, no two Web sites are alike; some are exceptionally good at providing information, while others fall far short.

Most early versions of congressional Web sites were, and many still are, little more than electronic bulletin boards. One of the earliest academic studies found that congressional Web sites were little more than extensions of the lawmakers' strategies to advertise to their constituents (Owen et al.). Reporter Gebe Martinez was less kind, characterizing congressional Web sites as "somewhat haphazard, occasionally hokey and highly political" (Martinez). Other earlier studies also noted that most Members of Congress were doing inadequate jobs in communicating with their constituents through online communications (Congressional Management Foundation, 1999; Carter). While there was considerable variation, in content, most congressional Web sites had certain common features: the lawmaker's biography, basic constituent services information, contact information, recent press releases, information on legislation the lawmaker had sponsored or cosponsored, and some information about the state or district, with links to other sites.

In 2001, the Congress Online Project conducted a systematic analysis of the online communications efforts in Congress. It established a best practices model for congressional online communication, examined and graded all 605 Web sites, and later offered assistance to those congressional offices that requested it, some 175 altogether.

One of the early discoveries was that congressional offices made their own decisions on Web site content without consulting their audiences. The chief of staff, press secretary, legislative director, and systems administrator, and to varying degrees the Member, would determine what would go onto the Web site. What was missing was something very central to any communication program: an understanding of what its audiences wanted to see. The Congress Online Project found, through its interviews of House staffers, that none of the offices interviewed had ever asked constituents what they wanted to view on the congressional Web sites.

To determine what constituents wanted to see, Congress Online Project, with Thomas Opinion Research, conducted a total of eight focus groups in Washington, DC, Richmond, Virginia, Phoenix, Arizona, and Philadelphia, Pennsylvania, in early 2001. Focus group participants were shown four actual congressional Web sites, two House and two Senate (two Republican and two Democratic) and asked to rate and comment upon them. Participants expressed a general dissatisfaction with Congress as an institution. Moreover, they were frustrated with inadequate and infrequent communication from their legislators, felt that Members of Congress were not sufficiently accountable to their constituents, and wanted to have their own voices heard by those who represent them.

Focus group participants were not at all impressed with flashy sites that appeared to be no more than self-promotional advertisements for lawmakers. Clever graphics, blinking icons, chat rooms, and online videos were not considered important or were viewed as annoyances. The focus group participants wanted accountability: they wanted to know how lawmakers voted on important issues, what their public schedules were, what they did all day, and information on contacting them and their district offices. The feature they wanted most–information on how lawmakers voted on key issues–was seldom found on the congressional Web sites; nor were many lawmakers willing to post daily or weekly public schedules (Congress Online, 2001b).

As a baseline for evaluation, the Congress Online Project developed a set of best practices that would be applicable to congressional Web sites, centering on the audience, content, interactivity of the site, usability, and innovations (Table 2).

All 605 congressional Web sites were evaluated and graded using the best practices criteria. There was a wide variation in quality and content of the congressional Web sites, but most sites received poor marks. Only 2.5 percent of congressional Web sites received a grade of "A" (or 4.00), and the average for all Web sites was C− (1.76). Overall, House of Representatives Web sites, which comprised 79.5 percent of all sites, received a grade of C− (1.67), while Senate sites were slightly better, with a grade of C (2.12) (Table 3).

There was no discernible pattern of Web site quality based on party affiliation. Senate Democratic Member offices had the highest overall grade average (C+ or 2.61), while House Democratic Member offices had the lowest ranking sites (D+ or 1.58) (Table 4). One reason that

TABLE 2. Best Practices for Congressional Web Sites

1. **Audience**. The site demonstrates that the office has clearly identified its Web audiences (both those seeking information from the office and those that the office wants to target) and methodically built the site around those audiences.

2. **Content**. The site provides content that is specifically targeted to meet the needs of the defined audiences, is up-to-date, attracts new visitors and supports the goals of the office.

3. **Interactivity**. The site offers its visitors opportunities to express their views and fosters on- and offline communications.

4. **Usability**. The design and information architecture of the site enhances the audiences' experience by enabling quick and user-friendly access to information and services.

5. **Innovations**. The site employs creative features that enhance a visitor's experience by making it more interesting or easier to use.

Source: Congress Online, 2002a

TABLE 3. Grade Distribution for Congressional Web Sites

Grade	Member Offices		Committees		Leadership	Grade
	House	Senate	House	Senate	Combined	Dis. Total
A	0.9	4.0	9.1	4.8	27.3	2.5
B	5.5	14.0	18.8	-----	9.1	7.4
C	59.6	64.0	42.4	57.1	18.2	58.8
D	28.2	16.0	27.3	28.6	36.4	26.3
F	5.9	2.0	3.0	9.5	9.1	5.3
GPA	1.57	2.12	2.06	1.62	2.09	1.76

Source: Congress Online, 2002a
All numbers in percentage, except GPA

TABLE 4. Member Office Web Sites, by Party and Chamber

Grade	A	B	C	D	F	Totals	GPA
Senate Democratic Member Offices	5.9%	13.7%	64.7%	13.7%	-----	51	2.61
Senate Republican Member Offices	2.0%	14.3%	61.2%	18.4%	4.1%	49	2.10
House Democratic Member Offices	0.5%	4.3%	56.6%	30.2%	8.5%	212	1.58
House Republican Member Offices	1.5%	6.6%	62.3%	26.3%	3.5%	228	1.76

Source: Congress Online, 2002a

Senate office Web sites scored higher is that they have more funds upon which they can draw to design and develop Web sites, either doing them internally or hiring Web design vendors to assist them. In the House of Representatives, with less money available per office, Members frequently relied on prepackaged materials from the House Information Resources office, their own internal Web design, and to a lesser extent, on professional Web design vendors.

The Congress Online Project selected fifteen congressional Web sites as the best examples of online communication tools which were able to meet audience needs, provide specific and up-to-date content, had interactivity tools, were user-friendly, and employed creative features (Table 5).

TABLE 5. Best Congressional Web Sites, 2002

Senate Member Sites

Senator Jeff Bingaman (Democrat-New Mexico), (http://bingaman.senate.gov)

Senator Barbara Boxer (Democrat-California), (http://boxer.senate.gov)

Senator Kay Bailey Hutchison (Republican-Texas), (http://hutchison.senate.gov)

Senator Patrick Leahy (Democrat-Vermont), (http://leahy.senate.gov)

House Member Sites

Rep. Kay Granger (Republican-Texas), (http://kaygranger.house.gov)

Rep. Mike Honda (Democrat-California), (http://www.house.gov/honda)

Rep. Mike Pence (Republican-Indiana), (http://mikepence.house.gov)

Rep. Richard Pombo (Republican-California), (http://www.house.gov/pombo)

Standing Committees

Senate Budget Committee (majority), (http://budget.senate.gov)

House Committee on Energy and Commerce (majority), (http://energycommerce.house.gov)

House Committee on Energy and Commerce (minority), (http://www.house.gov/commerce_democrats)

House Committee on Rules (majority), (http://www.house.gov/rules)

Leadership Offices

Speaker of the House, (http://www.speaker.gov)

Office of the House Majority Whip, (http://majoritywhip.house.gov)

House Republican Conference, (http://GOP.gov)

Source: Congress Online, 2002a

CONCLUSION

By 2002, the public had better access to the workings of Congress than ever before, through full coverage of floor proceedings televised by C-SPAN, audio and video coverage of selected House and Senate committee hearings through the Internet, and thousands of pieces of legislation, documents, and reports were available. Citizens could contact their representatives by e-mail, visit their official Web sites, and in many instances, sign up for electronic newsletters; with some lawmaker Web sites, they could join policy discussion groups and participate in online preference polls. Millions of people have sent e-mail messages, visited congressional Web sites, and downloaded official reports and documents. These improved communications and knowledge tools were a boon to the general public, but even more so for the attentive public, activists, and those who follow and try to influence Congress for a living.

Despite this progress, Congress still has miles to go to improve its online capabilities. Much depends upon the attitude and priorities set by the Members and their senior staff. Many offices have quickly embraced new technologies and have discovered that online communication can lead to great efficiencies, cost savings, better management of limited staff, and improved communication with constituents who are increasingly turning to electronic means of connecting with Congress. Many more offices, however, still have to learn those lessons.

Events are forcing Congress to rethink and reevaluate its communications policies and practices. The threat of anthrax contamination has compelled Congress to try a pilot study of digitizing postal mail. Begun in the summer of 2002, the program, if expanded, could mean that postal mail from constituents would be electronically scanned and sent to individual congressional offices in digitized form. There is a great potential for saving money and promoting electronic efficiency, but also the potential for the loss of a human or personal touch in the communications received. With laptop computers, cell phones, PDAs and other equipment commonplace, will Congress have to reconsider its ban on "electronic devices" in its chambers? After the September 11, 2001, terrorist attacks and the anthrax contamination in Senate and House office buildings, there has been a greater reliance on electronic mail and a quick acceptance of Blackberry wireless e-mail devices. Cell phones and pagers are commonplace on the floor, but are supposed to be turned off; likewise, Blackberries are now frequently found in the chambers and in committee meetings. There have been Members, particularly younger lawmakers and those who have served in state legislatures, who are perplexed by the ban on laptops on the floor of both chambers; thirty-four state legislatures permit laptop computers in their voting chambers (Legislators Online).

Many of these technology issues have been successfully addressed by private enterprise, driven by competitive forces and the need for efficiency, accuracy and quick turnaround of communication. Congress, several steps behind the private sector, through fits and starts, is attempting to catch up and to meet the rising demand and volume of electronic communication. The Congressional Management Foundation, a partner in the Congress Online Project, has provided training and assistance to over 175 congressional offices that have wanted to improve the design and content of their Web sites. In less than a year after the major report of the Congressional Online Project (2002a), there have been noticeable improvements in many of the congressional Web site; however, still much needs to be done to keep current and new Members of Congress aware of the importance of this dynamic form of communication.

As best practices models are refined and as technology improves, so will the demands and expectations of congressional online communications. Future research could provide annual audits of congressional Web sites, highlight and illustrate those offices which are doing exceptional well in communicating online, run a series of consumer tests on the effectiveness and value of Web-based information, and above all, determine if and how online communications make a difference in the complex, and often fractious, relationship between citizens and their representatives.

REFERENCES

Browning, Graeme. 2002. *Electronic Democracy: Using the Internet to Transform American Politics.* 2nd. ed. CyberAge Books.

Bulkeley, William M. 2001. "EchoMail Can Sort, Answer Deluge of E-Mails." *The Wall Street Journal,* November 15.

Carter, Matthew. 1999. "Speaking Up in the Internet Age: Use and Value of Constituent E-Mail and Congressional Web Sites." *Parliamentary Affairs* (July), 464-479.

Casey, Chris. 1996. *The Hill on the Net: Congress Enters the Information Age.* Academic Press.

Congress Online Project. 2001a. Kathy Goldschmidt, Nicole Folk, Mike Callahan, and Richard Shapiro. *E-Mail Overload in Congress: Managing a Communications Crisis,* available at ⟨http://www.congressonlineproject.org⟩.

Congress Online Project. 2001b. Dennis W. Johnson. *Constituents and Your Web Site,* available at ⟨http://www.congressonlineproject.org⟩. Thomas Opinion Research analysis available at ⟨http://congressonlineproject.org/focusgroups.pdf⟩.

Congress Online Project. 2002a. Kathy Goldschmidt, Nicole Folk, Mike Callahan, Richard Shapiro, and Brad Fitch. *Congress Online: Assessing and Improving Capitol Hill Web Sites,* available at (http://www.congressonlineproject.org).

Congress Online Project. 2002b. *Congress Online Newsletter* (July), available at (http://congressonlineproject.org).

Congress Online Project. 2002c. *Congress Online Newsletter* (August), available at (http://congressonlineproject.org).

Congressional Management Foundation. 1999. Katherine Bainbridge. *Building Web sites Constituents Will Use.*

Congressional Management Foundation. 2000. *Setting Course: A Congressional Management Guide,* 107th Congress edition.

Crabtree, Susan. 2000. "Changes Are Virtually Certain in Congress' Future." *Roll Call,* available at (http://www.rollcall/election/gtc2.html).

CyberCongress Accomplishments During the 104th Congress. 1997. Computer and Information Services Working Group, Committee on House Oversight, available at (http://www.house.gov/cha/publications/cybercongress/body_cybercongress.html).

Dreier, David. 2002. "We've Come a Long Way . . . Maybe" in James A. Thurber and Colton C. Campbell, eds. *Congress and the Internet.* Prentice-Hall.

Frantzich, Stephen E. 1982. *Computers in Congress: The Politics of Information.* Sage Publications.

Frantzich, Stephen E. and John Sullivan. 1996. *The C-SPAN Revolution.* Univ. of Oklahoma Press.

Griffith, Jane Bortnick. 1999. *Information Technology in the House of Representatives: Trends and Potential Impact on Legislative Process.* Congressional Research Service, available at (http://www.house.gov/rules/infotech99.htm).

Griffith, Jane Bortnick and Walter J. Oleszek. 1997. *Electronic Devices in the House Chamber.* Congressional Research Service, available at (http://www.house.gov/rules/e-devices.htm).

Josephson, Matthew. 1992. *Edison: A Biography.* John Wiley & Sons.

"Legislators Online," 2001. *Federal Computer Week.*

Martinez, Gebe. 1996. "Congress Now Posts Its Politicking on Internet Computers." *Los Angeles Times,* September 4, A1.

McAllester, Matthew. 1997. "Enlightening Lawmakers: The U.S. Congressional Internet Caucus Is Spreading the Word of the World Wide Web Among Colleagues." *Newsday,* October 8, C3.

McCarthy, Ellen. 2002. "Guiding the House to the 21st Century." *The Washington Post,* April 11, E8.

Office of Inspector General, U. S. House of Representatives. 1998. *Significant Improvements in the Management and Operations of the Office of the Chief Administrative Officer,* Report No. 98-CAO-19, available at (http://house.gov/IG/ cao19.pdf).

Office of Inspector General, U. S. House of Representatives. 1997. Letter of Transmittal from John W. Lainhart, IV, Inspector General, accompanying *HIR Management Practices Undermine the House's Ability to Keep Pace with Technological Changes,* Report No. 97-CAO-09, available at (http://house.gov/IG/97cao09.pdf).

Owen, Diana, Richard Davis, and Vincent James Strickler. 1996. "Congress and the Internet." *Harvard International Journal of Press/Politics,* vol. 2, 10-29.

Ruskin, Gary. 1997. "America Off-Line: Gingrich's Unfulfilled Internet Promise," *The Washington Post,* November 16.

Safir, Barbara. 1997. "Bit by Bit, Congress Is Opening Up to the Information Age," *The Washington Post,* June 2, A17.

Stepanek, Marcia. 1997. "Congressional Caucus Works to Plug Lawmakers into Internet." *Fort Worth Star-Telegram*, December 22, 23.

EUROPE

E-Government:
What Countries Do and Why:
A European Perspective

Kuno Schedler
Lukas Summermatter

Institute for Public Services and Tourism, University of St. Gallen, Switzerland

SUMMARY. This primarily descriptive contribution focuses on seven European countries. A heuristic e-government model is presented, which serves as a reference frame for structuring the information avail-

---

Dr. Kuno Schedler is Professor of Business Administration with special consideration of Public Management, and Director of the Institute for Public Services and Tourism at the University of St. Gallen, Varnbuelstrasse 19, CH-9000 St. Gallen, Switzerland (E-mail: kuno.schedler@unisg.ch).

Lukas Summermatter, lic. oec. HSG, is a research associate at the Institute for Public Services and Tourism at the University of St. Gallen, Varnbuelstrasse 19, CH-9000 St. Gallen, Switzerland (E-mail: lukas.summermatter@unisg.ch).

[Haworth co-indexing entry note]: "E-Government: What Countries Do and Why: A European Perspective." Schedler, Kuno, and Lukas Summermatter. Co-published simultaneously in *Journal of Political Marketing* (The Haworth Press, Inc.) Vol. 2, No. 3/4, 2003, pp. 255-277; and: *The World of E-Government* (ed: Gregory G. Curtin, Michael H. Sommer, and Veronika Vis-Sommer) The Haworth Press, Inc., 2003, pp. 255-277. Single or multiple copies of this article are available for a fee from The Haworth Document Delivery Service [1-800-HAWORTH, 9:00 a.m. - 5:00 p.m. (EST). E-mail address: docdelivery@haworthpress.com].

able from individual countries. In this examination, we assume that the differences between countries also have their roots in the motivational situation of the relevant political entities, as well as in the problem perception of the various governments. We have subjected the strategies communicated by the national government which results in a "motive barometer" for the soft factors behind e-government.   *[Article copies available for a fee from The Haworth Document Delivery Service: 1-800-HAWORTH. E-mail address: <docdelivery@haworthpress.com> Website: <http://www.HaworthPress. com> © 2003 by The Haworth Press, Inc. All rights reserved.]*

KEYWORDS. Electronic government, e-government framework, eEurope, politics, law, information society, technological development, soft factors

E-GOVERNMENT

E-Government: A New Perspective for an Old Issue

The introduction of information and communication technology (ICT) in administration is not a new topic. In the German-speaking region, which is our home ground, research work has been done and published under the heading "Administration IT" for many years. The leading lights are primarily the publications by Lenk and Reinermann, but also those by Brinkmann (1974) about the early automation of administration, and later by Grimmer (1986). In the wake of the new opportunities provided by the Internet, these technologies have gained a completely new significance. Under the heading of "e-government," they are now one of the topics most frequently debated in administration. E-government may be regarded as the new guideline for administration IT. In this context, the new concepts are based on existing, sometimes already highly advanced developments in administration. However, what makes e-government different in comparison to previous administration IT? We maintain that in essence, the reason is twofold: for one thing, technology now allows for adaptable applications which were previously not known in this form. Customer-oriented solutions can be established and, above all, maintained in a decentralized manner, at the place where the service is to be provided. The former bottleneck of centralized IT is becoming less important so that the offices' own initiatives hardly encounter any obstacles. Also, the general framework of conditions is completely different in different administrations. Not the least of these differences was the debate of the 1980s about an increasingly customer- and results-oriented administration ("New Public Management"), which was one of the conditions that paved the way for a new method of employing IT.

The Development of a Conceptual Frame for E-Government

The interaction-oriented basic model that is used here structures, and describes the structure of, comprehensive e-government. External interaction partners of the government may be politicians, parliaments and courts, citizens and groups as decision-makers in the democratic process, corporations as suppliers or cooperation partners, citizens and groups as customers and recipients of services provided by the administration, as well as other external administrative units. But internal interactions, those which take place entirely inside an administrative unit, are also remolded by e-government applications and integrated into an overall system.

For the purpose of deriving the model, a distinction is first made between areas which cover administrative action as a whole. To structure the "political decision-making and production process," Schedler (2001, 38) uses and names the elements *"Decide, Produce, Deliver."* The structural patterns for these areas are the interactions which take place there and can be supported by e-government applications. Thus, a great number of e-government applications are allocated to each area. This allocation gives rise to the core elements of comprehensive e-government.

In this fashion, four core elements can be derived for e-government: electronic Democracy and Participation (eDP), electronic Production Networks (ePN), electronic Public Services (ePS), and–by way of an interlinking element–electronic Internal Cooperation (eIC).

The element eDP–electronic Democracy and Participation–denotes the electronic representation and support of democratically legitimizing decision-making procedures, as well as their preparation. The interaction partners are, at one end, citizens and groups as creators of political opinions and as decision-makers, and, at the other end, the political organs which are given democratic legitimacy by them. The administration supports the operative management of political processes. In addition, the electronic support of the interactions between politics, parliament and the administration is also assigned to eDP; parliamentary inquiries directed at certain administrative units are cases in point.

ePN–electronic Production Networks–stands for the electronic support of cooperation between public and private institutions and between public and other public institutions for the joint provision of services. In particular, this refers to electronic production networks for the fulfillment of public tasks. Private companies act as suppliers and cooperation partners of the administration. Cooperation between administrative units is concerned with horizontal and vertical links in administration, i.e., an interlinkage within and between various levels of government. This interlinkage is particularly relevant when public tasks can only be fulfilled with the involvement of different governmental areas and levels.

ePS–electronic Public Services–serves to describe the electronic provision of public services. The recipients of these services may be individuals or groups; the term "group" may denote companies and lobbies.

In addition to the three elements described above, which relate to the interaction of the administration with the outside world, we consider the element of eIC–electronic Internal Cooperation–which covers the area of internal processes and communication procedures. This electronic support may involve, e-mail systems, the Internet, as well as numerous intranet applications. In an integrated system, many working processes are represented as electronic workflows (Figure 1).

Deviating from *relational concepts* (B2G, C2G, etc.) that are frequently encountered at an international level, we assume that one and the same individual or one and the same organization is able to take on

FIGURE 1. Basic Model for E-Government

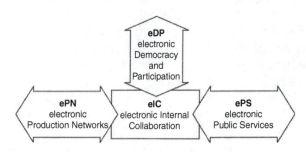

differing roles in their contact with government, and that these roles are characterized by greatly varying demands as regards quality. The "A-to-B" relation is thus often not sufficiently expressive. Table 1 provides an overview of the interaction partners of the administration and their roles in the four core elements of the e-government model.

The four elements have been explained in detail elsewhere (Schedler 2001; Schedler et al. 2001). Each of the elements has its own peculiarities with regard to implementation and the achievable potentials for the value creation of the state. However, it is only in joint operation that they constitute a basic model for e-government. This is why e-government is best implemented and designed in administration if all four elements are taken into consideration.

The Environment of E-Government

To understand the development of e-government in various European countries, it is necessary to analyze the e-government elements in their respective specific contexts. To generalize, we chose four areas to

TABLE 1. The Interaction Partners' Roles in the Four Core Elements

		Core elements			
		eDP	ePN	ePS	eIC
Interaction partners	**Private individual**	Citizens		Customer/ service recipient	
		Politicians			
		Electorate			
		Lobbyists			
	Companies	Sponsors	Suppliers	Customer/ service recipient	
		Lobbyists	Partners		
	NGOs/NPOs	Lobbyists	Partners	Customer/ service recipient	
	Parliament	Legislator			
		Decision-maker			
	Judiciary	Dispenser of justice			
	Other admin. units		Suppliers	Customer/ service recipient	
			Partners		
	Own admin. units				Suppliers
					Partners
					Customers

be examined for our model: politics, law, society, and technological developments outside administration.

Politics: The general political conditions cover the structures in which e-government is supposed to be implemented, as well as the presence of this issue in the political process. Elements such as the distribution of power between the executive, legislative and the people, but also the degree of decentralization and differentiation of political/administrative decisions are of significance here, as is the involvement of citizens in the decision-making process. According to the OECD (2000), the trigger and driving force of e-government is a critical volume of attention on the part of politics. Finally, it is interesting to discover what set of requirements political bodies have formulated for e-government.

Law: The implementation of e-government calls for legal prerequisites both in material and formal terms (cf. Herwig 2001, for continental Europe). Unresolved issues with regard to the legal framework are apt to delay the implementation of e-government quite considerably. Thus, unresolved legal aspects have so far been regarded as the main obstacle to development (Mies 2000, 7). It is therefore a question of creating mechanisms which identify and accelerate the necessary legal adaptations (NECCC 2000). This concerns, among other things, digital signatures and data protection, as well as formal/procedural rules for the validity of documents, etc.

Society: This general condition stands for the population's general attitude toward technology (cf. Jaufmann and Kistler 1991) and innovation, particularly toward the Internet. In relation to e-government, this influence factor describes the potential and actual use of electronic services. This depends on the infrastructure that is available to the population, on its security requirements (cf. Shutter et al. 2000, 24 et sqq. and 31), but also on comparable developments in the private sector (cf. Schily 2001, 2; Deloitte Consulting et al. 2000, 5). In addition, the demands made on the new facilities must be known so that the latter can be designed in a sensible manner. Financial incentives, too, may make the use of such services more attractive (Al-Kibsi et al. 2001, 72 et sqq.). And of course, the digital divide is an important issue with social aspects.

Technological development: Represents the speed of technical progress in the environment of government and the thrust of new developments.

DEVELOPMENTS IN EUROPE

In this chapter, we describe five countries whose general conditions we assumed to be different: the United Kingdom, Switzerland, France, Denmark, and Germany. In all these countries, external technological development plays an important part but will no longer be specially mentioned because it progressed more or less identically in all the countries under review.

United Kingdom

General Conditions

Blair and Cunningham (1999) presented a program to Parliament which provided, among other things, that 50% of all administrative dealings should be transacted online by 2005, and 100% by 2008. This excludes processes which cannot be made available online owing to operational or political reasons. As early as March 2000, Tony Blair revised this goal. Now, all the services were supposed to be online, i.e., available through PC, telephone or digital TV, by 2005 (The Prime Minister's Office 2000). With this aim in view, the first UK online report (Pinder et al. 2000) developed an e-government strategy which contains a comprehensible vision, clearly defined tasks and responsibilities, as well as a first action plan (Central IT Unit 2000). The recommendations of the annual UK online reports are implemented in the action plan (Office of the e-Envoy 2002b). Monthly reports provide information about the implementation plan of individual measures (Office of the e-Envoy 2002a).

Particular mention must be accorded to the establishment of the Office of the e-Envoy, together with an e-Minister, in September 1999. The appointment of an e-Envoy and an e-Minister can be traced back to a recommendation from the report of the Performance and Innovation Unit (1999), *e-commerce@its.best.uk*. The Office of the e-Envoy is responsible for all the "e" issues, both in e-business and in e-government, which we regard as perfectly typical of the UK, where the separation of the private and public sectors is less pronounced than in continental Europe.

The *Electronic Communications Act 2000* enables the use of electronic signatures, thus paving the way toward changes in legislation which still insists on the use of paper.

One of the conclusions that Grabtree (2001) drew in his report on the influence of the Internet on electoral behavior is that the political parties make great efforts to canvass voters through the Internet but that the public largely ignores them. A mere 2% of Internet users are certain that they would use the Internet to find information about the election campaign. Members of the electorate also prefer to retrieve information about the election from traditional media sites, such as the Website of the BBC, rather than obtaining their information directly from the Websites of the political parties.

Coleman (2001), too, has recognized a certain political apathy on the part of the electorate but thinks that the Internet has the potential to rekindle society's interest in politics.

Extremely interesting results concerning the use of ICT in the political environment are supplied in a report by the Hansard Society (2002). For instance, MPs in Northern Ireland and Scotland already receive more e-mails than letters from their constituents, whereas MPs in Westminster receive only half as many e-mails as letters. All in all, however, the quality of the e-mails as compared to that of letters is considered to be poorer. More than half of British citizens would like their MPs to have updated Websites. Twenty-eight percent of the interviewees would also like to make online contributions to the debates of the British Parliament. With regard to regional parliaments, the wish to participate in debates varies from less than 10% in Wales to more than 40% in Northern Ireland.

The UK Online Report 2001 reveals that a digital divide is also noticeable in the UK, which has increased in the past few years, particularly in respect of incomes (Pinder et al. 2001, 26), although the number of Internet users rose from almost 33% to more than 56% in the two years to May 2002 (Nua Internet Surveys 2002). Concerning the usage of government online services, Great Britain is far behind the global average. Only 13% of the population have used government online services in the past twelve months. One reason may be that nearly 60% of the population consider government online too unsafe (Mellor et al. 2002, 44).

Communicated Strategy

It must be stated in advance that the UK is among those countries in Europe which has the smallest number of direct-democracy elements of civic participation. The interest in e-government as a means of promoting just that participation is therefore correspondingly great. Interestingly, however, the intensive debate about the possibilities of e-democracy which is being conducted by both political and academic circles in the UK is hardly reflected in the government's strategies.

The UK's e-government strategy (Central IT Unit 2000) is primarily concerned with an improvement in the access and user-friendliness of government services, i.e., on ePS. It aims to establish separate transaction portals for private individuals and companies. Besides, further access channels are intended to be opened, some of them routed through private companies. For the desired increase in quality and customer benefit to be achieved, cooperation within the public sector for the joint provision of services is supposed to be reinforced–a factor in the element ePN. The gathering of information from different sources is supposed to result in new, user-friendly services. The prerequisites for this–shared standards and infrastructures–are supposed to be created jointly. Internal cooperation–eIC–is also considered in this strategy. The major players are interconnected through an intranet and provided with access to the Internet and to e-mails.

In the area of electronic Democracy and Participation (eDP), the strategy merely states that in the future, the general public will have access to substantially more information about the political process.

Germany

General Conditions

At least for an outside observer, the reforms in Germany would appear to be influenced to quite a considerable extent by those in the UK. Blair's social democratic reform program, The Third Way, which deliberately involves elements of the free market economy, evidently impressed the (equally social democratic) German federal government. Activities in Germany are defined by the vision *BundOnline 2005*, which was presented by Federal Chancellor Schröder (2000) in September 2000. In this vision, he announced the intention of making all the services of the federal administration which can be provided on the Internet available online by the year 2005. After a detailed analysis, a specific course of action to achieve this goal was presented in the *Umsetzungsplan für die eGovernment-Initiative*, i.e., an implementation plan for the e-government initiative, a year later (Die Bundesregierung 2001). This contains specific ideas as to what services will be available online in which year, what technical requirements must be satisfied for the purpose, and what will be the financial cost.

The implementation plan also provides for an adaptation of the relevant legal foundations. The prerequisites for the use of electronic signatures have already been created, and changes were made to the legal foundations with regard to the notification in court proceedings (e-mail and fax are also taken into consideration) and with regard to administrative proceedings.

As regards the use of e-government facilities, the Germans have substantially more security reservations than other nationalities. About 82%–after Japan the second highest proportion among the 27 countries that have been reviewed–consider the Internet to be too deficient in security for them to use administrative services online. The average is 63%. This is likely to be the explanation for the low proportion of 24% of the population who have used online services of the administration during the last twelve months, with an average of 30% in all 27 countries (Mellor et al. 2002, 18). For the time being, it remains unclear what the causes of this difference from other European countries may be. It is conceivable that a culture that prefers to take its bearings from formalities and rules assesses the security aspect more sensitively than a market- and contact-oriented culture.

A study by Perillieux et al. (2000) reveals that there is no such thing as a digital divide in Germany but that there are alarming signs that it may be opening up. Distinctions were primarily made in terms of the sociodemographic factors of sex, age, education and residential area. In May 2002, there were 26.7 million German Internet users above 14 years of age. These, however, are not evenly distributed across Germany. In the Western Länder, about 43% are connected up to the Internet, in the East only 37% (Initiative D21 et al. 2002).

Communicated Strategy

The strategy of the German federal government (Die Bundesregierung 2001) is characterized by the Federal Chancellor's announcement (Schröder 2000) that all the services capable of being offered on the Internet would be available online by 2005. The strategy thus aims at the element ePS. However, the necessary internal measures have also been mentioned (element eIC); for instance, it is intended to establish a transaction processing system.

The strategy says little about ePN although some model projects point in this direction, for example, the development of a joint procurement platform for all the allocation agencies at federal, Länder and communal levels.

Nothing is stated in the strategy about democracy and participation. Individual initiatives to increase the participation of citizens can only be found–if at all–in the communities. Germany's political elite at the national level, however, does not appear to perceive any necessity for an extension of democracy through the Internet.

France

General Conditions

France is regarded as the most centralist country of Western Europe, which raises the expectation that the development of e-government, too, is largely controlled by Paris. And indeed, Jospin (1997) declared in his then capacity as Prime Minister that the entry of France into the information age was one of his government's *top priorities*. This official commitment at the highest level, which was reinforced by the Government Action Program for an Information Society (Comité interministériel pour la société de l'information 1998), ensured that obstacles in the way of the dissemination of the Internet were quickly removed. The entire Program for an Information Society (1997-2001) was subsidized with about 9 billion francs (approx. €1.37bn) (Premier ministre-Service d'information du Gouvernement 2001).

Numerous legal foundations were adapted. For instance, electronic signatures were placed on a par with handwritten signatures, and the law concerning the treatment of personal data was amended. Between 1998 and 2001, the French administration produced almost 3,500 administrative Websites, on which about 900 forms are available online (Premier ministre-Service d'information du Gouvernement 2001, 5). The French citizens acknowledged this with rapidly rising user numbers, which meant that in a European comparison, France was not yet able to catch up with the Scandinavian top runners in 2002, but managed to overtake countries such as Germany and the UK. This is the more surprising as the safety of government online services is a very important issue for the French and only 15% of the adult population perceive government online services as safe (Mellor et al. 2002, 18 et sqq.).

Since 2001, the second stage of the *administration électronique* has been running with the clear aim of making all the administrative transactions, including fiscal and social security payments, available online for private individuals, associations and corporations (Comité interministériel pour la réforme de l'État 2001, 7. Translated by the authors).

The French government is also addressing the problem of the digital divide. Seven thousand public terminals are supposed to be made available in public libraries, post offices, employment offices and other strongly frequented places by 2003. Internet access through wideband technology is supposed to be made possible throughout France, particularly also in regions that have so far been poorly served (Premier ministre-Service d'information du Gouvernement 2001, 7).

Communicated Strategy

The French e-government strategy used for the purposes of this study is part of the Government Program for an Information Society (Comité interministériel pour la société de l'information 1998). Chapter 3 deals with the contributions of the information technologies toward the modernization of public services. The French government focuses on two aims: first on a simplification of access to the authorities, and second on an internal modernization of state operations. The first aim consists of various measures which can all be assigned to the element ePS. For instance, the most important public data are supposed to be offered on the Internet free of charge, and the general accessibility of administrative units by e-mail is supposed to be ensured. The second aim is meant to be achieved by an interlinkage of the administration, by a modernization of existing information systems, and by advanced training for civil servants. These measures derive from the element eIC, with the interlinkage of the administration also serving the joint provision of services and thus the element ePN.

The strategy does not refer to efforts for the promotion of political participation and the reinforcement of democracy. Evidently, the French government does not consider this to be an urgent problem that should be tackled by means of e-government.

Denmark

General Conditions

The Scandinavian countries tend to be regarded as pragmatic Europeans who prefer decentralized solutions. Moreover, they favor a contact-oriented culture which looks for many solutions by directly involving the people concerned. The foundation stone for e-government development in Denmark was laid by the IT Policy Plan of 1997. In this plan, the central points–protection of civil rights in the information age, the promotion of the whole population's IT capacities, a revitalization of interactions between citizens and the administration to realize the vision of an open public sector, and the solution of the security problems–were declared to be strategic aims (Ministry of Research and Information Technology 1997).

Thanks to the formulation of an extensive vision which sets the goal to provide "the best and most efficient public services in the Nordic countries" in Denmark (Forskningsministeriet 2000)–later, the prime minister reformulated the aims to "Best IT Nation in the World"–the resources could be concentrated on a clear-cut aim. In an e-government project that has been run by representatives of the central, regional and local authorities, individual objectives have been specified and combined into an e-government strategy (Den Digitale Taskforce 2002c). The project is conducted by the IT-Technical Center of the Ministry of Science, Technology and Innovation and by the Digital Task Force, which is part of the Ministry of Finance. The IT-Technical Center is meant to ensure that the "IT policy of the government is developed and implemented based on a technically solid and modern basis" (Den Digitale Taskforce 2002b). The Digital Task Force supports the Joint Board, which is made up of representatives of administrative units from all government levels. The Task Force brings interested parties together and works as a catalyst for the solution to cooperation and coordination problems (Den Digitale Taskforce 2002a). This course of action is typical of the contact culture of a Scandinavian country: the involvement of all government levels and interested parties, with government agencies acting as catalysts.

In May 2001, the Law on digital signatures (Lov om elektroniske signaturer) was enacted. In order to promote the use of digital signatures, the issuance of 200,000 digital signatures to inhabitants and companies was given financial support. Simultaneously, new services were developed which require the use of a digital signature (*Denmark* 2001).

The Danish population is less worried about the security of the Internet. Forty percent describe the Internet as safe. This may well be the reason why 53% of the population have used online services of the administration in the past twelve months, with an overall quota of Internet users of 64% (2001: 63%). The Danes do not only look for information (47%), they are also prepared to furnish it: no fewer than 20% have conducted online transactions with the administration. This development is based on a big confidence in government online services (Mellor et al. 2002, 22 et sqq.).

The digital divide is undoubtedly smaller than in other countries, yet there are significant differences with regard to Internet use between older and younger people, as well as between urban and rural areas. There is hardly any difference between the sexes (Blauenfeldt 1999).

Communicated Strategy

The Danish e-government strategy (Den Digitale Taskforce 2002c) sets four goals. The first designates e-government as part of the emerging information society and calls upon it to make a contribution to the promotion of that society. The second aim is for the entire public sector to use the new technologies to process cases and jointly settle other administrative concerns. This is intended to make cooperation between individual units more efficient. This corresponds to the element ePN, with cooperation being limited to the public sector. Moreover, the entire internal communication is supposed to be conducted electronically. This should also enable administrative units to share knowledge and to fulfill tasks with a substantially higher degree of flexibility. Thus functions can be observed wherever they can be carried out best and most efficiently. This aim serves to promote activities in the element eIC. The fourth aim demands that services should be made available in a comprehensive and customer-oriented manner, which must be assigned to the element ePS. Here, too, there are not explicit propositions concerning democratic and participative decision-making processes which should be affected by e-government.

Switzerland

General Conditions

Switzerland is certainly among the "late movers" in the field of e-government in Europe, and international organizations rate it at a correspondingly low level (cf. Ronaghan 2002, 37 et sqq. or eEurope et al. 2002, 8 et sqq.). In 1998, the Swiss federal government adopted a strategy for an information society in Switzerland in which electronic communication with the authorities constitutes a focal point (Bundesrat 1998). Subsequently, an interdepartmental Coordination Group Information Society (Koordinationsgruppe Informationsgesellschaft 1999) was set up, which presented its first report in April 1999. This report said that electronic communication with the authorities hardly went beyond Website presentations. A study conducted by Prognos (2001) revealed that all the cantons, but only 33% of the communities, had Websites of their own. It was also documented that only a fifth of the cantons had an e-government strategy, and that half of them intended to develop or adopt such a strategy in the course of 2001. In a survey conducted in autumn 2002, 72% of the respondent cantons said they have a strategy, or at least parts of a strategy like a vision or goals (Schedler et al. forthcoming).

At the federal level, the federal government adopted an e-government strategy in early 2002 (Informatikstrategieorgan Bund 2002). In his evaluation report, Lenk (2002, 31) criticizes the lack of a clear leadership organization, say, along the lines of the British e-Envoy.

A new project entitled *Vote électronique* (e-voting) is meant to provide citizens with the possibility of casting their votes in elections and referendums, or of signing an initiative, on the Internet (Bundesrat 2001). However, new possibilities of civic participation and political discussion are not considered to be of primary, high priority.

From a legal angle, the foundations were created for the recognition of electronic signatures. This was done in a regulation; a corresponding bill has passed the consultation process (Bundesamt für Justiz 2001) and is now debated in a committee of the National Council. It will not become effective before spring 2004.

With regard to the number of Internet users, Switzerland has 46% and is thus in the European midfield (Nua Internet Surveys 2002). According to Prognos (2001), however, the Swiss are willing to contact their administrations through the Internet. Thus, 60% of a community with a Website have visited that Website in the last twelve months. Seventy-four percent of all interviewees would like to communicate with the administration by e-mail.

In Switzerland, too, society is in the process of being divided up with regard to the possibilities and capacities of using the new technologies, with the divide running along the dimensions of education, age and sex. Only 22% of the people who left school after the compulsory part of the education system use the Internet regularly, whereas more than 70% of university graduates regularly use the Internet (Koordinationsgruppe Informationsgesellschaft 2002).

Communicated Strategy

The above-mentioned federal e-government strategy stipulates three thrusts: (1) create the prerequisites for e-government, (2) promote service excellence, and (3) produce a network. The first thrust mainly refers to the e-government element electronic Internal Collaboration (eIC). The aim is to enable smooth cooperation within the administration.

The second thrust focuses on the element electronic Public Services (ePS). Access to government services is supposed to become easier and more transparent. Varied and user-friendly transaction possibilities are supposed to made available step by step. In line with services provided by the Confederation, the services and facilities on offer will primarily be for companies and organizations.

The third thrust aims at the element electronic Production Networks (ePN), with particular store set by an improvement in cooperation between the administrations of the three levels of government.

In the course of the project, the element electronic Democracy and Participation (eDP), i.e., e-voting, was devalued in terms of priorities, not least because the procedures of voting and evaluation are very efficiently and effectively organized in Switzerland without any "e," and there is hardly any demand for further action. However, individual pilot projects are being conducted to clarify some important issues.

"European Proclamations"

Motives for the implementation of e-government can arise from objectives that are set within an administration, but also from outside pressure. Strategy papers contain such information. They are usually based on an analysis of the internal and external environments, and they define the aims to be reached. They are ideally suited as objects of study to provide answers to our questions. It must be taken into account that strategy papers are also used for political purposes and may be colored by political considerations. In this respect, an analysis of proclaimed strategies has its limitations: only the communicated motives can be analyzed.

To obtain a "European picture" of e-government, we analyzed seven e-government strategy papers from Denmark (Den Digitale Taskforce 2002c), Germany (Die Bundesregierung 2001), France (Comité interministériel pour la société de l'information 1998), the UK (Central IT Unit 2000), Ireland (Taoiseach 2002), Luxembourg (Commission Nationale de la Société de L'Information 2001) and Switzerland (Informatikstrategieorgan Bund 2002), respectively. Some e-government strategies were integrated in papers concerning the information society. In these cases, only the relevant passages were taken into consideration.

A similar survey was conducted at our Institute earlier on, but it focused on German-speaking Europe and all the government levels (Schedler et al. 2002). In that study, the motives were identified by means of a qualitative content analysis; these motives served as a grid for the present study. There are two classes of motives: on the one hand, the strategic aims of image promotion, support of administrative reform, rationalization/increase in efficiency, a contribution to the information society, and the promotion of political participation, and on the other hand, the responses to internal and external circumstances such as external technical developments, internally existing technologies, existing knowledge/know-how, personnel, customer requirements, and the competition between locations.

Overall, we regard it as important to state that the e-government projects involve two fundamental motivation scenarios: they can be launched in response to changes in the internal and external environments of the political/administrative system, but they may also contain a strategic component in that e-government is implemented to pursue certain purposes. Needless to say, both motivation scenarios are also apt to appear in tandem.

When scrutinizing the strategic papers, we notice that the texts worked with greatly differing terminologies and concepts. To make a structure and quantifiable evaluation possible, the researchers involved had to furnish an interpretation. To achieve a minimum measure of objectivity nonetheless, we summarized typical statements concerning individual motives in a table. Even so, it must be noted that the method retains a certain amount of subjectivity. In our view, however, the study is perfectly capable of registering trends with regard to the communicated motivation scenarios and of providing indications as to the background against which success and failure can be assessed at a later date.

With the help of a frequency analysis, we investigated the weight which individual motives have for a country's overall strategy; for this purpose, we recorded the position which they were accorded in the respective papers: each paper was combed for paragraphs containing statements about the aims and motives of e-government. The paragraphs thus identified were allocated to the individual categories and weighted in accordance with the total number of paragraphs of the whole document.

The results are graphically represented in Figure 2.

FIGURE 2. Motives for E-Government*

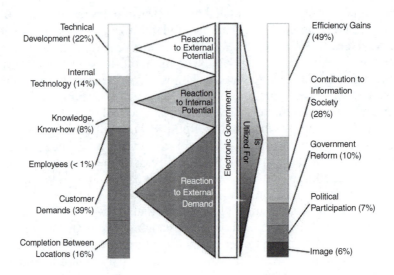

*Analysis of the Institute for Public Services and Tourism at the University of St. Gallen (IDT-HSG) 2002

All in all, we set out with the basic proposition that e-government was a development that was very strongly driven by the new technical possibilities. Moreover, we assumed e-government would primarily be used for the solution of problems which exist in a country anyway. This would mean that any communities about to implement e-government would place particular emphasis on these points in their strategy papers. These figures now reveal that these are important elements, but by far not the only ones.

CONCLUSIONS

How Can These Results Be Interpreted?

One thing that is conspicuous is the fact that motives of democratic participation have received a markedly low degree of attention in all the public proclamations. This is all the more astonishing since particularly on the Internet, intensive debates are often conducted about the possibilities of reinforcing democracy thanks to the use of ICT. This conclusion was drawn both on the strength of our observations of individual countries (Chapter 2) and on the basis of the content analysis of the strategy papers (Chapter 3).

Secondly, it is obvious that all the countries under review largely concentrate on the provision of services, i.e., on the element of electronic Public Services. This matches with the discovery in the content analysis that e-government strategies are often reactions to customer requirements.

Although gains in efficiency are reported as being one of the main motives for e-government implementation, and although from a scientific point of view, the greatest potential for an increase in efficiency is to be found in the element ePN, this element is not accorded priority. Some countries are at least trying to improve cooperation between their administrative units. Further-reaching potentials, however, would exist in interlinkages with the private and tertiary sectors, about which hardly any information is available.

Quite surprising are the significant differences in the countries' perception of IT safety. With Germany at 82 percent, France at 76 percent, the UK at 58 percent, and Denmark at 54 percent of alleged "unsafety," the range is wider than could be expected. After all, technical solutions are fairly comparable. One possible explanation is a cultural phenomenon: people's awareness about possible misuse of ICT–or in other words, trust in government. The latest Transparency International Corruption Perceptions Index 2002 correlates slightly with the above ranking, with Denmark on Rank 2, UK on 10, Germany on 18, and France on 25 (Côté-Freeman et al. 2002, 18). This phenomenon, however, needs more research and can only hint to possible cultural associations.

For the practical use of e-government, it is clear that the strategies to which the general public has access establish some focal points but that in other areas, propositions are (accidentally or purposely) unavailable. With the decentralized development which is typical of and inevitable for e-government, it remains unclear, for the time being, what is expected from administrative units with regard to an increased involvement of citizens. It remains unclear, too, to what extent e-government is considered to be part of a comprehensive reform or if–like so many reforms in the past–it will remain just another isolated building site. It does not come as a surprise that ultimately, the employment of e-government should result in gains in efficiency.

REFERENCES

Al-Kibsi, Gassan, Kito de Boer, Mona Mourshed, and Nigel P. Rea (2001) Putting citizens on-line, not in line. *McKinsey Quarterly, Special Edition On-line tactics* 2: 64-73.

Blair, Tony, and Jack Cunningham (1999) *Modernising Government* [online]. Prime Minister and the Minister for the Cabinet Office. [cited 05.09.2002]. Available from World Wide Web: (*http://www.archive.official-documents.co.uk/document/cm43/4310/4310-05.htm*).

Blauenfeldt, Andreas (1999) *Danskeres internetvaner* [online]. znail survey. [cited 06.09.2002]. Available from World Wide Web: (*http://www.znail.dk/survey/*).

Brinckmann, Hans et al. (1974) *Verwaltungsautomation. Thesen über die Auswirkungen automatisierter Datenverarbeitun auf Binnenstruktur und Aussenbeziehungen der öffentlichen Verwaltung.* Darmstadt: Toeche-Mittler.

Bundesamt für Justiz (2001) *Elektronische Signatur-elektronischer Geschäftsverkehr* [online]. Bundesamt für Justiz. [cited 06.09.2002]. Available from World Wide Web: (*http://www.ofj.admin.ch/themen/e-commerce/intro-d.htm*).

Bundesrat (2001) *Bericht über den Vote électronique: Chancen, Risiken und Machbarkeit elektronischer Ausübung politischer Rechte* [online]. 09.01.2002]. Available from World Wide Web: (*http://e-gov.admin.ch/vote/e-demo-dt-09.01.02.pdf*).

Bundesrat (1998) *Strategie des Bundesrates für eine Informationsgesellschaft in der Schweiz.* Bern.

Central IT Unit (2000) *E-government: A Strategic Framework for Public Services in the Information Age.* London: Cabinet Office.

Coleman, Stephen (2001) *2001: Cyber Space Odyssey.* London: Handard Society.

Comité interministériel pour la réforme de l'État (2001) *Relevé de décisions* [online]. Comité interministériel pour la réforme de l'État. [cited 04.09.2002]. Available from World Wide Web: (*http://www.internet.gouv.fr/francais/textesref/cire2001/decisionscire2001.pdf*).

Comité interministériel pour la société de l'information (1998) *Préparer l'entrée de la France dans la société de l'information* [online]. Premier ministre-Direction du Développement des Médias. [cited 04.09.2002]. Available from World Wide Web: (*http://www.internet.gouv.fr/francais/textesref/pagsi.htm*).

Commission Nationale de la Société de L'Information (2001) *eLuxembourg. Le plan d'action du Gouvernement.* Luxembourg: Le Gouvernement Luxembourgeois.

Côté-Freeman, Susan, and Karen Förnzler (2002) *Transparency International Annual Report 2002.* Berlin: Transparency International.

Deloitte Consulting, and Deloitte & Touche (2000) *At the Dawn of e-Government: The Citizen as Customer.* New York: Deloitte.

Den Digitale Taskforce (2002a) *The Digital Task Force* [online]. Den Digitale Taskforce. [cited 06.09.2002]. Available from World Wide Web: (*http://e.gov.dk/sitemod/design/layouts/default/index.asp?pid=1720*).

Den Digitale Taskforce (2002b) *IT-Technical Centre* [online]. Den Digitale Taskforce. [cited 06.09.2002]. Available from World Wide Web: (*http://e.gov.dk/sitemod/design/layouts/default/index.asp?pid=1730*).

Den Digitale Taskforce (2002c) *Towards E-Government–Vision and Strategy for the Public Sector in Denmark.* Copenhagen: Den Digital Taskforce.

Denmark (2001) Paper presented at the 35th ICA Conference, Berlin.

Die Bundesregierung (2001) *BundOnline 2005: Umsetzungsplan für die eGovernment-Initiative.* Berlin: Bundesministerium des Innern. Stabsstelle Moderner Staat–Moderne Verwaltung.

eEurope, and Cap Gemini Ernst & Young (2002) *Web-Based Survey on Electronic Public Services (Results of the Second Measurement. April 2002).* Brussels: European Commission.

Electronic Communications Act 2000 (2000) [online] Her Majesty's Stationery Office. [cited 06.09.]. Available from World Wide Web: (*http://www.hmso.gov. uk/acts/acts2000/20000007.htm*).

Forskningsministeriet (2000) *Digital Denmark–Conversion to the Network Society* [online]. Forskningsministeriet. [cited 05.09.2002]. Available from World Wide Web: (*http://www.detdigitaledanmark.dk/english/index.html*).

Grabtree, James (2001) *Whatever Happened to the E-Lection.* London: ISociety.

Grimmer, Klaus, ed. (1986) *Informationstechnik in öffentlichen Verwaltungen. Handlungsstrategien ohne Politik.* Basel: Birkhäuser.

Hansard Society (2002) *Technology: Enhancing Representative Democracy in the UK?* London: Hansard Society.

Herwig, Volker (2001) *E-Government: Distribution von Leistungen öffentlicher Institutionen über das Internet.* Edited by Norbert Szyperski, Beat F. Schmid, August-Wilhelm Scheer, Günther Pernul and Stefan Klein. Vol. 8, *Reihe: Electronic Commerce.* Köln: Eul.

Informatikstrategieorgan Bund (2002) *Regieren in der Informationsgesellschaft: Die eGovernment-Strategie des Bundes: Anhang 2: eGovernment-Projekte des Bundes.* Bern: ISB.

Initiative D21, and eMind@emnid (2002) *Studie: Deutsche Internet-Teilung* [online]. Initiative D21, eMind@emnid,. [cited 04.09.2002]. Available from World Wide Web: (*http://www. emind.emnid.de/downloads/studien/2002641Final_eMind@emnid_ PresseInfo_D21_ NONLINER.pdf*).

Jaufmann, Dieter, and Ernst Kistler, eds. (1991) *Einstellungen zum technischen Fortschritt: Technikakzeptanz im nationalen und internationalen Vergleich.* Frankfurt/Main, New York: Campus Verlag.

Jospin, Lionel (1997) *Préparer l'entrée de la France dans la société de l'information.* Hourtain: Discours prononcé lors de l'inauguration de l'Université de la Communication.

Koordinationsgruppe Informationsgesellschaft (1999) *1. Bericht der Koordinationsgruppe Informationsgesellschaft (KIG) an den Bundesrat.* Biel: KIG.

Koordinationsgruppe Informationsgesellschaft (2002) *4. Bericht der Koordinationsgruppe Informationsgesellschaft (KIG) an den Bundesrat.* Biel: KIG.

Lenk, Klaus (2002) Electronic Government. In *Bundesaktitivitäten für die Informationsgesellschaft. Evaluation der Strategie un der Umsetzung,* edited by Claudia Giannetti, Klaus Lenk, Patrick Mendelsohn, Andy Müller-Maguhn, Seamus Ross, Pascal Verhoest and Rolf H. Weber, 31-35. Bern: The Center for Science and Technology Studies (CEST).

Mellor, Wendy, and Victoria Parr (2002) *Government Online–An International Perspective* [online]. Taylor Nelson Sofres. [cited 22.11.2002]. Available from World Wide Web: (*http://www.tnsofres.com/gostudy2002/download/J20244_ Global_ Summary_revised.pdf*).

Mies, Helmut (2000) *e-Government: Eine Modeerscheinung oder "digitale Revolution" und Zukunft der Städte?* Chemnitz: PricewaterhouseCoopers.

Ministry of Research and Information Technology (1997) *Action for Change: IT Policy Plan 97/98* [online]. Ministry of Research and Information Technology. [cited 06.09.2002]. Available from World Wide Web: (*http://www.fsk.dk/fsk/ publ/1997/ action97/index.htm*)

NECCC (2000) *Critical Business Issues in the Transformation to Electronic Government*. Las Vegas: The National Electronic Commerce Coordinating Council.

Nua Internet Surveys (2002) *How Many Online?* [online]. [12.09.2002]. Available from World Wide Web: (*http://www.nua.com/surveys/how_many_online*).

OECD (2000) *Government of the Future*. Paris: Organisation for Economic Co-operation and Development.

Office of the e-Envoy (2002a) *Monthly Reports* [online]. Cabinet Office. [cited 06.09.2002]. Available from World Wide Web: (*http://www.e-envoy.gov.uk/oee/oee.nsf/sections/ ukonline-top/$file/montprog.htm*).

Office of the e-Envoy (2002b) *UK Online Action Plan* [online]. Cabinet Office. [cited 06.09.2002]. Available from World Wide Web: (*http://www.e-envoy.gov.uk/oee/ oee.nsf/sections/ukonline-actionplan/$file/table.htm*)

Performance and Innovation Unit (1999) *e-commerce@its.best.uk*. London: Cabinet Office.

Perillieux, René, Rainer Bernnat, and Marcus Bauer (2000) *Digitale Spaltung in Deutschland: Ausgangssituation, Internationaler Vergleich, Handlungsemp fehlungen*. Berlin: Booz·Allen & Hamilton und Initiative D21.

Pinder, Andrew, and Patricia Hewitt (2000) *UK Online Annual Report 2000* [online]. Cabinet Office. [cited 06.09.2002]. Available from World Wide Web: (*http://www.e-envoy.gov.uk/oee/oee.nsf/sections/reports-anrep1-top/$file/default.htm*).

Pinder, Andrew, and Patricia Hewitt (2001) *UK online annual report 2001* [online]. Cabinet Office. [cited 06.09.2002]. Available from World Wide Web: (*http://www.e-envoy.gov.uk/oee/oee.nsf/sections/reports-anrep2001-downloads/$file/ annrep2.pdf*).

Premier ministre-Service d'information du Gouvernement (2001) *Four Years of Government Measures to Promote the Information Society* [online]. Premier ministre-Service d'information du Gouvernement. [cited 06.09.2002]. Available from World Wide Web: (*http://www.internet.gouv.fr/francais/textesref/agsi4years.pdf*).

Prognos (2001) *ICT im öffentlichen Sektor in der Schweiz*. Basel: Prognos.

Ronaghan, Stephen A. (2002) *Benchmarking E-Government: A Global Perspective*. New York: United Nations Division for Public Economics and Public Administration, American Society for Public Administration.

Schedler, Kuno (2001) eGovernment und neue Servicequalität der Verwaltung? In *eGovernment: eine Standortbestimmung*, edited by Michael Gisler and Dieter Spahni, 33-51. Bern, Stuttgart, Wien: Paul Haupt.

Schedler, Kuno, and Maria Christina Scharf (2001) Exploring the Interrelations Between Electronic Government and the New Public Management. *IDT Working Paper* Nr. 2.

Schedler, Kuno, and Lukas Summermatter (forthcoming) *E-Government Barometer: Stand und Entwicklung von E-Government in der Schweiz.* St. Gallen: Institut für Öffentliche Dienstleistungen und Tourismus der Universität St. Gallen.

Schedler, Kuno, and Lukas Summermatter (2002) Was treibt das e-Government? In *eGovernment 2: Perspektiven und Prognosen,* edited by Dieter Spahni, 105-22. Bern: Haupt.

Schily, Otto (2001) *Auf dem Weg zu einer modernen Verwaltung, "BundOnline 2005."* Paper presented at the Messe "Effizienter Staat," Berlin.

Schröder, Gerhard (2000) *Internet für alle-Schritte auf dem Weg in die Informationsgesellschaft.* Paper presented at the Kongresses der Initiative D21 "Leben, lernen, und arbeiten in der Informationsgesellschaft" auf der EXPO, Hannover.

Shutter, Jay, and Ellen de Graffenreid (2000) *Benchmarking the eGovernment Revolution: Year 2000 Report on Citizen and Business Demand.* Austin, San Francisco: Momentum Research Group.

Taoiseach (2002) *New Connections: A Strategy to Realize the Potential of the Information Society.* Dublin: Government of Ireland.

The Prime Minister's Office (2000) *Government to Speed Up Provision of Online Services* [online]. The Prime Minister's Office. [cited 06.09.2002]. Available from World Wide Web: (*http://www.pm.gov.uk/output/page1951.asp*).

Index